CLOTHING AND FURNISHINGS

Clothing and Furnishings

*Women's suits, walking costumes and dresses, wrappers,
shawls, underwear, corsets, shoes, trimmed hats;
bridal dresses and sets; men's furnishings
and boys' clothing; laces and embroideries*

LORD & TAYLOR
1881

Illustrated Catalog and Historical Introduction

AMERICAN HISTORICAL CATALOG COLLECTION

THE PYNE PRESS
Princeton

All Rights Reserved

Copyright © 1971 by The Pyne Press

No part of this publication may be reproduced
or transmitted in any form or by any means,
electronic or mechanical, including
photocopy, recording, or any information storage
and retrieval system, without permission
in writing from the publisher.

First edition

Library of Congress Catalog Card Number 74-162360

ISBN 0-87861-013-8

Printed in the United States of America

Note to the reader. Reproduction of copy and line drawings is as faithful to the original as is technically possible. Broken type and lines which are uneven or broken can be spotted; these are original! You will understand that manufacturers or merchants of such products as tinware, clothing, weathervanes and guns were not dedicated to the fine art of printing or involved in the business of publishing. All American Historical Catalog Collection editions are photographed from the best available copy, are printed on an especially receptive offset paper, and are strongly bound.

687
L88c

CATALOGUE

OF

Silks,	Bedding
Dress Goods,	Laces,
Cloths,	Embroideries,
Millinery,	Handkerchiefs,
Ribbons,	Perfumes,
Suits,	Cloaks,
Hosiery,	Shawls,
Gloves,	Shoes,
Underwear,	Gentlemen's
Infants' Clothing,	Furnishing,
White Goods,	Boys' Suits,
Linens,	Carpets,
Domestics,	Upholstery, Etc.

LORD & TAYLOR,

NEW YORK.

Broadway and Twentieth Street.
Grand and Chrystie Streets.

44446

In ordering from this Catalogue please refer to it as No. 26.

There are two ways in which to supply your wants:—one, to find a reliable merchant, and make use of him whenever you have need; the other, to go in search of so-called "bargains," offered by adventurers. In the one case, you will get your money's worth of honest goods—no more; in the other, you will be served with spurious goods, and only learn your loss when your purse is empty.

We have two stores, one on Grand Street, the other on Broadway; to some extent the stocks in these stores are suited to the neighborhoods in which they are located but both are embraced in this Catalogue, presenting therein a stock, which, for variety, quality, magnitude and range from low-priced to high-priced, is rarely if ever elsewhere found; these stocks are supplied direct from the manufacturing centers at home and abroad through connections formed during a business existence of fifty years.

LORD & TAYLOR

New-York, May 1st, 1881.

THE best means of judging goods are samples of the goods themselves. Write for samples of whatever you may want; when, from the nature of the goods, samples cannot be cut, information is given in other ways.

When ordering goods make a first choice, and, if two of the samples be satisfactory, a second choice also, to save time in case your first is gone when the order is received; do not cut the Catalogue, but refer to it by page and number.

Remit by check, P. O. order, registered letter, or draft on New York. Goods are sent C. O. D. when desired, but this is a more costly mode of remitting. Include in the amount the postage on the articles; it may be determined by reference to page 3.

Errors occur through a lady using at first her own name and afterwards that of her husband, or vice versa: to avoid this a married lady should use her husband's full name.

Prices fluctuate according to the wholesale market, but when goods are marked down, between the times samples are sent and orders received, absent buyers have the same advantages as those present.

Accounts are opened, payable monthly, with those making themselves known to us as responsible.

Any article that is unsatisfactory may be returned. We take pleasure in affording this guarantee in the hope that discretion and care will be shown in ordering goods, so that we may know beforehand exactly what you want. Study the samples and the catalogue, and state your wants clearly and fully.

LORD & TAYLOR,

RATES BY MAIL AND EXPRESS.

A package of goods (if under four pounds) may be sent by mail at one cent per ounce or sixteen cents per pound; and may be "registered" for ten cents additional, but must not contain any writing, except the name and address of the sender on outside of wrapper (for example: Mrs. John Smith, Akron, Ohio), and must be easy of inspection.

AVERAGE WEIGHTS IN OUNCES.

Item	About	Item	About	Item	About
Collar	2	Lace, doz. yards,	4	Shawl, single,	25
Cuffs,	4	Napkins, doz.,	24	" double,	50
Corset,	17	Pillow and Sheet Shams, set,	22	Slippers, pair,	15
" Cover,	4	Quilt (Marseilles),	60	Shoes, pair,	20
Chemise,	12	" (Honeycomb),	43	Suit, Boys'	50 to 75
Drawers,	9	Ruffling (without frame),	22	" Ladies'	50 to 75
Diaper, piece,	30	Robe, Night,	20	" Misses'	25 to 50
Doylies, doz.,	11	Skirt, Walking,	18	Towels, doz.,	30 to 60
Embroidery, yard,	3	" Train,	25	Table Linen, yard,	12
Fringe, yard,	5	Sacque, Toilet,	8	Shirts and Drawers, Gents',	
Flannel, yard,	6	Slip, Infant's,	8	each,	15
Gloves, pair,	3	Skirt, "	3	Upholstery, Cretonne, yard,	15
Hose, pair,	4	" Flannel, Infant's,	8	Vest and Drawers, Ladies'	13
Handkerchiefs, doz.,	15	Silk, yard,	7	Flannel Wrapper,	40

The following are approximate Express-Charges from New-York to places reached by the Adams, American, United States, Delaware, Lackawanna & Western, Baltimore & Ohio, Union, Central, and New Jersey Express Companies.

In	1 lb.	1 to 2 lbs.	2 to 3 lbs.	3 to 4 lbs.	4 to 5 lbs.
Mass., R. I., Conn.,	$0.25	.25	.25	.25 to .30	.25 to .35
N. Y., N. J., Pa., Del., Md.,	.25	.25 to .30	.25 to .35	.25 .45	.25 .50
Ohio, Ind.,	.25	.25 .30	.35 .45	.35 .55	.35 .60
Mich., Ill.,	.25	.30	.35 .45	.40 .60	.50 .70
Wisconsin,	.25	.30	.35 .45	.45 .60	.50 .70
Iowa,	.25	.30	.45	.55 .60	.60 .70
Minnesota,	.25	.30	.45	.60	.70 .75
Missouri,	.25	.30	.35 to .45	.45 to .60	.50 .70
Kan., Neb., Dak.,	.25	.30	.45	.60	.70

In	5 to 7 lbs.	7 to 10 lbs.	10 to 15 lbs.	15 to 20 lbs.	20 to 25 lbs.
Mass., R. I., Conn.,	.25 to .35	.25 to .45	.25 to .50	.25 to .50	.25 to .55
N. Y., N. J., Pa., Del., Md.,	.25 .55	.25 .60	.25 .65	.25 .75	.25 .90
Ohio, Ind.,	.40 .60	.45 .65	.50 .75	.50 .90	.65 1.00
Mich., Ill.,	.50 .75	.55 .90	.60 1.10	.70 1.25	.80 1.50
Wisconsin,	.55 .75	.65 .90	.75 1.10	.90 1.25	1.00 1.50
Iowa,	.65 .95	.70 1.15	.80 1.25	1.00 1.75	1.20 1.75
Minnesota,	.75 1.00	.90 1.25	1.00 1.60	1.25 2.00	1.40 2.25
Missouri,	.55 .75	.65 1.00	.75 1.20	.90 1.50	1.00 1.75
Kan., Neb., Dak.,	.75 1.00	.90 1.15	1.10 1.25	1.25 1.75	1.50 1.75

The rates of the Southern Express Company are somewhat higher.

The cost of sending money by the above-named Expresses, **any distance, is**, under $20, fifteen cents; $20 to $40, twenty cents; $40 to $50, twenty-five cents.

The lowest rate for ordinary Freight by Railroad is " for 100 lbs."

INSTRUCTIONS FOR MEASURING.

Take the following measures over the dress, rather closely:

1. Around the bust, at the largest part, under the arms, A A A A.
2. From sleeve-seam to sleeve-seam across chest, being the width between shoulders across chest, B B.
3. From sleeve-seam to sleeve-seam across the back, being width between shoulders across back, C C.
4. From sleeve-seam under arm straight down to waist-seam, D D.
5. Length of sleeve on the inside seam, E E.
6. Length of sleeve outside, viz.: from junction of sleeve-seam with shoulder-seam, at back of shoulder, to point of elbow, thence to wrist, K F F.
7. Around waist, G N G G G G.
8. Around neck at collar-seam, H N H H N H.
9. Around hips at the largest part, R R R R.
10. Length of shoulder-seam from collar-seam to sleeve-seam, H K.
11. From neck to waist-seam in front, N N.
12. From neck to waist-seam at the back, N G.
13. Length of skirt in front, N P.
14. Length of skirt at back, G Q.

If the bust-measure is taken too high in front **and** too low behind, or otherwise than as directed, **an error** of one or two inches will result.

If you stoop when measured for length **of skirt, the** measure will be two to six inches short.

A waist-lining, made to fit as you would like it, would be preferred.

LADIES' COSTUMES.

The new dresses are made with smooth-fitting basques and elaborately draped over-dresses, which are now always united to the lower skirt.
Basques are usually single-breasted and fit smoothly around the hips in princess style. There is usually some fullness added at the middle forms in the back. Some basques are pointed, back and front, and often a flat drapery is added in panier style. Other basques are in long surtout style. These basques extend plainly to the middle forms of the back which are cut out quite short, disclosing the elaborate draperies of the tournure. Vests are simulated by trimming or are laid on flatly in gay bayadere stripes or in fine shirring or pleating. A plastron or Pompadour square of similar trimming is as often used as a vest. A great deal of shirring is seen on the new basques. Sometimes they are entirely formed of fine shirring, and the sleeve is shirred its entire length or only at the bottom and top, while the middle part forms a puff. Sleeves are rather longer and cuffs are very simple. Buttons are not conspicuous, often being hidden in the vest of shirring or fine pleats. Skirts are narrow and the lower-skirt is oftener pleated than plain. Box-pleated and kilt-pleated skirts are often bordered by a wide band of bayadere stripe or other trimming. Other skirts are bordered by narrow plaiting and others are finished by double ruching, The entire front of the under-skirt is often disclosed and it is then elaborately trimmed with five or more flounces. The flounces most used are shirred at the top and pressed into fine pleats at the bottom. Sometimes an over-skirt is draped on one side and left open to display the under-skirt which on that side is flounced to the belt.
Over-dresses are always fastened to the under-skirt. They are no longer bordered but there are a great many revers, retroussé pieces, sashes and panels of gay trimming. Over-skirts are both short and long and their draperies are of the most elaborate and intricate description, exquisitely graceful, formed of numberless curves and soft wrinkles. There seems to be very little regularity in the methods used by skilled modistes who arrange these draperies to suit the height and style of the figure.
When cross-over or bayadere stripes are employed in combination with plain fabrics the over-skirt and basque are of the plain material, while the **striped goods is used for the vest or plastron, revers and cuffs and collars.**

Most skirts are non-bouffant, but a few new dresses show puffed draperies at the back. All costumes, except dinner and evening dresses, are short, and these are often short.

There is a great deal of gay facing and piping on the new costumes. Handkerchief scarfs are still worn. Black cashmere dresses are trimmed with soft surah silk and they are quite popular. Black silk is trimmed with heavily jetted or plain Spanish lace and with steel passementeries and fringes, and it is often embroidered with wreaths and clusters of flowers in natural colors. Changeable satin surah dresses are trimmed with ombré satin surah or black lace over the under color of the changeable goods. Graceful bows of long loops are placed often at the waist-line, on the cuffs, back of the jacket, and suitable places among the pleating of the drapery.

The following are some of the styles we make to order this season. Our resources and facilities are so complete and extensive that we guarantee a perfect fit, if our directions for self-measurement on page 4 are followed, or an old waist-lining is sent.

1 Suit of black cashmere. Plain waist with folds and bows of cashmere on front, panier back, sleeves trimmed with bows; over-dress slashed in front and caught with large silk bow, long square back, fully draped; short skirt with deep side-pleating. Price, $16.

LORD & TAYLOR, NEW YORK.

2 Walking-dress of navy-blue cloth. Hunting jacket trimmed with braid; box-pleated skirt with pointed over-dress looped high on side and fastened with lapel and buttons, back short and full. Price, $12.
   LORD & TAYLOR, NEW YORK.

3 Traveling-costume of coachman's drab, with rows of stitching trimming. Double-breasted English jacket with rolling collar, sleeves trimmed with braid and buttons; apron-front over-dress with revere looped on side with heavy cord and tassel, back draped full and short; skirt of large kilt-pleats trimmed on bottom with rows of braid and cloth, panel on each plait. Price, $25.

LORD & TAYLOR, NEW YORK.

4 Walking-costume in the new shades of cloth trimmed with rows of stitching. Half-fitting jacket with long, pointed hood; over-dress pointed front and back and draped on sides; skirt trimmed with rows of stitching. Price, $28.

LORD & TAYLOR, NEW YORK.

5. Walking-dress of blue flannel trimmed with soutache braid. Front of waist made to give princess effect, postillion back; pointed shawl-front overdress, draped pretty full in back and looped high on side with large buckle; skirt with deep side-pleating in front and shirred in back. Price $35.

LORD & TAYLOR, NEW YORK.

6 Walking-costume of dark green Assabet cloth: Close-fitting jacket, cut short on hips, postillion back trimmed with soutache braid and large buttons, pointed revere collar fitting high in neck, plain sleeves with rows of braid; full, round apron-front over-dress draped very high on hips with plain pleated back ; narrow side-pleated flounce on skirt, headed with rows of braid. Price, $35.

LORD & TAYLOR, NEW YORK.

7 Walking-costume of striped écru cloth, trimmed with rows of stitching. Jacket with rolling collar and revers finishing in a cuirass front, and trimmed with large buttons and loops; diagonal front of over-dress confined with silk girdle; back simply draped; deep side-pleated flounce finished with braid trimming on skirt. Price, $38.

LORD & TAYLOR, NEW YORK.

8 Havelock costume in all the new shades. Cape trimmed with cardinal satin and finished with satin to match cloth ; French waist with deep shirred satin collar, sleeves trimmed with satin ; short apron-front over-skirt to show pleatings on skirt, back draped short and full. Price, $55.

LORD & TAYLOR, NEW YORK.

9   Suit of colored silk.   Plain waist with postillion back; over-dress shirred in front and at the sides, silk scarf attached in front and finished with jet balls, back draped; under-skirt trimmed with five large, single, box-pleats in front, and two narrow pleated flounces at back.   Price, $28.

LORD & TAYLOR, NEW YORK.

10 Walking-dress, silk or satin-de-Lyon, in black or colors. Plain waist with panier back, revere collar, and sleeves finished with folds of silk twisted and confined with a bow; pointed front over-dress, draped low on sides; long, square draped back; side-pleated flounce about nine inches deep on skirt. Price, $29.

LORD & TAYLOR, NEW YORK.

11 Dress of colored silk or black satin-de-Lyon. Plain French waist with bow of silk on back, standing collar, revers on front of waist; cuffs trimmed with two fine pleatings and fastened with a knot of silk; front of over-skirt draped diagonally to show kilt-pleated front of skirt, which is finished at the side with revers and fastened with silk bows; back of skirt draped long and plain, bottom of skirt trimmed at the back with narrow shirred flounce. Price, $30

LORD & TAYLOR, NEW YORK.

12 Suit of black satin-de-Lyon. Long, close-fitting basque, collar, cuffs and pockets trimmed with passementerie; skirt trimmed in front with three deep pleated flounces stitched half way; bottom finished with narrow box-pleating; over-dress draped in front and looped with a bow to show pleating, back draped short and full. Price, $45.

LORD & TAYLOR, NEW YORK.

13 Walking-dress of black Henrietta cloth, with crape. Plain basque with standing collar and revers of crape, cuffs of crape, back slashed and looped in bows, front trimmed with deep bias of crape; apron-front over-dress draped high and trimmed with crape, back of silk fully draped; skirt enentirely of crape and finished with narrow box-pleating of Henrietta. Price, $48.

LORD & TAYLOR, NEW YORK.

14 Mourning-dress of Imperial serge. Revers and plaitings of crape on waist and sleeves; demi-train skirt with rose-pleating on train and two rows of box-pleating on front, left side trimmed with three large pleats of crape fastened half way with knot of same, drapery on left side very high to show pleats and fastened with large bow and ends of crape finished with crochet ball, back of skirt draped full. Price, $90.

LORD & TAYLOR, NEW YORK.

15 Long dress of Italian lace and organdie to be worn over colored slip. Half-fitting basque with jabot of lace and ribbon loops down front, sleeves and basque finished with heading and deep edging of lace; front of skirt made of insertion with three rows of lace gathered on bottom; panier back of organdie finished with insertion and lace; demi-train made of insertion and edging. Price, $65.

LORD & TAYLOR, NEW YORK.

16 Costume of iron-frame grenadine: scarf trimming on waist and cording of silk, sleeves with side-pleating and reversible cuffs; skirt with large pleats running across front and caught with shirring in centre, finished on sides with paniers and revers trimmed with silk bows, two box-pleatings on bottom. Price, $50.

LORD & TAYLOR, NEW YORK.

17. Walking-dress of brocade grenadine with Spanish lace, and trimmings and loops of satin: plain waist; skirt with double paniers, back long and draped, two pleatings on bottom. Price, $68.

LORD & TAYLOR, NEW YORK.

18. Dinner-dress of bronze satin-de-Lyon and brocade. Princess back of brocade and basque front of satin-de-Lyon; collar and square front of brocade; waist finished with crystal ornaments and fringe, sleeves trimmed to match.; front of skirt of brocade with sash drapery of satin-de-Lyon fastened at side with knot and ends of same; back of brocade with side-drapery of satin-de-Lyon; train finished with rose-pleating of satin-de-Lyon. Price, $190.

LORD & TAYLOR, NEW YORK.

19. Bridal-dress of white brocade and satin-de-Lyon. Princess back and basque front of brocado, neck cut square and filled in with lace, sleeves of brocade with insertions of crystal trimming; front of skirt of brocade cut in squares to show pleatings on bottom, back finished with very narrow shirred trimming, panier sides of crystal and pearl fringe; garnitures for waist, sleeves and skirt of orange-blossoms. Price, $200.

LORD & TAYLOR, NEW YORK.

The following are made to order:

CASHMERE, BLACK AND COLORED.

20 Walking-dress: plain waist with postillion back, trimmed with material; reversed pleats of material down front of skirt giving effect of puffs, sides long and plain and finished with deep hem, short, full drapery on back; side-pleating and box-pleating each four inches deep on bottom of skirt, $16.

21 Walking-dress of black cashmere: plain basque with revere collar and cuffs of cashmere; over-skirt pointed in front and looped high on left side with silk bow showing three deep side-pleatings on under-skirt, full back drapery; one side-pleating on back of skirt, $18.

22 Walking-dress, short: collar, revers and cuffs of brocade; long round apron-front over-dress trimmed with fringe, plain full back; narrow side-pleating on bottom with deeper box-pleating above, $20.

23 Walking-dress: close-fitting basque with silk collar and cuffs, and silk pockets at back; front of skirt with shirring and revers of silk, double panier sides of material trimmed with silk, long, square back with fold of silk, two box-pleatings on bottom, $22.

24 Walking-dress, short: French waist with silk belt and bow; over-dress shirred in front and caught with large silk bow, back softly draped; three deep pleatings on front of skirt, also trimmed with silk, $25.

25 Walking-dress: back of waist en-panier finished with large silk bow, waist trimmed with silk collarette and bow, deep silk cuffs on sleeves; short apron-front over-skirt with silk revers opening to show skirt; skirt plain in front trimmed at bottom with box-pleating of cashmere six inches deep, long full drapery at back, $30.

26 Walking-dress of black serge trimmed with black-and-white stripe and steel buttons: plain basque front with belt of stripe coming from side seams, pocket of serge and stripe attached to belt, back slashed and fastened with silk balls, plain sleeves opened at back, pleating **of serge** on hips to form pocket with **trimming** of stripe arranged diagonally; **drapery** on front and back of skirt fastened at side with steel buttons; front of skirt box-pleated half way; and for nine inches at back, deep band of stripe running under pleats and showing in the spaces, $35.

27 Walking-dress of armure cloth: close-fitting jacket with silk collar and cuffs; apron-front skirt with deep bias fold of silk bound with heavy silk and tape fringe, shawl-draped back; one box-pleated flounce five inches deep on bottom of skirt, $36.

28 Walking-dress of black camels-hair: basque with vest front of silk, two silk girdles across front fastened with passementerie ornaments, revers at back caught with large bow showing silk lining, deep pointed collar and cuffs of silk; front and sides of skirt of silk, two box-pleatings at bottom; over-dress with panier sides finished with jet and silk fringe, two silk girdles with passementerie ornaments across front, back slightly looped, $43.

29 Walking-dress of black worsted polka-dot: polonaise front with basque effect at back; skirt of fine satin stripe with three narrow flounces shirred and pleated alternately; drapery short to show skirt, $55.

30 Walking-dress of camels-hair: paniers of surah satin on sides of waist, finished at the back with large twist of same, the back of the basque below this twist in two large box-pleats, steel buttons and ball trimmings on waist; skirt drapery caught high in front with satin scarf finished with steel balls; four graduated side-pleated flounces finished on bottom with fold of satin, on front of skirt, the lower flounce headed with deep fold of satin continuing around the skirt, $56.

31 Walking-dress of Jersey goods made with polonaise and faced with red silk: skirt of satin-de-Lyon with deep kilt-pleating, $58.

FLANNEL.

32 Walking-dress of dark-green flannel: pleated waist with belt, deep collar with three rows of gold braid, sleeves trimmed to match; long round-front over-dress with deep hem and four tucks, full pointed back; box-pleating with heading on skirt, $16.

33 Walking-dress of black or colored flannel: close-fitting jacket trimmed with rows of stitching, long pointed hood with silk tassel; over-skirt looped high on side and finished with deep hem and stitching; skirt finished with narrow pleating, deep hem and stitching, $19.

34 Walking dress of blue flannel: basque with short front and sides and long pointed back, finishing in revers, waist and sleeves trimmed with stitching and buttons; front of over-skirt with three clusters of tucks in spaces finished at sides with revers fastened with buttons, short drapery at back; kilt-pleatings on back of skirt and side-pleating six inches deep on front, $22.

35 Walking-dress of grey-flannel: pleated waist, collar and cuffs of black-and-white velvet stripe, lined with rose colored silk; long apron-front over-skirt looped high on side and trimmed with rows of stitching; skirt with full shirred back and three deep tucks and pleatings on bottom; belt of velvet stripe with panier sides of flannel, to be worn over waist, $22.

CLOTH.

36 Walking-dress in new shades of cloth: hunting jacket trimmed with braid; over-dress and skirt combined, drapery looped high on left side and fastened with lapels and large buttons, deep knife-pleating on bottom of skirt, $19.

37 Walking-dress of light-mixed brown cloth: side-pleatings down front of basque, large buttons and chenille ornaments on back, sleeves trimmed with shirring of cloth pleated at back; drapery looped high on right side of skirt, shawl-drapery on back finished with rows of stitching; side-pleatings nine inches deep on skirt, $22.

38 Walking-dress of light-mixed brown fancy cloth: English walking-jacket trimmed with fancy buttons and loops of silk cord, cuirass front with deep revere collar; skirt, double-panier sides edged with rows of stitching and crossing diagonally in front, heavy silk girdle across front, back draped to fall in point at back, **deep pleating finished with stitching on bottom, $35.**

39 Walking-dress in new shades of cloth. double-breasted English jacket trimmed with rows of stitching and silk-girdle on sides; apron-front drapery and long sash ends for back; three flounces on skirt laid on plain without shirring or pleating and edged with rows of stitching, back kilt-pleated half way, $35.

40 Suit of navy-blue cloth for house or street: close-fitting double-breasted jacket; double-pointed apron-front over-skirt caught at side with large buckle; back draped to match; deep side-pleatings edged with soutache braid on skirt, $38.

COLORED SILK.

41 Walking-dress of striped silk: basque trimmed with material; apron front over-skirt, long full back trimmed with pleatings, side-pleaitngs on bottom, $15.50.

42 Walking-dress: plain round basque with surplice collar and shirred satin ruffle; front of skirt trimmed with large box-pleats and shirrings of satin between, short panier drapery with fold of satin, back trimmed with box-pleated ruffle and soft drapery, $26.50.

43 Walking-dress of navy-blue silk: plain waist, with panier back and trimming of material on front and sleeves; drapery on skirt long and full and caught up in front with large bows, deep side-pleating on bottom, also in brown, maroon and gray, $29.

44 Walking-dress of olive-green silk and brocade: waist of silk with scarf of brocade shirred in spaces for front trimming, back slashed and finished with satin bows and brocade; sides of skirt with paniers of silk and brocade and pipings of green satin, back of silk and brocade draped together, bottom with side-pleatings in spaces headed with reversed pleats, $40.

45 Walking-dress of olive-brown satin: duchess waist with fine graduated pleatings down front confined with pleated belt and bow, long postillion back with ends caught in center by rainbow jet to form bow; skirt with short scarf front drapery and large bow and slide of rainbow jet at right side, five tucks in front, finished at bottom with box-pleating, back in four large box-pleats, $65.

46 Walking-dress of steel-colored silk, duchess costume: waist, neck and sleeves

COLORED SILK—Continued.

trimmed with bias fold of material and steel clasps, back with large shirred bow fastened with silk girdle and steel buckles; skirt with scarf front drapery caught at side with large steel buckle and ends finished with steel balls, front trimmed with three panels of box-pleatings and box-pleating on bottom, back drapery of three deep shirred flounces, $75.

47 Evening-dress of blue brocade and satin-de-Lyon: plain waist with drapery on bottom to effect vest, trimming of satin; skirt of blue satin, drapery of brocade high on sides and falling in a point in front, loops and ends of satin finished with blue crystal balls, long sash of brocade draped at back to show two rows of satin side-pleatings on bottom, $75.

BLACK SILK AND SATIN.

48 Walking-dress of satin-de-Lyon: jacket of brocade trimmed with large buttons; skirt trimmed with brocade and silk pleating on bottom; drapery of satin-de-Lyon, $38.

49 Walking-dress of satin-de-Lyon: basque trimmed in front with pleatings of same and jet buttons, back trimmed with loops of satin and jet tassels, sleeves to match; over-dress shirred and draped high in front and caught with loops of satin and jet tassels to show side-pleatings with revers of satin; back draped very full; box-pleats of satin on bottom of under-skirt, $35.

50 Walking-dress of satin-de-Lyon: plain basque with jetted cord and tassel on back; over-dress shirred in front and at sides and draped at the back; front of skirt with two deep flounces shirred in spaces; back with narrow box-pleating, $40.

51 Walking-dress of surah satin and Sicilian checked brocade: jacket of brocade looped on the hips to form points in front which are finished with crochet and steel balls, back slashed and caught up with loops of brocade and finished with balls, front and sleeves trimmed with buttons to match trimming; over-dress of checked brocade shirred in front and looped very high with slide and balls of amber and jet, back draped; skirt of surah satin with three clusters of fine tucks across

front, shell trimming and box-pleats of satin on bottom, back composed of three large box-pleats, $85.

52 Long-dress of satin-de-Lyon: back of basque slashed and ends finished with steel balls, trimmed with steel and jet ornaments; short skirt with apron-front drapery caught up at side with scarf of material and steel balls, back composed of two large double box-pleats without drapery, rose-pleating on bottom, $180.

MOURNING.

53 Walking-dress of cashmere: plain basque with postillion back; over-dress shirred in front and on sides, back draped to fall in two points, trimmed with tape fringe; box-pleating and shell-trimming on skirt, $18.

54 Walking-dress of crape cloth: English jacket trimmed with large buttons; long panels on sides of skirt finished with bias folds of material, five rows of French pleatings on front, sash ends knotted at the back, three narrow pleatings on bottom of skirt, $20.

55 Walking-dress of Henrietta cloth: polonaise draped very high on hips, neck and sleeves trimmed with material; narrow pleatings headed with three bias folds two inches wide on bottom of skirt, $22.

56 Cashmere: close-fitting double-breasted jacket with deep collar, cuffs and pockets of crape; apron-front over-skirt with fold of crape, plain short back; two alternate folds of crape and cashmere on front of skirt and one on back, box-pleating on bottom, $25.

57 Henrietta-cloth: deep basque with postillion back; over-dress trimmed with fringe: three knife-pleatings on bottom of skirt, $30.

58 Walking-dress of Imperial serge: pleated waist with deep shirred collar, sleeves with reversible cuffs; pointed front over-dress caught at side with silk girdle and shaped shawl-style at back; deep box-pleatings on skirt, $40.

59 Walking-dress of tamise cloth: waist trimmed with collarette of crape, and sleeves with double cuffs of same; fold of crape on over-dress; narrow pleating headed with bias fold of crape **nine inches deep** on skirt, $50.

60 Walking-dress of Chudda cloth trimmed with large buttons and mourning fringe: short English jacket with large pockets and revere collar of crape; diagonal drapery on skirt trimmed with deep fold of crape; kilt-pleating and three bias folds of crape on skirt, $65.

BUNTING, BLACK AND COLORED.

61 Walking-dress of black bunting with rows of white silk stitching on waist and over-dress to be worn with belt: waist pleated back and front; long apron-front skirt, with short sash ends for back, two narrow side-pleatings on bottom, $17.50.

62 Walking-dress of black French bunting with lace trimmings: plain waist trimmed with crochet buttons and lace; over-dress draped to effect double panier on sides and trimmed with lace, back draped; skirt trimmed in front with narrow side-pleatings and two side-pleatings on bottom, $25.

63 Walking-dress of seaside buntings in black or colors, made over silk skirt: plain waist slashed in back and looped with gros-grain ribbon bows, sleeves trimmed with cuffs and pleatings of bunting; skirt drapery trimmed with narrow pleatings and looped to show side-pleatings down front of skirt, long full shawl-back; narrow box-pleatings on bottom of skirt, $39.

64 Short walking-dress of white French bunting: pleated waist made with yoke, waist and sleeves trimmed with white crystal trimming; diagonal drapery on front of skirt caught at side with scarf of same, scarf finished with white crystal balls, short, full drapery at back; rose-pleating on bottom of skirt, $58.

65 House-dress of cream-colored French bunting: basque pointed front and back and cut short on hips, large silk bow on back, square neck filled in with Spanish lace, front of waist and sleeves trimmed with lace; long court-train skirt, trimmed with fine French pleatings and shell heading, front draped with bunting and trimmed with lace, $75.

GRENADINE.

66 Walking-dress: silk or satin skirt with one or two rows of box-pleatings or side-pleatings on bottom; draperies of material; fancy basque or same skirt with polonaise of grenadine $25.

67 Walking-dress with postillion basque: over-dress draped diagonally in front and finished with pleatings of material; on bottom of skirt one row of box-pleating and one row of side-pleatings, $30

68 Walking-dress of figured striped silk and mohair grenadine: waist trimmed with French lace, edging and satin bows; double apron-front skirt, with lace trimming, long, draped back; four rows of fine side-pleatings and lace edging, and three rows of same on back of skirt, $50.

69 Walking-dress of silk polka-dot brocade grenadine, trimmed with French lace: plain basque, back slashed and looped with satin bows and trimmed with French lace; skirt with double panier sides trimmed with lace and draped to show satin pleatings down front, back draped, bottom trimmed with narrow satin box-pleating and one of grenadine, $60.

70 Walking-dress of brocade grenadine with lace and satin trimmings: skirt draped and trimmed with lace, two narrow side-pleatings at bottom, $80.

BRIDAL DRESSES.

71 White silk and brocade: princess dress with draperies of brocade trimmed with fringe; narrow box-pleatings or side-pleatings on bottom of skirt; fancy basque, $80.

72 Creamy-white satin-duchess: basque long in front and back and trimmed on sides with pearl lace and fringe one half yard in depth; three-fourth sleeves of lace, surplice neck with pearl trimming; pearl lace drapery on front of skirt, double panier sides of satin finishing at back with three large pleats of satin running from waist to the rose-pleating which finishes the bottom of skirt, $135.

73 White brocade: square train finished at bottom with heavy silk cording; basque effect in front trimmed with crystal ornaments, square neck with large box-pleats of satin at back fifiishing in revers and filled in with dotted-net or Breton lace; three fourth sleeves with white crystal trimming on back finished with

BRIDAL DRESSES—Continued.

lace and pleatings; front of skirt of brocade, sides of satin-de-Lyon revered from front to give effect of shell trimming; rose-pleating of satin around front of skirt; garniture of orange-blossoms for neck, sleeves and skirt, $180.

RIDING HABIT.

74 Ladies' cloth in dark-blue, green, grey and black: plain French waist with postillion back, $55.

SWISS AND ORGANDIE.

These dresses are made of either organdie or Swiss

75 Walking-dress of Swiss: long basque edged with Italian lace; full round over-dress looped high on sides and trimmed with lace; short skirt finished with three narrow shirred flounces, $15.

76 Short princess dress of Swiss with Italian lace: plain waist with trimming of lace to effect square neck, shirred ruffle edged with lace on sleeves; double apron-front drapery of Swiss, back to match; two side pleatings on skirt, $18.

77 Short dress of Swiss: basque with polonaise, back looped and trimmed with lace and insertion; double apron-front drapery; kilt-pleating on underskirt, $25.

78 Evening-dress of white organdie: French waist of organdie and languedoc insertion, three-fourth sleeves made with insertion of lace and puffs of organdie finished with lace edging; over-dress caught up on side to show skirt-front of lace insertion; narrow, fine pleatings of organdie edged with lace at bottom of skirt, $35.

79 Short dress of organdie: half-fitting basque with edging and embroidered insertion; short apron-front over-skirt with sash back; skirt, with five shirred flounces of embroidery, $40.

80 Princess-dress of Swiss with Italian lace: waist trimmed with edging to give effect of basque front, back with three rows of insertion: drapery of Swiss with lace edging on front of skirt caught at side with large bows of white satin and flowers, very full drapery at back; alternate flounces of box and side-pleatings on bottom, $45.

81 Train-dress of organdie trimmed with Breton lace: basque trimmed around with lace and loops of ribbons; three-fourth sleeves of organdie and lace insertion; drapery on left side of skirt looped high to show seven graduated rows of insertion and edging; two rows of shirred flounces headed with puffing of organdie on bottom of skirt $48.

READY-MADE SUITS.

The following are kept in stock in diminishing quantities as the season advances. The bust measure and skirt length only are guaranteed, the other measures are in proportion; if other measures are necessary to insure a fit, the garment will need to be made to order.

1 Walking-dress of écru flannel, trimmed with fancy buttons: half-fitting jacket, double drapery on front of skirt with plain back; narrow box-pleating on front of under-skirt, and deep kilting on back, $14.

2 Walking-dress of olive-green cloth: plain basque with large cuffs and pockets of naterial: drapery looped high on right side, full short back falling in a point on left side; large side-pleating on back of skirt and narrow pleatings on front, $16.

3 Walking-dress of grey cloth: half-fitting jacket; full round apron-front over-skirt finished with hem and headed with five narrow tucks, draped at back and falling in a point at the right side; side-pleating nine inches deep on bottom of skirt, $18.

4 Walking-dress of navy-blue flannel: long basque in cuirass style fitting close over the hips and trimmed with plaid; over-dress with bias folds of plaid; one box-pleated ruffle of plaid on skirt, $22.
5 Walking-dress of black cloth: double-breasted close-fitting jacket trimmed with rows of stitching; large box-pleats on front of skirt and side-pleats on back with rows of stitching on bottom; drapery high in front finishing in revers at sides and joining back drapery, trimmed with stitching and with heavy silk cord and tassels in front, $24.
6 Walking-dress of garnet serge: plain waist trimmed on front and sleeves with brocade velvet; front of skirt with eleven rows of fine side-pleatings graduated and band of brocade on each side; side-pleating six inches deep on bottom, $25.
7 Walking-dress of brown flannel: short walking jacket with hood, trimmed with colored embroidery and silk cord and tassels; side-pleatings on bottom of skirt; long full drapery finished with deep hem and stitching, $25.
8 Walking-dress of fine summer camels-hair cloth with olive-silk trimming; basque with silk vest and piping of silk on bottom, revere cuffs and loops of silk on sleeves; front of under-skirt of large box-pleats of silk and camels-hair alternating and running half way, the back trimmed with narrower double pleats of camels-hair; front of over-skirt looped high on left side and trimmed with deep fold of silk, and on right side meeting with back drapery which is pointed and trimmed to match, $29.
9 Walking-dress of black armure cloth: tight-fitting basque with vest of worsted brocade, standing collar and reversible cuffs of brocade; shawl-draped over-skirt with band of brocade; two rows of knife-pleatings on skirt, $45.
10 Walking-dress of light écru silk-and-wool plaid combined with solid colors of darker shades; tight-fitting basque cut away in front, showing fine shirring of darker shade of satin giving vest effect, and finishing on sides with satin revers, back in two large double box-pleats, neck and sleeves trimmed with same shade of satin; under-skirt of same shade of satin trimmed with shirring of satin twelve inches wide and at bottom with narrow shirred ruffle headed with five rows of shirring and two very narrow puffs; diagonal draped over-skirt of plaid falling in two points in front showing the shirring on under-skirt, $47.

LADIES' WRAPPERS.

Ladies' wrappers are in princess style and princess front with flowing watteau backs. They are often of cashmere or silk. Cashmere is trimmed with silk. They may be shirred back and front and trimmed with many full ruchings of creamy lace. Mirecourt and any cheaper lace in Mechlin design is used. Beautiful dressing sacques in pale tinted cashmere are embroidered in flowers in natural tints and shades. Only the bust measure and front length guaranteed in the first seven enumerated.

1 Calico, $0.75.
2 Calico: princess back and Spanish flounce with edged-fold, ruffle on neck and sleeves, $1.25.
3 Cambric: princess back, double flounce, trimmed around neck and down front with edged-fold and ruffle, $2.25.
4 Lawn: princess or Gabrielle back, two ruffles edged with lace on bottom, ruffle around neck and down front, $3.25.
5 Flannel: empress train, pockets, cuffs, and collar corded, $4.50.
6 Cashmere: pockets, cuffs and collar of silk or satin plain or quilted, $6.
7 Cashmere, princess style: collar, cuffs, pockets and fold down front of satin stripe and silk, $8.

No. 10, $12.

No. 11, $15.

LORD & TAYLOR, NEW YORK. 33

LADIES' WRAPPERS—Continued.

8 Flannel, all colors: revers on back; collar, cuffs and pockets of plaid, $9.
9 Flannel, all colors: pipings of cashmere on collar, cuffs and pockets, $10.
10 Flannel, in all colors, with sailor-collar: pockets, cuffs and collar, trimmed with gold lace, $12.
11 Flannel, in all shades: front, collar, cuffs and pockets of brocade, $15.

16 Cashmere, all colors, with languedoc lace : shirred trimming down both sides of the front ; double box-pleated flounce on bottom, with shell trimming of lace above ; full trimming of lace, $48.
17 Cashmere, in all colors : front of puffed satin elaborately trimmed with Mirecourt lace ; triple watteau hood, lined with satin ; trimmed with cord and tassel, $48.

No. 12, $15.

12 Flannel, all shades: hood lined with plaid, collar, cuffs and pockets of plaid, $15.
13 Plaid, all-wool: watteau back, hood lined with satin, $17.
14 Nainsook, white : side-plaiting on bottom with embroidered flounce above; insertion and edging and blue ribbon bows down front, $25.
15 Plaid, all-wool: hood lined with satin, sashes finished with tassels, $25.

No. 13, $17.

18 Black cashmere : embroidered trimming to form sacque ; front of pearl silk and black ruffles alternating, with Spanish lace falling over ; watteau back with bows of pearl and black, mixed, $56. May be had in all colors.
19 Black moire stripe silk : front of cardinal shirred satin trimmed with Spanish lace; hood lined with cardinal satin ; triple watteau box-plaited flounce, $70. Made with different colored fronts.

No. 14, $25.   No. 15, $25.

No. 16, $48.   No. 17, $48.

No. 18, $56.   No. 19, $70.

MISSES' SUITS.

Dresses of flannel will be used in standard blue flannel as well as in all other colors. They are made in smoothly-fitting princess shape and are trimmed either with a plain or striped material of contrasting color. A dress of brown flannel is combined with cream: it is then made with a vest of the cream, a group of five tucks is placed on each side of the front and extended on either side down the back to the kilt-pleating which borders the dress and is alternately of the brown and cream, the curved fold, called the jacket-piece which finishes the upper part of the dress, of brown, falls over the pleating and is surmounted by a second fold in cream color. A grey flannel is thus combined with cardinal, a navy-blue with black-and-white stripe. Roman stripes often trim a dress in this way. Coquettish little hoods are often seen on children's dresses. A good many dresses are double-breasted.

In ordering, give measure around the chest and on inside of sleeve, the **length in front and the age of the child.**

No. 1.   No. 2.

1 Gingham: double-breasted; three box-pleatings all around.

3 years,	$1.75	6 years,	$2.50
4	2.00	8	2.75
5	2.25	10	3.25

2 Gingham, trimmed with embroidery: tabs edged with embroidery in the back.

3 years,	$2.50	6 years,	$3.25
4	2.75	8	3.50
5	3.00	10	4.00

LORD & TAYLOR, NEW YORK.

No. 3

No. 4

3 Sailor suit of dark-blue flannel; double box-pleats, with four rows of white braid all around skirt; blouse trimmed to match.

    6 years, $6.50   10 years,   7.00
    8   6.75   12   7.50
           14 years, 8.00

4 Dark blue flannel: double-breasted, with two rows of braid on each side.

    3 years, $4.50   6 years, 5.00
    4   4.75   8   5.50
    5   5.00   10   6 00

No. 5.   No. 6

5 Piqué, princess dress, trimmed with woven-edge embroidery.

 4 years, $5.75 8 years, 6.50
 6   6.00 10 7.25

6 Piqué: skirt with ruffles of open-work embroidery and row of insertion above; jacket with vest front and ruffle of embroidery and insertion all around.

 10 years, $15.00 12 years, 15.50
   14 years. 16.00

LORD & TAYLOR, NEW-YORK. 39

No. 7.   No. 8.

7 Piqué, two-piece suit: plaiting of material on skirt with ruffle of embroidery and insertion above; jacket with vest front trimmed with embroidery to match skirt.

    8 years, $6.25   12 years, 7.50
    10   7.00   14   8.00

8 Piqué, princess dress: double-breasted, trimmed with embroidery on each side of front; back made to form a jacket.

    4 years, $4.25   8 years, 5.00
    6   4.50   10   5.50

No. 9.   No. 10.

9 Piqué, trimmed with very rich embroidery: double-breasted front with ruffle of embroidery and insertion on each side to simulate a jacket; three ruffles of embroidery headed with a row of insertion across the front of skirt.

    4 years, $16.00   8 years, 17.50
    6   16.75   10   18.25

10 Piqué, princess dress: front made to form a jacket; two ruffles of embroidery headed by a row of insertion on the 3, 4, 5 and 6 years sizes; three ruffles on the 8 and 10 years sizes; center of back trimmed in the same manner.

    3 years, $4.50   6 years, 5.50
    4   4.75   8   6.25
    5   5.00   10   6.75

LORD & TAYLOR, NEW-YORK. 41

No. 11.   No. 12.

11 Organdie, trimmed with vermicella lace: back and front trimmed alike; side-plaiting with edging and insertion all around skirt.

    6 years, $12.00   8 years, 12.50
        10 years, 13.00

12 Organdie, trimmed with Italian lace: front with puffs and insertion; back with yoke of puffs and insertion and four rows of insertion below; two ruffles edged with lace and row of insertion in each.

    4 years, $5.75   6 years, 6.00
        8 years, 6.50

13 Double-breasted princess dress of dark-blue flannel trimmed with grey flannel; box-pleating around bottom headed with a band of grey.

   3 years, $3.00   5 years, 3.50
   4   3.25   6   3.75
         8 years, 4.00

14 Dresses of dark-blue flannel trimmed with grey, garnet trimmed with écru, and grey trimmed with brown: box-pleating of both shades at the bottom; vest of the contrasting shade.

   3 years, $3.50   6 years, 4.25
   4   3.75   8   4.75
   5   4.00   10   5.25

15 Dress of fine dark-blue flannel piped with cardinal: three box-pleats front and back, cuffs and collar of dark-blue and cardinal, gilt buttons with red figures.

   3 years, $4.50   6 years, 5.25
   4   4.75   8   5.75
   6   5.00   10   6.25

16 Dresses in different shades of fine all-wool cloth: upper part in box-pleats slightly fitted to the figure, sailor collar, sash on back, flounce laid on in box-pleats; trimmed with chain-stitching of contrasting color.

   3 years, $3.75   5 years, 4.50
   4   4.00   6   5.00
         8 years, 5.75

17 Dresses in different shades of fine all-wool cloth: upper part in box-pleats slightly fitted to the figure, flounce laid on in box-pleats, sash on back; collar, cuffs, sash, and band on the bottom of flounce of contrasting colors.

   3 years, $4.00   5 years, 4.75
   4   4.25   6   5.25
         8 years, 6.00

18 Dresses of various shades of cloth: the upper part with two groups of fine tucks back and front; the lower part in kilt-pleats of two contrasting colors.

   4 years, $10.00   8 years, 12.00
   6   11.00 10   13.50

19 Sailor suits in dark-blue flannel: box-pleated skirt with strap of flannel stitched with old-gold on each pleat; blouse waist, sailor collar pointed in front and trimmed with three rows of gold braid.

   4 years, $7.00 10 years, 8.75
   6   7.50   12   9.50
   8   8.00   14   10.25

20 Dress of armure and camels-hair cloth with silk and velvet brocade: vest of brocade with five tucks on each side, back the same; lower part in double box-pleats with brocade above; sash of material, 6 to 10 years, $20 to 25.

21 Three-piece suit of dark-blue flannel: double-breasted waist with box-pleat on each side, one box-pleat in back, collar and cuffs stitched with old-gold and red; over-skirt stitched with old-gold and red; kilt-pleating on skirt.

   10 years, $8.75 14 years, 11.00
   12   9.75 16   12.00

22 Dress of dark and light-grey and écru shades of de biege trimmed with fancy striped material or plaid, (can be made entirely of the plain goods if desired): tucked-ruffles and box-pleatings on back, apron-front; box-pleated waist with belt and pocket at the side;—or full over-dress with two or three tucked ruffles on skirt, 12 to 16 years, $18 to 25.

23 Piqué dress with jacket front, and kilt-pleats in back: sizes 3 to 6 years have two ruffles of embroidery across front, sizes 8 and 10 years have three ruffles.

   3 years, $2.50   6 years, 3.50
   4   2.75   8   4.00
   5   3.00   10   4.50

24 Piqué dress buttoned in the back: front trimmed with edging and insertion to form a jacket; three ruffles of embroidery headed by a row of insertion across front and back; pleatings of piqué on sides.

   4 years, $5.25   8 years, 6.25
   6   5.75 10   6.75

25 Piqué princess dress with embroidery: pleated vest in front, edging and insertion all around jacket; three rows of insertion and one of edging on back from neck to waist forming point at waist; two ruffles of embroidery headed by a row of insertion all around skirt (8 and 10 years sizes have three ruffles).

   3 years, $7.75   6 years, 9.50
   4   8.25   8   10.50
   5   8.75   10   11.50

26 White organdie princess dress trimmed with Italian lace: six ruffles edged with wide lace up the front and five at the back; waist part with puffs and rows of insertion, paniers on sides, 16 years, $21.50.

27 White organdie dress in two pieces: front of skirt with tucked ruffles edged with lace, puffs and rows of insertion on back of skirt, vest of puffs and insertion, waist buttoned at back, $19.

CLOAKS.

It is an era of many styles in cloaks, especially of the mingling of several styles in one garment. The ulster is made in loose sacque shape, with large dolman sleeves, which, instead of flowing are shirred close to the wrist. The neck is finished by a flat collar of pleating, and a nine-inch pleating is placed around the bottom, and the cloak becomes the dolman-ulster, a graceful négligé garment, which retains the length and the most desirable characteristics of the ulster, while it has lost something of its masculine appearance. The Havelock, a mantle with dolman sleeves, is shown for spring in plain and mixed cloths. It is lined with plain or pin-head checked surah, and the pointed hood which is seen on these garments is finished with a heavy cord and tassels and lined with similar silk, and the front and lapels of the garment are finished with buttons covered with silk.

Most garments in dark and grey-mixed cloths are trimmed with pleating and shirred ruffles of the material. A great deal of shirring is seen on the new wraps, as the soft cashmere-like nature of the goods used render such trimming graceful. All the handsome cloaks are lined with surah in some bright shade like pale-blue, gold-color or red. Cloth-wraps with gay under-surfaces, are piped with a narrow edge of color in dull red, old-gold or blue, and plain dark-blue, and other cloths are similarly finished with piping of satin in contrasting shades. Gay Roman stripes are used to trim these wraps and to line the hoods. The dragoon jacket is a close-fitting, single-breasted coat, with a belt and chatelaine bag of the material, all other pockets being dispensed with.

Satin-de-Lyon, satin surah and brocaded satin are the materials of handsome wraps. A new dolman in graceful design was made of silk grenadine brocaded with velvet. It was handsomely trimmed with a shirred back of satin, and a fullness of box-pleats was added below the waist at the back. Full frills and ruchings of Spanish lace edged the garment, and handsome steel ornaments were placed at intervals above the lace, and hanging ornaments of steel were added. Handsome black wraps are trimmed with Spanish or French lace, and with jet or steel passementeries. Plainer black wraps are of repped cashmere and are trimmed with lace and jet, or silk passementeries.

The garments illustrated are kept in stock in the following sizes: bust-measure 32, 34, 36, 38, 40: this only is guaranteed, if other measures are necessary to insure a fit the garment will need to be made to order.

The Ulster is in favor as the most convenient, comfortable and useful garment yet devised for traveling, riding and driving.

LADIES' SIZES.

Bust Measure.	Length in back.
34 inches.	54 inches.
36 "	56 "
38 "	56 "
40 "	58 "
42 "	50 "

No. 1, $16.

1 Dolman-ulster, made from light mixed cloth: three seams in back, double-breasted and straight in front, three small capes; corded colored silk around entire garment, loose sleeves, pockets in front, $16.
2 Ulster of small checked cloth; double-breasted; close-fitting back, loose front, pockets on sides, six buttons down front and on cuffs, $17.
3 Walking-coat, in invisible checks, all-wool: plaits set in at back and stitched down and trimmed with fancy buttons; bust sizes 32, 34, 36, 38, $c.

No. 2, $17.

4 Walking-jacket ("Dragoon,") from light mixed cloth: plain, tight-fitting, single-breasted, buttoned all the way down; cuffs and neck finished with small box-plaiting of cloth, lined with satin; belt around waist with buckle, small satchel at side attached to belt with silk cord, $10.
5 English walking-jacket of mixed and plaid cloths, lined throughout with silk: double-breasted, rolling collar, closed in back, with lapels turned back; skirts of jacket cut open; hood lined with silk; seven rows of stitching around jacket and lapels; pockets in front; bronze and gilt buttons, $25.
6 Dolman of cashmere serge, all-wool, made in mantle shape; trimmed all around with silk and bead fringe headed with narrow lace and gimp; pointed

hood trimmed full with lace and beads, lined with shirred satin and finished at bottom with bow and ends; neck trimmed to match, $10.

7 Dolman of cashmere, cut to form mantle over arms; tabs in front, garment trimmed with fringe headed with lace and passementre ; long pointed hood, and neck trimmed to match, $18.

8 Dolman, from ribbed cashmere, cut to form sleeves: finished all around with two rows of fringe with lace and gimp above ; neck trimmed in same manner with bow in front ; buttons down the front ; round hood lined with satin, gathered around the bottom, trimmed with lace and finished with long satin ribbons and spikes at bottom, $27.

10 Dolman of black satin-de-Lyon: trimmed all around with fringe and two rows of lace above the fringe and one row of passementerie above lace; hood lined with black satin gaged and trimmed in same style as the dolmans with long strings of satin ribbon from end of hood ; neck to match, $40.

11 Dolman of black satin-de-Lyo cut to form sleeves over arms: trimmed all around with jet fringe, one row of Spanish lace above fringe headed with row of narrow lace and jet ornaments, bow of ribbons on each side ; hood lined with black satin shirred, trimmed with jet fringe, and finished at bottom with long bow and ends of satin ribbons with jet spikes ; neck trimmed with lace to match, $45.

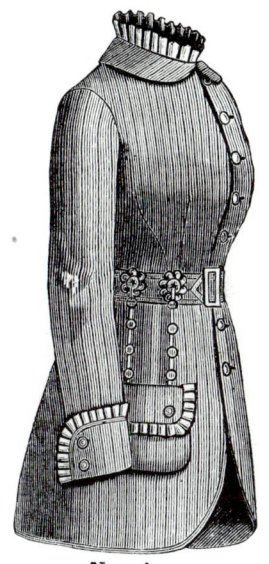

No. 3, $9.

No. 4, $13.

9 Havelock Dolman of navy-blue cloth, lined throughout with small black and white checked silk: sleeves turned back and faced with same silk ; two lapels on back with three buttons to match silk ; single-breasted with same buttons all the way down; long, pointed hood lined with same silk that lines the garment ; heavy cord and tassels to match, $30.

12 Cape of black ribbed silk: long tabs in front trimmed all around with fringe and heading of lace and passementerie ; hood lined with black satin, gaged and trimmed with lace and jet ornaments and finished at end with bow of satin ribbon, $18.

LORD & TAYLOR, NEW YORK.

No. 5, $25.

No. 7, $18.

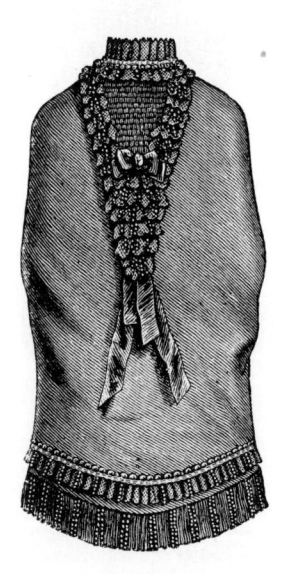

No. 6, $10.

No. 8, $27.

LORD & TAYLOR, NEW YORK. 47

No. 10, $40.

No. 9, $30.

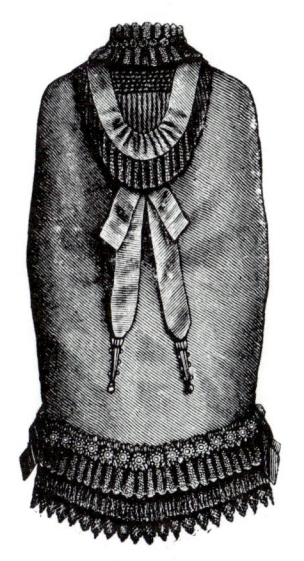

No. 11, $45.

No. 12, $18.

CHILDREN'S CLOAKS.

Most of the wraps worn by ladies are modeled in simpler styles for children. Single and double-breasted coats, Havelocks, and quaintest of all, dolmans, called Tom Thumb dolmans, are furnished for little ones and misses. Mixed cloth and invisible checks, with and without gay threads of color, are the materials of coats and Havelocks, but many of the more dressy little dolmans are made of drab, corded or figured cloth, lined with surah and trimmed with gay plaid velvet.

A double-breasted jacket in mixed écru cloth, with a close little hood lined with navy-blue silk, is finished by a rolling collar, small pockets and cuffs of the material. Another little sacque in invisible check is made with a deep cape collar of dark velvet, surmounted by a smaller one of the material, the cuffs and small pocket flaps are of the velvet. A little cutaway coat, more closely fitting than the others, is single-breasted, and is made with an English back, and the side forms are sloped into postillions, just below the waist, and fall over a group of side pleats which reach to the bottom of the garment.

In ordering give measure around the chest, the length of sleeve inside, and age of child.

1 Child's sacque of cream-colored cloth with very small check: hood lined with shirred satin of dark-blue or cardinal; back of sacque and hood trimmed with ornaments of silk cord the color of the cloth.
    4 years, $5.00   8 years, 6.00
    6   5.50   10   6.50

2 Walking-jacket of brown and grey mixtures with small check: pleatings set in at side-seams; finished with stitching and bone buttons.
    12 years, $6.50   14 years, 7.00
    16 years, 7.50

3 "The Havelock," made of light shades of checked cloth: hood lined with cardinal and black checked silk and finished with two tassels.
    8 years, $11.00   12 years, 13.00
    10   12.00   14   14.00
    16 years, 15.00.

4 Dolman shaped, ("Tom Thumb") of light-tan and cream-colored cloths, with deep collar or hood: trimmed with bright colored Scotch plaids, and lined with silk in a variety of shades.
    8 years, $18.00   12 years, 22.00
    10   20.00   14   25.00
    16 years, 28.00

LORD & TAYLOR, NEW YORK. 49

No. 1.

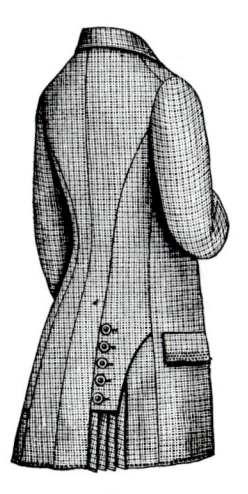

No. 2.

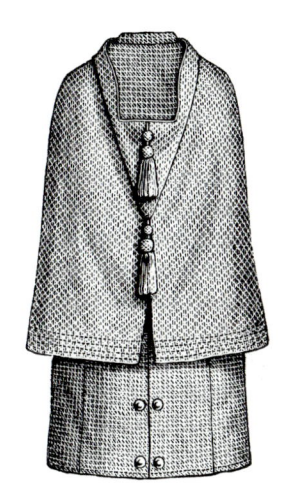

No. 3

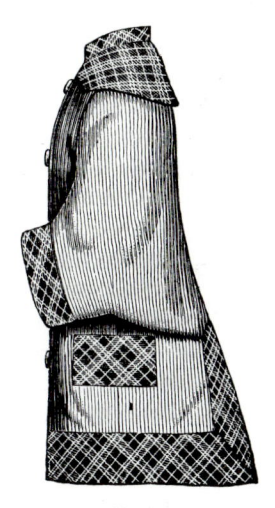

No. 4

MILLINERY.

New bonnets are in fancy braids of various kinds. Tuscan lace braids, rough-and-ready straws, leghorn and chips are all used. Sun-burned Tuscany straw, in numberless fine open work patterns, is often mingled with gold, silver or steel lace, and sometimes with strips of uncut velvet. Cut steel is everywhere used and though it has not replaced jet, all jet now used is mixed with steel or tinsel. Bonnet crowns of black net are wrought with cut steel beads, and bonnets are made of steel cord sewed in spirals over the frame.

Flowers and feathers are both used. One does not displace the other. The bandeaux of roses, clusters of poppies and chrysanthemums have very little foliage. Light coral shades, écru and old-gold are all seen on new bonnets. Cigar shades, évêque or bishop's purple, acajou or mahogany color give relief to lighter tints. Steel-grey is combined with gold and with sage green. Reséda or mignonette green is a favorite color in millinery, and mignonette flowers in various shades are very popular. Ombré is a feature of all materials in trimmings this year. Feathers, flowers and soft satin merveilleux trimmings are all used.

Light trimmings of lace, dotted net or soft satin surah are employed for all new hats. Bonnet strings are very wide, some as wide as sash ribbons. Strings of piece material are often used in place of ribbons. Medium poke shapes, small capotes and cottage bonnets are preferred. A few round hats are shown.

A graceful little bonnet in fancy Tuscan braid is trimmed with jabots of cream-white Mirecourt lace, with shaded pompons and ostrich tips in pale-pink. A Tuscan braid mingled with steel lace is trimmed with a shaded feather of pink running into cream. A bandeau of full-blown roses in pink and cream is placed across the top and partly veiled by a strip of steel lace. A large black chip hat is tastefully trimmed with ombré satin surah in fancy pattern. The brim is edged with a broad plume of cardinal-color which gradually shades into pale-pink. A quaint leghorn, poke-shape, is trimmed with old-gold and shaded chrysanthemums mingling gold écru and cream. The brim is lined with gold-colored satin, a broad band of cardinal velvet is set inside, over which falls a full pleating of creamy lace.

We keep a large stock of hats and bonnets, both trimmed and untrimmed; but the greater part of our trimmed work is made to order. Our facilities are large and very short notice is required.

HATS AND BONNETS.

UNTRIMMED.

1. Cantons, $0.25
2. Milans, 0.50 to 1.50
3. Imitation chip hats, 0.50 to 1.00.
4. Imitation chip bonnets, 0.50 to 1.00
5. Chip hats and bonnets, all shapes, 1.25 to 2.75
6. Tuscan hats and bonnets 1.50 to 6.00
7. Leghorn hats and bonnets, 0.75 to 2.25
8. Fancy Swiss braids 1.25 to 5.50
9. Fancy mixed black and white hair 1.00 to 2.25
10. Misses' school hats, 0.25 to 1.50
11. Misses' school hats trimmed 0.50 to 2.00
12. Boys' cloth caps, 0.85 to 2.50
13. Boys' straw hats, 0.50 to 2.25
14. Infants' lace hoods, 0.75 to 4.00
15. Infants' lace caps, 0.65 to 2.50

TRIMMED:

1. Straw bonnets, $2.50 to 10.00
2. Chip bonnets, 4.50 to 20.00
3. Fancy lace bonnets, 7.00 to 25.00
4. Fancy lace and steel bonnets, 8.00 to 20.00
5. Silk bonnets, 4.00 to 15.00
6. Crape bonnets, 2.50 to 20.00.

FLOWERS, FEATHERS, &C.

Flowers of all the new shades in great variety, ostrich tips and plumes both plain and shaded. New designs in jet, gilt, steel and pearl ornaments.

TRIMMED HATS.

No. 1

No. 2

1. Fancy Swiss straw lace trimmed across the front with daisies, fancy ribbon across the top, with strings of the same material, $5. 6. 7.

2. Black chip, edged with Swiss lace: cluster of pansies on left side, with loop of straw-colored satin and gros-grain ribbon in front; folds of black velvet carried around on right side and across the back terminating under the string, $7. 9. 12.

No. 3

No. 5

3   Fancy Swiss straw lace, trimmed with bronze surah ribbon: bows on right side fastened with ornaments in form of hairpin; strings of same material brought across the crown, with cluster of shaded bronze poppies and buds in front; inside trimmed with puffing of satin to match, $5, 6, 7.

5   Écru chip, "St. George" walking hat, faced over brim with écru shaded gauze plush, and shaded plume to match; bow of shaded ribbon in front with spear ornament, $6, 8, 10.

No. 4

No. 6

4   Black chip, trimmed with fancy shaded satin merveilleux; three black ostrich tips drooping over left side and one drooping back, $10. 12. 15.

6   Black chip "Pixley," edged with steel straw braid mixed: trimmed with ostrich plumes and tips and dagger ornament, $15. 18. 20. 25.

LORD & TAYLOR, NEW YORK. 53

No. 7

No. 8

7 Straw-colored Swiss lace mixed with steel: wreath of flowers across the front with fancy ostrich pompon, and plaid ribbon seven inches wide to match, all the trimmings in antique shades, $8. 12. 15.

8 White Tuscan straw: rolling brim faced with dark cardinal gauze plush, edged with fancy steel braid, trimmed with cream-colored satin and with three ostrich tips, cardinal shaded to cream falling over the flaring side of brim, $5. 6. 8.

RIBBONS.

Ombré effects are the leading feature in new ribbons and take the place of damassé or brocaded styles. These shaded ribbons are often plaided with gay colors and crossed with many threads of gold forming a broken plaid on an ombré ground. Some ribbons are in stripes of different colors which are each graded in ombré style, while other ribbons show a dark center of navy-blue, black or myrtle-green and are finished on either side by a shaded edge in flame color or cardinal, beginning at a shade so dark it can scarcely be distinguished from the center, and shading into the lightest tint.

WIDTHS.

| Nos. 1½ | 2 | 3 | 4 | 7 | 9 | 12 | 16 | 22 | 30 | 40 |

Price per yard.

BLACK SATIN AND GROS-GRAIN.
Quality A:
No.   9   12   16   20   30
Price, 0.32 .40 .50 .57 .65
Quality B:
No.   5   7   9   12   16   22   30   40   60
Price, 0.15 .22 .28 .33 .40 .50 .55 .60 .70
Quality C:
No.   4   5   7   9   12   16   22   30   40
Price, 0.12 .14 .17 .22 .27 .33 .37 .43 .50
Quality D:
No.   4   5   7   9   12   16   20
Price, $0.08 .12 .14 .17 .23 .27 .35

COLORED SATIN AND GROS-GRAIN.
Quality E:
No.   5   7   9   12   16   22   40
Price, 0.17 .20 .25 .30 .37 .50 .55
Quality F:
No.   4   5   7   9   12   16   22
Price, 0.09 .12 .14 .16 .22 .28 .35

BLACK GROS-GRAIN.
Quality G:
No.   5   7   9   12   16   22
Price, 0.15 .20 .28 .35 .45 .55
Quality H, Italian Faille:
No.   3   4   5   7   9   12   16   20   30   40
Price, 0.15 .18 .22 .28 .35 .45 .55 .60 .70 .80

COLORED GROS-GRAIN.
Quality I:
No.   5   7   9   12   12
Price, 0.12 .14 .17 .22 .27

FANCY RIBBONS.
All colors and designs, 0.20 .30 .40 .50 .75 .85 1. 1.25 to 1.50

SATIN SURAH RIBBON.
No.   12   16   22   30   40   60 100 200 300
Price, 0.25 .35 .50 .65 .75 .85 1.00 1.10 1.25

SATIN SURAH RIBBON, SHADED.
No.   30   40   60 100 200 300
Price, 0.75 .90 1.10 1.25 1.50 1.75

SASH RIBBONS, ETC.
1   Gros-grain, 6 inches, 0.50 to .65
              7   .60   .75
2   Satin and gros-grain :
    6 inches, 0.90 to 1.50
3   Brocade, 6 inches, 1.00 to 4.00
              7   1.70   4.50
4   Roman and fancy, 0.60 to 2.00
5   Ribbons with corded edge and satin edge:
No.   1½   2   4   5   7   9   12
Price, 0.03 .04 .06 .07 .09 .12 .17
6   Satin ribbons with plain and feather edge.
7   Taffeta.

SHAWLS.

Handsome square shawls with entire centers in steel-gray or black have gay borders and elaborate corner designs of double palm-leaves in rich India camels-hair. These shawls draped into graceful dolmans by artistic hands will be favorite wraps for spring and summer, and are far less expensive than solid India wraps.

The Langtry shawl—sold only by this house—with plain center of cream-white, pale-blue, cardinal or beige has a border in India camels-hair or in odd antique style and will be a pleasant shoulder covering for cool summer evenings at watering places. These wraps with black centers and antique borders are especially liked by elderly ladies. Gay little shawls in Roman stripes will be used for evening wraps and for country wear.

Fleecy Berlin wool shoulder shawls in white, pale-blue and rose are as much used as ever.

FOR EVENING WEAR.

1 Berlin, red, blue, or white, $3. 4. 5. 6. 7.
2 Berlin, open-worked, fancy fringe, 2.25 2.50 3. 3.50 4. 5. 6.
3 Shetland, white, blue, red, 1.50 2.25 2.50 3. 3.50 4.
4 Persian, white matelassé center, with Persian border, 16.
5 Persian, white center, with Persian border, 10. 12. 14.
6 Tsatlee silk shoulder-shawls, 9. 10. 11.50 12. 14.

FOR OUT-DOOR WEAR.

1 Fancy striped, all colors, $7.
2 Persian matelassé, gold and black, gold and brown, gold and blue, plain gray, 15. 16. 17.
3 Plaid, all colors, 4. 5. 6. 7. 8. 10.
4 Scotch plaid, all clans, 5. 5.50
5 Scotch plaid, long, all clans, 5. 6. 7. 8. 10.
6 Domestic, square, all colors, 2.50 3. 3.50 4. 4.50
7 Domestic, long, all colors, 4.50 5. 6. 7. 8. 9.
8 Himalayan, subdued colors, 10.

9 Reversible: velvet, drab, brown, or gray on one side, fancy stripe or plaid on the other, 8. 10. 12. 14. 16.
10 Paisley broché, scarlet or black center, 10. 12. 15. 18. 20. 22. 25.
11 Paisley broché, long, 15. 18. 20. 22. 25. 28. 30. 35. 40. 45. 50. 55. 60. 65. 70. 75.
12 Broché, striped, 8. 10. 12. 15. 18. 20.
13 Broché, striped, long, 12. 15. 18. 20.
14 French camels-hair, India colors, 15. 20. 25. 30. 35. 40. 45. 50.
15 Cashmere, black, square, 3. 4. 5. 6. 7. 8. 9. 10. 11. 12.
16 Cashmere, black, long, 4.50 5. 5.50 6. 7. 8. 9. 10. 11. 12. 14. 16. 18. 20. 22. 25.
17 Cashmere, black, embroidered, square, 10. 12. 15. 18. 20. 22. 24. 25. 30. 35. 40. 45. 50. 55. 60.

INDIA SHAWLS.

1 Camels-hair, $35. 40. 45. 50. 55. 60. 65. 70. 75. 100. to 300.
2 Valley Cashmere, 150. 185. 200. 250. 275. 300. 325. 350. 400. to 1,000.
3 Stella, black and scarlet, 38. to 275.
4 Breakfast shawls in black, scarlet, blue, gray, drab and cardinal, 25. 35.
5 "Langtry" in all colors, 25. 35.

SILKS, SATINS AND VELVETS.

Gros-grain has now a formidable rival in surah, the soft twilled silk which has been used in neckties. New black gros-grain however is now almost as soft as surah. It has been the special object of the merchant to secure these fabrics in qualities which are as yielding and as pliant as the finest cashmere, yet so elastic that practically they cannot be wrinkled. A yard may be crumpled in the hand, yet it returns as smooth as if it had not been disturbed. This is true of the best qualities of gros-grain. The use of inferior qualities, sold under attractive prices, has tended to depreciate all qualities, and has brought into market its new rival the twilled surah.

Black satin surahs take the place of dresses of black satin, and are largely used for all purposes where satin was formerly employed. For visiting dresses satin surahs are in stylish condor browns, laurier—the red of our mountain laurel,—dark myrtle-green, garnet and other colors. There are many varieties of these soft draping fabrics. Beautiful changeable satin surahs, which call to mind the old-fashioned Turk satin or Levantine silk dear to the hearts of our grandmothers, are among the new importations. The satin surface in tints of maize, pearl-grey, drab, dark Russian green, navy-blue and black is woven over brilliantly contrasting grounds of Vandyke red, canary color, ruby, old-gold, French blue, salmon-pink, or porcelain-green. But the gay under-surfaces only show through the sheer of the more quiet colors. These rich fabrics form the veritable chameleon costume, in shadow showing only the dark or neutral-tinted satin surface, but in strong light throwing out splendid gleams of the brilliant color beneath. A flood of sunlight will suddenly transform a quiet dress of drab satin into a gay toilette gorgeous with ruby color.

New brocades in quaint Eastern figures are often mingled with threads of tinsel. In one pattern in medium design, but with thickly-wrought surface can be traced the curious head, curving tusks and winding trunk of the elephant. Cream-white brocades are mingled in large, handsome patterns with threads of gold or silver, and these stately damassés will be used for bridal dresses united with plain satin.

Ombré-shaded satins, bayadere and Roman stripes, are used for garniture to take the place of brocades. The ombré satin grades a color from selvage to selvage, and it is said one hundred different tones of color are seen in the same fabric, beginning with the lightest tint and ending with the darkest shade. Often the satin is in broad stripes in ombré style of medium colors, or a shaded goods is crossed by narrow stripes also shaded. Bayadere stripes show Roman colors mingled with maize or condor brown and other neutral colors. There is a good deal of gold in these stripes, and many bands in chiné effect. Threads of gold tinsel and bands of gold tinsel cloth add gorgeous garniture to coloring already Oriental. Persian stripes, gay plaided grounds with little set figures of overshot, are shown in all the gay tints and shades of the season, so marked by brilliant coloring and novel effect.

Gros de l'Indes is a soft India silk which is crossed in broken plaids by gay lines in contrasting colors and stripes of dark velvet, and often by threads of gold. Gay surah silk in Moorish colors and styles show a plaided ground in which garnet, gold, sultaine, pale-blue, and bronze are variously mingled, scattered over with double polka-dots of black velvet. Many new figured velvets mingle patterns of uncut velvet on a darker ground of cut velvet. Louisine silks and foulard silks are among the low-priced goods. The former have stripes, checks, dashes and bars of a single thread, and combine many gay Madras colors, yet with quiet effect. Foulard silks are in dark grounds with polka-dots of cream or white. The soft silks are made in dresses entirely of one material with facing bows and scarf sashes of solid color. Black brocaded grenadines are usually in Mexicaine grounds. They are blocked with black velvet or strewn with large or small figures of tulips, pansies and other patterns in black plush. The window pattern in grenadine consists of four blocks of grenadine outlined and surrounded by double lines of plush. Sometimes the grenadine blocks which form the window are in gold. Tasteful black grenadines are strewn with tiny ferns in velvet. Brocaded and striped grenadines are often used for the basque alone, while the skirts are of plain iron grenadine or smooth sewing silk grenadine with the brocaded or striped goods for trimming.

Messrs. Bonnet & Co., of Lyons, France, have made us their agents in this market for their "Duchesse" black silks: we recommend this silk as being beyond all others the best silk made—in fact, the standard of excellence.

BLACK SILKS AND SATINS.

Silks for Dresses.

1. Bonnet, *Duchesse*. Made of the best quality of French raw-silk, without the addition of any substance for the purpose of increasing its weight. The prices, therefore, vary according to weight alone. It is of a fine soft satin finish and durable; the standard of excellence. 19 to 23 inches, $1.15 1.25 1.50 1.75 2. 2.25 2.50 2.75 3. 3.25 3.50 3.75 4. 4.25 4.50 4.75 5. 5.50
2. Poncet, *gros de France*. Well known in the Paris and Lyons markets as first-class in all respects. 24 to 25 inches, 2. 2.25 2.50 2.75 3. 3.25 3.50 4. 5.
3. Bellon, *cachemire de soie*. Showy, soft and durable. We keep only the finer grades. 21 to 24 inches, 1.50 1.75 2. 2.25 2.50 2.75 3. 3.25 3.50
4. Teillard, *gros-grain*. Durable and of good finish. We keep only heavy grades suitable for cloaks, etc. 23 to 25 inches, 2. 2.25 2.50 2.75 3. 3.25 3.50
5. Tapissier, *cachemire de soie*. A well-known and approved brand. We keep only the finer grades. 23 to 24 inches, 1.75 2. 2.25 2.50 2.75 3. 3.25 3.50
6. Guinet, both *cachemire de soie* and *gros-grain*. A well-known and popular silk. 20 to 22 inches, 1.25 1.50 1.75 2. 2.25 2.50 2.75 3.
7. Westminster, medium-grain. A French silk of good quality and finish. 20 to 21 inches, 1.50 1.75 2. 2.25 2.50 2.75 3.
8. American, both *cachemire* and *gros-grain*. More durable than any foreign brand of equal value. We guarantee this silk not to cut in the least or to pull apart on any ordinary strain. 18 to 22 inches, 1. 1.25 1.50 1.75 2. 2.25 2.50
9. Lord & Taylor, American, cashmere finish. Made of the best quality of French and Italian raw-silks, without the addition of any substance for the purpose of increasing its weight. The prices, therefore, vary according to weight alone. It is of a fine soft finish and of a good luster. We guarantee this silk not to cut in the least, to pull apart on any ordinary strain, **or to wear shiny.** 27 inches, 3.50 4. 4.50 5.

The foregoing are in stock in full assortments. Many others are kept in varying amounts, mostly at low and medium prices.

Satins for Dresses.

1. Linen-back, 18 to 24 inches, 0.75 to 3.
2. All-silk, 21 to 27 inches, 1.75 to 7.

Silk for Trimmings.

1. Gros-grain; 18 to 22 inches, 0.70 .80 .85 .90 1. 1.10 1.15 1.20 1.25 1.50
2. Gros de Rhin; 18 to 22 inches, 0.70 .80 .85 .90
3. Taffetas:
 18 to 22 inches, 0.75 .80 .90 1. 1.10 1.25
 24 inches, 1.25 1.50 1.75 2.

Silks for Linings, etc.

1. Foulards, lustrines, serges, etc., in great variety; 24 inches, 0.50 to 1.50
2. Quilted silk for lining cloaks, etc.; 24 inches, 1. 1.25 to 1.50

Novelties.

1. Satin-de-Lyon, satin face, gros-grain back, soft and durable:
 19 to 27 inches, 1.50 to 5.
 60 inches, for circulars, 9. to 13.
2. Radsimeres
3. Gros d'Ecosse
4. Gros d'Afrique
5. Damassés, gros-grain ground
6. Damassés, satin-de-Lyon ground
7. Damassés, satin ground
8. Moires, plain
9. Moires, silk-striped
10. Moires, satin-striped
11. Armures
12. Pekin stripes, plain
13. Pekin stripes, watered designs

COLORED SILKS AND SATINS.

For Dresses, Trimmings, etc.

1. French, gros-grain or faille, all colors and shades; 18 to 24 inches, $1. to 3.
2. American gros-grain or faille, all colors and shades; 18 to 24 inches, 1. to 3.
3. Satins, plain colors; 18 to 24 inches, 1. to 5.

Novelties.

1. Brocades, satin ground, plain
2. Brocades, gros-grain, plain colors
3. Brocades, gros-grain, fancy colors
4. Gros-grain and satin stripes, two or three colors
5. **Gros-grain and satin stripes, fancy colors**

WHITE SILKS AND SATINS.

1. Plain, 18 to 27 inches, $1. to 8.
2. Damassés, 19 to 24 inches, 1.50 to 5.
3. Damassés, colored designs on white-satin ground, 20 to 24 inches, 2.50 to 5.
4. Satin, plain, 18 to 27 inches, 1. to 8.
5. Satin, striped, 19 to 24 inches, 1.25 to 3.

BLACK SILK-VELVETS.

PLAIN.
1. Silk-face:
   17 inches, $1. 1.25 1.50
   19   1.60 1.75 2. 2.25 2.50 2.75 3.
   24   2.50 2.75 3.
   27   2.75 3. 3.50 4.00 5.00
2. All-silk, Lyons:
   27 inches, 7. 8.
   28   9. 10. 11. 12.

DAMASSÉ.
1. All-silk, Lyons, 20 inches, 3.00 to 6.00

STRIPED.
1. Satin-striped, 20 inches, 2.50

COLORED SILK-VELVETS.

PLAIN.
1. Silk-face, all colors:
   17 inches, $1.50 1.75 2.
   19   2. 2.25 2.50 3. 3.50
2. All-silk, Lyons, 7.00

DAMASSÉ.
1. Pompadours, Lyons, 20 inches, 4. to 6
2. Brocades, Lyons, 20 inches, 4.50 to 6.

STRIPED.
1. Striped, 20 inches, 2.50

VELVETEENS.

1. Plain, black:
   22 inches, $0.50 .60 .75 1.
   27   1.50
2. Plain, colored:
   22 inches, 0.50 .60 .75 1.
   27   1. 1.25
3. Brocades, 22 inches, 1.
4. Striped, 20 inches, 0.65 .75 .85

DRESS GOODS.

It has been the special object of the manufacturers to produce soft goods of the finest wool with the least weight, yet with the net-corded surface and fine armure figure formerly seen only on the heavy stuff fabrics. These soft, corded and figured wools and materials of mixed cheviot style are leading features in all dress-goods. The under-surface of gay color is often seen in these pliant stuffs. Many of the new woolens are sheer, and almost transparent. Nun's veiling and fine French bunting are shown in the colors of last year and in new olive, maize and grey.

In garniture, the bayadere and vertical stripes are used in place of brocades of former years. Checker-board materials in black and white, black and red, drab and white, blue and drab and other combinations are quite popular. All these garnitures are of wool pronounced by lines of silk in some of the gay mingling colors. These trimmings are preferred on street costumes to pure silk, as they produce more quiet effects than the glitter of silk and tinsel united to the gay Oriental colors which are nearly always used in garniture. Satinet is a soft twilled substance of silk-and-wool which comes in all shades and is popular for trimmings.

POPULAR GOODS.

1	Armures, about	24 inches,	$0.15 to	$0.25
2	Baskets,	24	.18	.30
3	Brocades,	24	.20	.40
4	Cashmeres,	24	.25	.35
5	Momie cloths,	24	.20	.30
6	Melange suitings,	24	.25	.30
7	Damassés,	24	.40	.50
8	Camels-hair,	45	.50	.75
9	Buntings,	24	.20	.50
10	Fancy plaids,	43	.50	1.00

STAPLE GOODS.

PLAIN COLORS.

11	Camels-hair,	45 inches,	0.85 to	3.00
12	Victoria cords,	46	1.25	2.00
13	Imperial cords,	46	1.00	2.00
14	Coutill cords,	45	1.25	1.75
15	Armures,	46	.75	2.00
16	Serges,	45	.50	1.50
17	Albatross,	30	.50	.75
18	Albatross,	45	.90	1.00
19	Nun's veilings,	45	1.25	1.50
20	Sicilians,	45	1.00	2.00
21	Surah satinettes	24	1.25	1.50
22	Cashmeres, 36	40	.40	1.25
23	Buntings, 24	45	.50	1.00

MIXED COLORS.

24	Camels-hair,	46 inches,	0.75 to	2.00
25	Zulu suitings,	46	1.00	2.00
26	Cheviots, French,	46	.90	2.00
27	Cheviots, Scotch,	46	.90	2.00
28	Cashmeres,	46	.60	1.00
29	Albatross,	43	.85	
30	Debeiges,	24	.25	.50
31	Debeiges,	44	45	1.25

PLAIDS.

32	French,	about 45 inches,	0.75 to	2.50
33	English,	45	.75	1.50
34	American,	24	.25	.75

STRIPES.

35	Bayadere,	about 45 inches,	2.00 to	3.50
36	Roman,	24	.60	1.50
37	Vertical,	24	.25	2.00

GRENADINES.

1 Evening shades, brocades and stripes
   24 inches, $1.00 to 3.00
2 For street wear, all colors, 24 inches
   0 50 to 2 00
3 Canton crapes, all colors:
   24 inches, 2.00
   30   3.00

MOURNING.

Imperial serge, nun's veiling and French bunting are all used in deep mourning. Our new fabrics for summer mourning are plain and armured Bayonnaise, sewing-silk, byzantine and Florentine grenadines.

For first mourning we use Henrietta cloth and imperial serge heavily trimmed with crape. Lustreless surah trimmed with crape is also used for handsome dresses. Armure and iron-frame grenadine will be worn.

Drap eté and fine camels-hair is made into mourning wraps and trimmed with bands of crape. Outside jackets or mantles are often of solid crape or of the material of the dress suitably trimmed.

Box-pleating and side-pleating of black crape and of crêpe lisse is used at the neck and sleeves. White bands of fine folded muslin or of crêpe lisse are edged with footing. Wide scarfs and fichus of crêpe lisse or mull are hem-stitched and edged with footing. Dead finished black pins and sleeve-buttons are almost the only jewelry worn in mourning.

Crape is now renovated so that it can hardly be distinguished from the new fabric. All grades and varieties are thus done over.

All requisite articles for full or partial mourning are kept in stock, or made to order. Complete outfits supplied at very short notice.

DRESS-GOODS.

1 Grenadine, iron frame, silk and wool, 22 inches, $0.50 .65 .75 .85 1. 1.25 1.50 1.75 2.

2 Grenadine, armure, all silk, 22 inches, 1.25 1.50 1.75 2.00 2.25 2.50

3 Grenadine, fancy, 22 inches, 0.65 .75 .85 1. 1.25 1.50 1.75 2.

4 Grenadine, Lyons, brocade, all silk, 22 inches, 1.25 1.50 1.75 2. 2.25 2.50 3. 3.50

5 Buntings:
22 inches, 0.18. 20 .25 .30 .35 .40 .45 .50 .55
46   0.65 .75 .85 .90 1. 1.12 1.25 1.50 1.75 2.00

6 Lace buntings:
22 inches, 0.45 .50 .55 .60
46   0.75 .85 1. 1.25

7 Albatross buntings:
24 inches, 0.40 .45 .50
46   0.75 .85 .90 1. 1.10 1.25

8 Damassé and Brocade, 24 inches, 0.75 .85 1. 1.25 1.50 1.75

9 Cashmeres, jet and medium shades:
36 inches, $0.50 .55 .60 .65 .75 .85 .90 1.
40 inches, 0.55 .60 .70 .75 .85 .95 1. 1.12 1.25
45 inches, 0.75 .85 .90 1. 1.12 1.25 1.50 1.75 2. 2.25 2.50

10 Merinos:
    38 inches, 0.65 .75 .90 1.00
    40 .75 .85 .90 1.00 1.25
    45 1.25 1.50 1.75 2.00 2.25 2.50
11 Camels-hair:
    45 inches, 0.75 .85 .90 1. 1.12 1.25 1.50 1.75
    48 inches, 0.85 .90 1. 1.12 1.25 1.50 1.75 2. 2.25 2.50
    50 inches, 2. 2.25 2.50 2.75 3. 3.50 4. 4.50
12 Bayonnaise, plain, 45 inches, 0.75 .90 1. 1.15 1.25 1.50 1.75 2. 2.25
13 Bayonnaise, plaid, 45 inches, 0.85 .90 1. 1.15 1.25 1.50 1.75 2.
14 Satin de Gendre, 24 inches, 1.75 2.
15 Llama cloths, 42 inches, 0.50 .60 .75 .90 1. 1.25 1.50
16 Draps d'été, 48 inches, 1.25 1.50 1.75 2. 2.25 2.50 2.75 3.
17 Momie, 45 inches, 0.75 .85 1. 1.15
18 Abyssinians, striped, 45 inches, 1.15 1.25 1.50 1.75 2.
19 Armures, figured, 45 inches, 0.75 .90 1. 1.10 1.25 1.50 1.75 2. 2.50
20 Armures, striped, 45 inches, 1. 1.25 1.50 1.75 2.
21 Armures de Ecosse, 45 inches, 1.50 1.75 2. 2.25 2.50 2.75
22 Crêpes de chêne, silk-and-wool, 27 inches, 1.75 2.
23 Crape cloths, 40 inches, 0.40 .50 .60 .75
24 Crape cloths, all-wool, 45 inches, 1. 1.25 1.50 1.75
25 Henrietta cloths, silk-warp, 40 inches, 0.95 1. 1.12 1.25 1.50 1.75 2. 2.25 2.50 2.75 3.
26 Imperial serges, silk-warp, 36 inches, 1.50 1.75 2. 2.25 2.50
27 Empress cloths, 30 inches, 0.50 .60 .75 .80
28 Granite cloth:
    all-wool, 45 inches, 0.90 1. 1.25 1.50 1.75 2.
    silk-and-wool, 40 inches, 1.75 2. 2.25 2.50
29 English serges, all-wool, 40 inches, 0.75 .85 1. 1.12 1.25 1.50
30 Crape de soie, silk-and-wool, 40 inches, 1.75 2. 2.25 2.50
31 Damassé Saxon, silk-and-wool, 24 inches, 1. 1.12 1.15 1.25 1.50 1.75

CRAPE.

COURTAULD'S CRAPE, straight or bias.

1 4-4, measures 27 inches, $1.25 1.50 1.75 2. 2.25 2.50 2.75 3. 3.25 3.50 3.75 4. 4.25 4.50
2 5-4, measures 36 inches, 2.25 2.50 3. 3.50 4. 4.50 5. 5.50 6.
3 6-4, measures 42 inches, 2.50 3. 3.50 4. 4.50 5. 5.50 6. 6.50 7. 7.50 8. 10

MADE ARTICLES.

1 Mourning hosiery, see Hosiery.
2 Woven crape veils, $2.25 2.50 3. 3.50 4. 4.50 5. 5.50
3 Crape veils, on hand or made to order, 3.50 4. 5. 6. 8. 9. 10. 12 to 25.
4 Brussels-net veils, plain, 0.85 1.50 1.70 2. 2.50 3. 3.50
5 Brussels-net veils, trimmed with crape, 1. 1.50 1.70 2. 2.50 3. 3.50
6 Crape collars, 0.40 .50 .60 to 2.50
7 Crape cuffs, 1. 1.50 1.75 to 2.50
8 Crape bows, 0.30 .35 .40 50 to 1.75
9 Crape jabots, 0.30 .35 .40 50 to 1.75
10 Lisse bows, 0.30 .35 .40 .50 to 1.75
11 Lisse jabots, 0.30 .35 .40 .50 to 2.50
12 Lisse ties, 0.28 .35 .40 .50 .60 to 1.25
13 Mull ties, 0.25 .35 .40 .50 .60 to 1.35
14 Mull and lisse fichus, 0.70 1.25 1.70 2. to 3.50
15 Handkerchiefs, 0.15 .20 .25 .30 .35 .40 .50 .60 1.50 to 2.25
16 Linen collars and cuffs, per set, 0.25 .35 .40 to .75
17 Linen collars, each, 0.08 .10 .12 .15 to .40
18 Linen cuffs, pair, 0.16 .18 .20 .25 .30 to .50
19 Tarletan ruchings, 0.10 .13 .18 .25 to .50
20 Lisse ruchings, 0.25 .30 .40 to 1.
21 Crape ruchings, 0.55 .65 .75 .85 to 1.35
22 Widow's ruchings, 0.10 .13 .25 .30 to .50

Novelties constantly being received.

WHITE GOODS AND TIDIES.

French nainsooks are still the standard goods for small children's wear and for tasteful white morning dresses. Victoria lawn is now furnished with embroidered edges, and is liked by some ladies as it is less expensive than nainsook. Piqué is used as much as ever for children's and misses' white dresses, and a fine light quality with small cords is usually chosen. Lace striped piqué which was introduced last year is very popular this season.

Swiss muslins dotted or strewn with tiny sprays and fine striped or barred organdies will still be used for young girls. There is no material so becoming to youthful beauty as these muslins which make fresh, cool dresses for summer afternoons and are always in good taste and style. White has been used in silk in our ball-rooms this winter, almost to the exclusion of colors, and bids fair to be extensively worn in wash fabrics this summer.

MUSLIN.

NAINSOOK.
1. English, plain, sheer, 36 inches, $0.20 .25 .30 .35 .40 .45 .50 .55 .60
2. English, plain, heavy:
   32 inches wide, 0.14 .16 .18 .20 .22
   36   .25 .30 .35 .40 .45 .50 .55 .60
3. English, striped, 34 inches, 0.15 .18 .20 .25 .30 .35 .40 .45 .50
4. English, plaid, small and large, 0.18 .20 .25 .30 .35 .40 .45 .50
5. Domestic, plaid, 34 inches, 0.12 .15 .18 .20
6. French, nainsook, plain, sheer, 48 inches, 0.30 .35 .40 .45 .50 .55 .60 .70 .80 .90 1.
7. French, nainsook, plain, heavy, 48 inches, 0.30 .35 .40 .45 .50 .55 .60 .65 .70 .80 .90 1.

JACONET.
1. English:
   32 inches wide, hard finish, 0.12 .15 .18 .20 .25
   36 inches wide, soft finish, 0.25 .30 .35 .40 .45
2. French, 45 inches, 0.60 .70

ORGANDIE.
1. French, pearl-white:
   34 inches, 0.22 .30 .35 .40 .50
   69   0.35 .40 .45 .50 .55 .60 .65 .70 .75 .85 .90 1. 1.10 1.20 1.30 1.40 1.50
2. French, blue-white:
   34 inches, 0.16 .22 .30 .35 .40 .50
   69   0.35 .40 .45 .50 .55 .60 .65 .70 .75 .85 .90 1. 1.10 1.20 1.30 1.40 1.50
3. Plaid, 33 inches, 0.22
   Striped, 33 inches, 0.22

MASSALIA.
1. French, 36 inches, 0.30 .35 .40 .45 .50

MULLS.
1. Mol-mol, French, écru and white, 69 inches, 0.65 .75 .90 .1 1.15 1.30 1.50
2. Mol-mol, French, white and cream, 52 inches, 0.50 .55 .60 .65 .70 .75 .80 .90 1.
3. India-mull, 36 inches, 0.20 .25 .30 .35 .40 .45 .50 .65 .75
4. Mol-mol, French, all-silk, écru, white, blue, pink and black, 54 inches, 1.20
5. Mol-mol, French, silk and cotton, black and cardinal, 54 inches, 1.45
6. Mol-mol, French, pink and blue:
   36 inches, 0.55
   69   .85

SWISS.
1.   36 inches, 0.18 .20 .23
      42   .25 .30 .32 .35 .40 .45 .50
2. Scotch, plain, blue and white:
   34 inches, 0.20 .25 .30 .35 .40

MUSLIN—Continued,

3 Dotted, all size dots :
   34 inches, 0.20 .25 .30 .35 .40 .45
   .50 .60
4 Figured :
   34 inches, 0.20 .25 .28 .30 .35 .40 .45
   .50 .55 .60 .65
5 Dotted, écru, all size dots :
   34 inches, 0.30 .46 .50 .60
6 Figured, écru :
   34 inches, 0.30 .40 .50 .60 .70

TARLETAN.
1 White :
   54 inches, 0.10 .12 .14 .16 .18 .20 .25
   60   .25 .28 .30 .35 .40
   65   .45 .50 .55 .60 .65 .70 .75
           .80
2 Colored, pink, rose, buff, yellow, scarlet,
   crimson, black, light-blue, medium-
   blue, navy-blue, purple, orange,
   lemon :
   54 inches, 0.10 .12 .15 .18 .20 .25
   60   .30 .35 .40 .45 .50 .60

PERCALE.
1 French, white, 36 inches, 0.12½ .15 .25
   .30 .37 .45

LAWN.
1 Victoria, 36 inches, 0.15 .18 .20 .25 .30
   .35 .40 .45 .50
2 Bishop, 36 inches, 0.15 .20 .25 .30 .40
3 Persian, 34 inches, 0.25 .30 .35 .40 .45
   .50
4 India Linen, 36 inches, 0.20 .25 .30 .35
   .40 .45 .50 .60
5 Linen, 28 inches, 0.18 .20 .25 .30 .35
   .40 .45 .50 .55
6 Battiste, 32 inches, 0.35 .40 .45

SHIRRED MUSLIN.
1 French, plain, 33 inches 0.35 .40 .50
2 Revere, striped, 33 inches, 0.40 .50

CAMBRIC.
1 Jones's, light and heavy, 36 inches, 0.20
   .25 .30 .35 .40 .45 .50 .55
2 Long cloth, 36 inches, 0.30 .35 .40
3 Berkely, 36 inches, 0.20
4 Lonsdale, 36 inches, 0.13

INDIA TWILL.
1 Plain, 38 inches, 0.25 .30 .35
2 English, long cloth, striped, 40 inches,
   0.25 .30 .35 .40

GRENADINE-TARLETAN, WHITE.
1 French, 0.20 .25 .30 .35

PIQUÉ.
1 Fleecy-back, 27 inches, 0.35 .40 .45 .50
   .55 .60 .65 .70 .75 .80 .90 1.
2 Corded, French and English, 33 inches,
   0.20 .25 .30 .35 .40 .45 .50 .55 .60
   .65 .75.
3 Dimon, all sizes, 27 inches, 0.20 .25 .30
   .35 .45
4 White ground, colored figure, 33 inches,
   0.20
5 Lace, striped and open-work, 27 inches,
   0.12½ .15 .18 .20 .25 .30 .35 .40 .45

SATEEN JEANS, all colors.
1 English, 27 inches, 0.30 .35 .40 .45 .50
   .55

TUCKING.
1 Tucked-all-over, and clusters, 27 inches,
   .50 .60 .70 .75 .80 .85 .90 1. 1.10 1.25
   1.40 1.50 1.75
2 For children's skirts, 27 inches, 0.25
   .30
3 For children's dresses and ladies' skirts,
   36 inches, 0.35 .40 .45 .50 .60 .65 .75
   .80

COUTIL.
1 White, 54 inches, 1. 1.10 1.25 1.50 1.65
   1.75 1.80 1.85 1.90 2. 2.25 2.50 2.85
2 Drab, light and dark, 54 inches, 1. 1.10
   1.25 1.50 1.60 1.75 2. 2.20

DIMITY RUFFLING.
1 French, 18 inches, 0.25 .30 .40 .50 .60 .70

TIDIES.

ANTIQUE.
1 For chairs, all sizes, $0.50 .60 .70 .80 .90
   1. 1.15 1.25 1.30 1.50 1.75 2. 2.25
   2.50 2.75 3. 3.50 4. 4.50
2 Small, 0.25 .30 .37 .45 .50 .60 .70 .80
   .90
3 For chair-arms, 9 × 14 inches, 0.35 .45
   .50 .60 .70 .80 .90 1. 1.25 1.50
4 For sofas, 18 × 30 inches, 1.25 1 50 1 7
   2. 2.25 2.50 3. 3.50 4. 4.50 5.
5 For sofas and lounges, 18 × 56 inches,
   2.50 3. 3.50 4. 4.50 5. 5 50 6. 6.50
   7. 7.50 8. 9. .12
6 Antique squares, 5 inches, 0.04 .06 .10
   .12 .15 .20 .23 .25 .30 .32
7 Antique squares, 9 inches, 0.30 .35 .40
   .45 .50 .60

TIDIES—Continued.

ANTIQUE AND EMBROIDERED SATIN, combined in alternate squares.

1   18 inches square, 2.50   4.   4.50   5.   5.50
2   Centers for arms, 1.60   1.90

APPLIQUÉ.

1   For chairs, all sizes, 0.15 .20 .25 .30 .35 .40 .50 .60 .70 .80 .90 1. 1.25 1.50 1.75
2   For chair-arms, 9 × 14 inches, 0.35 .40 .45 .50 .60

IMITATION-GUIPURE, white or écru.

1	8 × 8 inches,	0.12
	12 × 14	.20
	13 × 13	.25
	20 × 20	.35
	20 × 27	.50
	27 × 27	.65
	32 × 32	1.00

NOTTINGHAM TIDIES.

1	7 × 7 inches,	0.07
	11 × 11	.10
	13 × 13	.13
	17 × 17	.20
	18 × 27	.25
	24 × 24	.30
	30 × 30	.40

2   Pillow shams, per pair, 36 × 36 inches, 1.00   1.20   1.40   1.50   1.80

GINGHAMS AND PRINTS.

Stripes in ginghams have succeeded the broken plaids worn last season. They are broken stripes of hair-lines in black, blue and other colors, and bands of grey with dashes of color in chiné effect. Fine Roman stripes are shown with many lines of gay Madras colors. A great deal of yellow is mingled with other shades in these ginghams, but it is so toned by the mingling colors that the effect is good, and not too gaudy. Seaside zephyrs and cheese cloths are all used this season. Fine cambrics in foreign and domestic patterns are in numberless tasteful designs, but the quaint Egyptian figures and the pretty flower patterns, which are imported this season, are so ornate and mingle so many colors that they should be made in simple styles. A good mold is a gathered belted waist, with a full round skirt, simply hemmed without flounces, and trimmed with the border when there is one, or if not, the waist may be simply piped with some pronounced color in the cambric, and the full skirt edged with two ruffles, not over a finger in depth, which are also piped with the same color. This design is especially recommended for simple domestic calico and for plain dresses of American seersucker gingham in fine stripes of blue, pink and white, or in brown and white, or blue and white.

Handsome momie cloth dresses or percale dresses with dark grounds, strewn with gay flowers, are made with long princess-fitting basques, on which vests are outlined by the gay border which comes with the goods, and a pelerine or round cape is trimmed with this flowered border. A daisy border is used for dark percales. The over-skirt may be arranged in many intricate draperies, which should be made so that it can be easily taken apart and laundered in a simple piece. The over-skirt is not trimmed, but finished with a plain hem. The lower skirt which is now the point of ornament in all costumes, is often formed of double box-pleating with stripes of gay bordering edging the bottom of the skirt, and extending down the center of the box-pleats.

Cheviot shirting in bright mixed grounds, crossed by checks and plaids, are used for men's and boys' shirts, and trimmed with fancy piping for children's dresses.

PRINTS.

1. French, 33 inches, $0.30
2. English, 33 inches, 0.25
3. Calicoes, 25 inches, 0.08 .09 .10
4. Momie-cloth, French, 33 inches, 0.25
5. Momie-cloth, Pacific, 33 inches, 0.20
6. Cretonnes, Pacific, 33 inches, 0.15
7. Foulards, Cocheco, 33 inches, 0.15
8. Dress-cambrics, 27 inches, 0.11

TURKEY-REDS.

1. Plain:
   25 inches, $0.12½ .15 .18 .25
   31   .30 .35 .40
   42   .50
2. Twilled:
   31 inches, 0.30 .35 .40 .45 .50 .55

BLACK PRINTS.

1. Cambrics, French, 33 inches, $0.30
2. Cambrics, domestic, 33 inches, 0.15
3. Prints, English, 33 inches, 0.25
4. Prints, domestic, 25 inches, 0.09

SHIRTINGS,

1. Cheviots, French, 33 inches, $0.30
2. Cheviots, English, 33 inches, 0.25
3. Cambrics, French, 33 inches, 0.30
4. Cambrics, English, 33 inches, 0.20 .25
5. Cambrics, domestic, 33 inches, 0.15 .18 .20
6. Cambrics, domestic, 27 inches, 0.10 .11
7. Prints, domestic, 25 inches, 0.08 .09 .10

GINGHAMS.

1. Madras-cloth (zephyr), French, 27 inches, $0.25 .28
2. Dress-ginghams, domestic, 27 inches, 0.15
3. Book-fold ginghams, domestic, 27 inches, 0.16
4. Seersucker, domestic, 27 inches, 0.16 .18 .20

CLOTHS.

Tricot cloths, fine diagonals and Sicilienne cords in light goods, which are as soft as cashmere, are the favorite choice for handsome woolen wraps. The tricot cloth, its fine figure simulating a closely knitted fabric, is especially liked in black, light-grey and écru for spring mantles, and in dark shades of color for ladies' suits. A new material in fine lengthwise cord, yet of such pliant wool that it makes the most graceful, clinging draperies, is a specialty of this house.

New cloths for jackets or ulsters in cheviot mixtures are woven with many threads of gay color, which are nearly covered by a neutral-tinted woof, so that though the fabric is touched by Oriental brilliancies of shade and tint the effect is refined and quiet: these mixed cloths will be used in light qualities for ladies' négligé shopping dresses, which are made entirely of one material, with a long double-breasted hunter's jacket with belt and chatelaine bag of the dress goods, and a short pleated under-skirt simply draped by a wrinkled apron. The Pemberton suitings, 54 inches wide at $1.25, will be, however, the most popular material for these dresses; they are smooth flannel-finished fabrics without a nap to roughen; the favorite colors are bronze, olive, dark-blue, prune, hunter's green, écru and quaint mixtures of greys and olives. with an underlying surface of gay threads

CLOAKINGS.

54 inches wide.

BLACK:

1	Sicilienne cords,	$2.50 to 4.00	
2	Raye cords,	3.00	
3	Armures,	2.00 to 4.00	
4	Baskets,	1.50	3.50
5	Diagonals,	1.50	6.00
6	Camels-hair,	2.25	3.50
7	Tricots,	2.50	3.00

COLORED, all shades.

1	Raye cords,	3.00	
2	Sicilian cords,	2.00 to 3.50	
3	Diagonals,	1.75	3.00
4	Baskets,	2.00	2.50
5	Cheviots,	1.25	3.50
6	Livery cloths,	1.25	5.00

INFANTS', white, blue and pink.

1	Baskets,	2.00 to 3.50	
2	Cords,	2.50	3.50
3	Diagonals,	2.00	3.00
4	White ground, with blue, pink and bluedots,	2.50	3.00
5	White corduroys	.75	1.25
6	White cordurettes	1.10	

LADIES' CLOTHS.

54 inches.

FOR SUITS AND HABITS, all colors and shades.
1. Plain, dull-finish, 0.95 1. 1.25 1.50
2. Twilled, dull-finish, 1.25 1.50
3. Plain, silk lustre, 150 to .350
4. Lord & Taylor's demi-finish, especially adapted for riding habits, 2.50
5. Pemberton cloth suitings, 1.25
6. Cheviots, Tweeds, Checks and Melton mixtures, 1.25 to 3.50

FOR ULSTERS, 27 and 54 inches.
1. Full line, ranging from 1.25 to 4.00

FOR WATERPROOFS, 54 inches.
1. Plaids, 1.50 to 2.50
2. Plain colors, .75 2.50

CORDUROYS.

22 and 27 inches.
1. All colors and size cords, 0.65 to 1.00

VELVETEENS.

22 and 27 inches.
1. Plain, black, 0.50 .75 1. 1.25 1.50
2. Colored, 0.75 1. 1.25
3. Brocades, 1.00

FARMER'S SATIN LININGS.

32 inches.
1. Black, 0.25 .40 .50 .60 .75 1.00
2. Colored, 0.50 .60 .70 .80
3. Stripes, 0.60 .70 .80

GENTLEMEN'S CLOTH.

54 inches.

COATINGS.
2. Broadcloths, Tricots, Diagonals, Granites, Baskets, 5.50 to 7.00

SUITINGS.
1. Cassimeres, Tweeds, Cheviots, 1.50 to 5.00
2. Cassimeres, for boys, 0.50 to 1.50

LADIES' AND CHILDREN'S HOSIERY.

New stockings for ladies are in gay horizontal Roman stripes mingled with many lines of gold-color. For summer wear there has been, however, for sometime a growing preference for fine Balbriggan hose in écru, or striped with delicate hair-lines, and for silk stockings in dark shades of solid color.

Children's stockings are usually ribbed and are as fanciful as possible. The foot in fine stripes of gay color is separated from the plainer top by bands of gold-color, blue or dull red. Black stockings are liked for children, with bright Madras stripes of blue, red or yellow, or strewn with small polka dots. Half-hose or socks are preferred during the warm weather for little ones under five. They are in lisle-thread, in the color, and often in open-work patterns.

COTTON.

For Ladies.

1. White, or unbleached, regular-made, 8 to 10 inches, $0.25 .40 .50 .55 .60 .70 .75 .85 1. 1.20; extra wide, .50 .60 1.25
2. Plain colors, 0.50 .65 .75 .85 1. 1.25 1.35 1.50 1.65 1.75; extra wide, 1.25 1.50
3. Novelties, embroidered, mixed or striped, .50 .65 .70 .75 .85 1. 1.25 1.35 1.40 1.50 1.65 1.75 2.

For Misses.

1. Plain colors:
5 inches, 0.45	.50	.55	.60	.80
5½	.50 .55	.60	.65	.85
6	.55 .60	.65	.70	.90
6½	.60 .65	.70	.75	.95
7	.65 .70	.75	.80	1.00
7½	.70 .75	.80	.85	1.05
8	.75 .80	.85	.90	1.10
8½	.80 .85	.90	.95	1.15

2. Plain colors, ribbed:
6 inches, 0.55	7½ inches, 0.70
6½	.60	8	.75
7	.65	8½	.80

3. Plain colors, ribbed and clocked:
6 inches, 1.30	7½	1.60
6½	1.40	8	1.70
7 inches, 1.50	8½	1.75

4. Novelties, embroidered, mixed or striped, 0.25 .30 .35 .40 .50 .60 .70 .80 .90 1. 1.05 1.10 1.15 1.20 1.25

For Children; Socks and ¾ Hose.

1. Socks, white:
4 inches,	.20	.23	.27
4½	.25	.34	.37
5	.28	.34	.42
5½	.30	.38	.42
6	.32	.38	.45
6½	.34	.42	.50
7	.36	.45	.50

2. ¾ hose, white:
4 inches,	.30	.40	.45
4½	.33	.43	.48
5	.33	.45	.50
5½	.36	.50	.53
6	.38	.55	.58
6½	.42	.58	.60

3. Socks and ¾ hose, plain colors:
4 inches,	.30
4½	.35
5	.45
5½	.40
6	.45
6½	.50
7	.50

4. Socks and ¾ hose, fancy stripes:
4 inches, 25.	.40
4½	.30	.45
5	.35	.50
5½	.40	.55
6	.45	.60
6½	.50

5. ¾ hose, stripes:
4 inches,	.30	.40
4½	.35	.40
5	.40	.45
5½	.45	.45
6	.45	.50
6½	.50	.55
7	.55	.60

LISLE-THREAD.

For Ladies.

1. White, or unbleached, $0.75 .85 1. 1.25. 1.50; extra wide, 1. 1.25.
2. Colored, plain or fancy; all staple and new colors, viz., écru, gendarme, turquoise, sky-blue, royal-blue, lilac, lavender, purple, black, etc., 1.25 1.50 1.75
3. Plain colors, 1.25 1.50 1.75
4. Plain colors, ribbed, all shades, 1.25
5. Opera-lengths, light tints, 2.75 3. 3.50
6. Embroidered-fronts, 1.25 1.50 1.75 1.90 2. 2.25 2.50 2.75 3.
7. Novelties, 1.25 1.35 1.40 1.50 1.75 2. 2.25 2.50 2.75 3.

For Misses.

1. Plain colors: Novelties, striped:
5 inches, 0.75	.85		1.05	1.30
5½	.80	.90	1.10	1.35
6	.85	.95	1.15	1.40
6½	.90	1.00	1.20	1.45
7	.95	1.05	1.25	1.50
7½	1.00	1.10	1.30	1.55
8	1.05	1.15	1.35	1.60
8½	1.10	1.20	1.40	1.65

MOURNING.

For Ladies.

1. Cotton, plain black, $1. 1.25 1.50 1.75
2. Cotton, striped, .75 .80 .85 1.25
3. Cotton, fancy, 1. 1.25 1.50 1.75
4. Lisle-thread, plain black, 1.25 1.50 1.75
5. Lisle-thread, striped, 1.25 1.50 1.65 1.75
6. Lisle-thread, fancy, 1.25 1.50 1.65 1.75 2.
7. Silk, see Silk Hose.
8. Novelties as they are produced.

For Misses.

1. Cotton, black or black-and-gray mixed, 0.50 .60 .70 .80 .90 1.
2. Cotton, striped, 0.50 .60 .70 .75 .80 .90 1.
3. Lisle-thread, striped :
5 inches,	0.75	7 inches,	1.10
5½	.85	7½	1.15
6	.95	8	1.20
6½	1.00	8½	1.25

SILK

For Ladies.

1. Spun-silk, plain colors, all staple and new colors and shades, $2.25 2.50 3.
2. Spun-silk, fancy, in endless variety, 2.50 to 4.50
3. Spun-silk, opera, 3.85 to 5.50.
4. Silk, in all colors, plain, 4.50 4.75 5
5. Silk, fancy ; a very large assortment, including a full line of mourning hose, 5. to 50.

6. Silk, ribbed, 3.25
7. Silk, opera, 6.50 to 10.

For Misses.

1. Spun-silk, plain colors; all colors and shades :
5½ inches,	1.80
6	1.90
6½	2.00
7	2.10
7½	2.20
8	2.30
8½	2.40
2. Spun-silk, ribbed ; all colors and shades :
5½ inches,	2.50
6	2.70
6½	2.90
7	3.10
7½	3.30
8	3.50
8½	3.70
3. Silk, all colors and shades, according to size and color, 3.15 to 5.50

For Children.

1. Silk ½ hose, plain colors :
   | Size, | 4 | 4½ | 5 | 5½ | 6 |
   | Price, | 1.60 | 1.75 | 1.95 | 2.05 | 2.20 |
2. Silk ½ hose, sandal-lace, plain colors :
   | 4 | 4½ | 5 | 5½ | 6 |
   | 1.80 | 1.95 | 2.10 | 2.25 | 2.40 |
3. Silk ¾ hose, sandal-lace, plain color :
   | 4 | 4½ | 5 | 5½ | 6 |
   | 2.00 | 2.20 | 2.40 | 2.60 | 2.80 |

LADIES' AND CHILDREN'S GLOVES.

Kid gloves are preferred in fine dressed leather. There is a tendency to the use of the darkest possible shades of a color and to light tints. Colors called black-blue, black-purple, ebony-brown and green-black are among the spring gloves. Nut-browns, steel-greys, olive and dark olive-greens, heliotrope and condor-colors in maize tints grading into deep tan-color, divide the choice. Mousquetaire buttonless gloves and button gloves are equally used. Button gloves are finished at the wrist by quarter-inch welts and button-holes of white kid which prevent dark gloves from crocking the hand.

The introduction of the long mousquetaire glove, which is only found in from six to ten-button lengths, has tended to increase the length of all handwear. Few gloves are worn shorter than four buttons, and six and eight buttons are as often chosen.

White castor will be a favorite riding or driving glove during the summer. Long-wristed French lisle thread in écru and drab, and English silk gloves in gold and black, are now kid-finished, and fit the hand as neatly as the finest leather.

Mitts in French filet lace in fine grades rival in texture costly chantilly lace. They are finished with and without fingers, and are a stylish and pleasant hand-covering for summer.

KID.

Dressed and undressed.

TRÈFOUSSE, Paris, unexcelled in shape, color and durability.

1	Ladies' two-button,	$1.65
2	three	1.90
3	four	2.20
4	six	2.70

Gants de Suède (undressed kid).

1	Ladies' three-button,	1.50
2	four	1.75
3	six	2.00
4	eight	2.50

DUPRÈS, Paris, unsurpassed for shape, elasticity and durability.

1	Ladies' two-button,	$1.40
2	three	1.60
3	four	1.85
4	six	2.10
5	eight	2.50
6	ten	3.00
1	Misses' two	.90
2	three	1.15
3	four	1.40
4	six	1.75

FOSTER'S new patent fastening, iscing wtth silk cord:

1	Ladies' three-hooks,	$1.75
2	five	2.00
3	seven	2.25
4	ten	2.75
5	fifteen	3.50

The foregoing brands are warranted: this guarantee applies to such gloves as shall tear when being first tried on; gloves returned that show signs of wear will not be exchanged.

ELITE, a real kid, which has given general satisfaction for several years, and can be recommended for ordinary wear:

1	Ladies' two button,	$1.00
2	three	1.25
3	four	1.50
4	six	1.75

COUPE JOUVIN, a superior quality of fine lambskin.

1	Ladies' two-button,	0.75
2	three	1.00
3	four	1.25
4	six	1.50
5	eight	2.10
6	ten	2.50

Gants de Suède, undressed kid, made expressly for Lord & Taylor:

  1 Ladies' three-button, 1.00
  2   four   1.25
  3   six   1.50

Ladies' mousquetaire "Sara Bernhardt" in white and colored undressed kid 2.50.

LEATHER GLOVES.

1. Ladies' castor beaver, in drab and black; suitable for traveling, driving, etc. :
two-button, $1.25
three   1.50
four   1.75
six   2.00

2. Ladies' white castor beaver, for riding :
three-button, 1.50
four   1.75
six   2.00

3. Ladies' chamois, natural color, stitched backs and plain:
three-button, 1.50
four   1.90

4. Ladies' doeskin gauntlets, 0.50 0.75 1.00

5. Ladies' white castor-beaver gauntlets, stitched backs, for riding or driving, 2.50

6. Ladies' dogskin :
two-button, 1.25 1.75 1.90
three   1.25 1.90 2.00

7. Misses' and boys' castor beaver, drab, 1.00

8. Misses' and boys' dogskin, browns and slates, 1.00

LISLE THREAD AND SILK.

1. English thread, first quality, kid-finish:
Ladies' two-button, $0.50
three   .55
four   .60
six   .75

2. French thread, first quality, kid-finish :
two-button, 0.50
three   .55
four   .60

3. Paris thread, regular made, long arm; clocked and lace tops, 0.90 1. 1.25

4. Berlin lisle-thread, regular made, lace tops, ladies' 0.35 .50 .55 .65 .75 to 1.25

5. Gauze lisle-thread :
two elastics, 0.50
three   .50 .65
four   .65 .75

6. Ladies' cotton :
two-button, 0.15 .25
three   .25 .35
four   .30 .50

7. English thread, for misses and boys :
two-button, 0.25 .40
three   .40 .45
four   .45 .50

8. Misses' and boys' cotton :
two-button, 0.15 .25
three,   .25 .35

9. French silk, first quality :
Ladies' two-button, 1.25
three   1.40
four   1.50
Misses' and boys'
two-button, 0.90
three   1.00

10. English silk, in black only:
Ladies' two-button, 0.75
three   .85
four   .95
six   1.00
eight   1.10

11. Paris silk, long arm, lace tops, in black only, ladies, 2.00

LACE AND SILK MITTS.

1. Ladies' woven: quarter length of forearm, in black, white, light-blue, flesh, cream, old-gold, mastic and pearl, 1. 1.25

2. Ladies' Paris, best French silk : short with half fingers, 0.75 1. 1.25 1.50 1.75 2.00 to 3.00

3. Ladies' Paris, short, without fingers, .50 .75 1. 1.25 1.50 1.75 2.00 to 3.00

4. Ladies' Paris, in quarter-length of forearm, with fingers, 0.75 1. 1.25 1.50 1.75 2.00 to 3.50

5. Ladies' Paris, quarter-length of forearm, without fingers; 0.50 .75 1. 1.25 1.50 1.75 2.00 to 5.00

5. Ladies' Paris, three-quarter-length of fore-arm, without fingers, 1.50 1.75 2. 2.50 3.50 to 15.00

7. Misses' and children's woven : in black, white, light-blue, pink, cream, old-gold, pearl, 0.55 .65 .75 1.

8. Misses' Paris, in black, 0.50 ,75 1. 1.25

9. Glove buttoners, 0.15 .25

10. Powder boxes, 0.50

11. Glove stretchers 0.25 .75

LACES.

Point duchesse and round point are the choice among rare laces. There is a revival of old point applique and of broad widths of real Valenciennes which is imported now in the lightest and most delicate patterns.

Woven lace, which has virtually succeeded the hand-made lace for ordinary occasions, is no longer a thing which any lady can object to wear. The word imitation has an ugly sound, but the woven lace of to-day, much of it in patterns run by hand, is so soft in texture, so exquisite in design that it is completely, in everything except in the process of making, a reproduction of hand-made lace.

Black Spanish lace has replaced French thread and is the favorite trimming for handsome satin and satin surah wraps. Black and white Spanish lace sleeves are much in vogue with full dress costumes. Cream-white Spanish shawls of silk lace to be worn fichu-like, are knotted carelessly in front and caught by a cluster of crimson roses. Graceful pointed hoods of white and black lace fastened with silken cords and tassels are in the pretty coquettish style of Spain. Point Imperial is a new and handsome lace, which is used for collar fichus and children's cloaks. Coraline lace is a dainty dotted pattern which is often mingled with Spanish and with Vermicelli. Point Newport, a delicate lace in Mecklin pattern, has succeeded Languedoc. Mirecourt, woven in cotton and in silk, with fine meshes and thickly wrought designs of roses or leaves which form its sharply scolloped edges, is very effective and washes well in cotton. Some lace is now tinted to a pale gold color. Large scarfs are still worn and are made of India-mull, silk-mull or of soft Breton net.

Fichus, jabots and breakfast bows which match breakfast caps were never more worn than now. They are made of coraline, rose-point or silk Mirecourt. The Vandyke is the new pointed collar of lace. Extra quality of Brussels net for bridal veils is now so exquisitely fine that its silken mist-like meshes seem hardly a thing of substance.

IMITATION LACES.

Prices per yard.

ITALIAN VALENCIENNES.

1	½ inch,	per yard, $0.03 .05 .07 .08 .10
		per doz., .20 .25 .30
2	1	per yard, .07 .10 .12 .15
		per doz., .50 .55 .65 .75
3	2	per yard, .15 .18 .25 .35 .40
		per doz., 1.00 1.25 1.60
4	3	per yard, .40 .50 .55 .75
5	4	per yard, .75 .85 1.00

ITALIAN VALENCIENNES INSERTION.

1	½ inch,	per yard, $0.03 .07 .10
		per doz., .20 .26 .30 .35
2	1	per yard, .10 .15 .18 .20
		per doz., .60 .75 .80 .95
3	1½	per yard, .18 .20 .25 .33
		per doz., 1.20 1.40 1.60
4	2	per yard, .25 .35 .43 .55
5	3	per yard, .40 .55 .65

IMITATION MALTESE.

1	1 inch,	$0.14 .16 .18
2	1½	.15 .20 .25
3	2	.25 .28 .30
4	3	.33 .40

IMITATION MALTESE INSERTION.

1	1 inch,	$0.08 .10
2	2	.15 .18

IMITATION DUCHESSE.

1	1 inch,	$0.12 .15 .18
2	1½	.16 .18 .20 .25
3	2	.25 .30
4	3	.35 .40 .45

IMITATION DUCHESSE INSERTION.

1	1 inch,	$0.15 .18 .20
2	1½	.17 .22 .25

IMITATION POINT.

1	2 inches,	$0.40 0.55
2	3	0.60 0.75 0.90
3	4½	1.00 1.25 1.60

IMITATION RUSSIAN.

1	1 inch,	$0.10 .12 .15
2	2	.13 .15 .18
3	3½	.20 .25 .33

IMITATION RUSSIAN INSERTION.

1	1 inch,	$0.07 .10 12
2	1½	.09 .12 .15

IMITATION BRETON.

1	¾ inch,	$0.05 .07 .10
2	1	.08 .10 .12
3	1½	.10 .12 .16 .18
4	2	13 .15 .17 .20
5	2½	.16 .18 .20 .25

IMITATION BRETON INSERTION.

1	1 inch,	$0.06 .08 .10
2	1¼	.09 .10 .12
3	1½	.12 .15 .18

IMITATION MECHLIN.

1	1¾ inches,	$0.20 .27 .30
2	2½	.27 .45 .60 .75
3	3	.75 .95

BLACK FRENCH.

1	½ inch,	$0.07 .09 12 .14
2	½	per doz., .75 .95 1.10
3	1½	.16 .18 .20
4	2½	.25 .28 .30 .33 .40
5	3½	.35 .38 .45 .50
6	4½	.55 .62 .65 .75

REAL LACES.

Prices per yard.

VALENCIENNES.

1	½	$0.18 .25 .30 .35 .45
2	1	0.55 .65 .75
3	1¼	1.00 1.25 1.50 2.00
4	2	1.37 1.55 2.00 2.50 3.25
5	2½	2.50 3.00 3.50 4.25
6	3	4.00 5.00 6.00
7	4	5.00 6.50 7.50

VALENCIENNES INSERTION.

1	½ inch,	$0.40 0.55 0.60
2	1	0.75 0.95 1.00 1.25 1.40
3	1½	1.25 1.50 1.75 2.00 2.50
4	2	2.00 2.25 2.75 3.00

MALTESE.

1	1 inch,	$0.35	.40		
2	2	0.75	.95	1.20	1.45
3	3	1.50	1.75	2.00	

MALTESE INSERTION.

1	1 inch,	$0.22	.25	
2	2	.35	.45	.60

RUSSIAN.

1	2 inches,	$0.56	0.65	0.75
2	3	1.20	1.50	

RUSSIAN INSERTION.

1	1 inch,	$0.45	0.50
2	2	0.75	1.00

CLUNY.

1	1 inch,	$0.20	.35	.40	
2	2	.25	.35	.45	.50
3	3	.40	.45	.65	.75

CLUNY INSERTION.

1	¾ inch,	$0.20	.28	
2	1½	.25	.35	.48
3	2½	.40	.45	.65

TORCHON.

1	½ inch,	$0.05	.07	.09	.11	.15
2	1	.12	.15	.18	.25	
3	1½	.18	.22	.25	.30	
4	2	.25	.35	.40		
5	3	.45	.48	.50	.55	

TORCHON INSERTION.

1	½ inch,	$0.08	.10	.12	.18
2	1	.12	.15	.18	.20
3	1¼	.31			
4	1½	.20	.22	.25	.27
5	2½	.28	.32	.42	

BRETON.

1	1 inch,	$0.18	.25	.30		
2	1¾	.14	.20	.35	.75	
3	2	.25	.30	.38	.45	.55
4	3	.30	.40	.55	.75	.95 1.20
		1.40				
5	4	1.30	1.45	1.75		

BRETON INSERTION.

1	1 inch,	0.18	.22	.28	.30
2	2	.30	.35	.40	
3	3	.38	.45	.55	

ENGLISH THREAD.

1	½ inch,	$0.20	.25		
2	1	0.28	.35	.40	
3	2	0.65	.75	.95	
4	3½	1.30	1.45	1.75	1.95

SPANISH.

1	1 inch,	0.25	.30	.38	
2	2	.37	.45	.50	
3	3	.40	.50	.60	.65 .75
4	4	1.10	1.25	1.35	

BLACK GUIPURE.

1	1 inch,	0.25	.28	.30
2	2	.45	.55	.65
3	3	.75	1.00	1.10
4	4	1.35	1.50	1.75
5	5	2.50	3.00	3.75

BLACK-GUIPURE INSERTION.

1	1 inch,	0.45	.50	.60
2	2	0.75	.85	1.00
3	3	1.30	1.60	1.75

BLACK THREAD.

1	1 inch,	0.50	.65	.75
2	2	0.95	1.15	1.30
3	3	2.25	2.50	2.75
4	4	3.25	3.75	4.50
5	5	5.50	6.00	6.75
6	8	10.00	15.00	
7	12	18.00	22.00	
8	15	20.00	25.00	30.00

POINT APPLIQUÉ.

1	1 inch,	0.85	.95	
2	2	1.45	1.75	2.00
3	3	2.25	2.50	3.00
4	4	3.00	3.50	4.00
5	8	10.00	18.00	
6	14	25.00	28.00	

POINT DUCHESSE.

1	1½ inches,	1.95	2.75	
2	2½	3.00	3.25	3.75
3	3½	4.00	4.50	5.00
4	4½	5.50	6.50	7.00 7.50
5	5½	8.50	9.00	10.50

POINT GAZE.

1	1½ inches,	3.00	4.00	5.50	
2	2½	8.75	9.00	11.00	
3	3	13.00	14.00	15.00	16.00
		18.00			
4	4	22.50	25.00	30.00	
5	12	65.00			

NETS AND VEILINGS.

Price per yard.

COTTON BRUSSELS NET.

1. White, plain.
   36 inches, 0.25 .30 .38 .50
   72   .45 .60
2. White, figured.
   27 inches, 1.60

ILLUSION.

1. White silk, 16 inches, .30 .40 .50 .60
2.   1 yard,   .40 .50 .60
3.   2   .80
4.   3   1.20
5.   4   1.50

BLACK-SPANISH NET.

1. 27 inches, 2.25 2.75 3. 3.50 4. 4.50

GUIPURE NET.

1. 27 inches, 1.75 1.90 2. 2.75 3. 3.50

THREAD NET.

1. 16 inches, 1.15 1.40 1.75 1.95 2.25 3. 3.75
2. 27 inches, 4.50 5. 6.

BLACK BRUSSELS NET.

1. 16 inches .30 .45 .50 .60
2. 36   .60 .75 1. 1.25 1.75 2.

PARASINA.

1. 18 inches, .35 .40
2. 27   .50

SCARFS.

Prices each.

1. Chintz-silk and Breton, $1.25 1.75 2.10
2. Breton, .75 1.25 1.65 2.25
3. Spanish, .75 1. 1.35 1.50 2. 2.50 3. 4. 7. 9.50
4. French, .85 1. 1.25 1.50 1.75 2.25 2.50
5. Imitation point, 1.50 1.75
6. Guipure, 2.30 2.75 3.25 3.75 4. 5. 6.50 8.
7. Thread, 10. 12.50 15. 20. 22.50 24. 28.
8. Point Duchesse, 9.75 10.75 12.50 14. 16. 18.50 22.50 25. 28.50 30. 35.
9. Mirecourt, 1.00

BARBS.

1. Thread, $1.15 1.35 1.75 2. 2.50 3. 3.50 3.75 4. 5. 6. 7. 8. 10. 12.50 17.

2. Point Appliqué, 3.25 4.50 5. 6.50 7. 7.75 8.25 10. 12.50 15.
3. Point Duchesse, 3. 3.75 4.50 5.50 6.25 7.50 8. 9. 11. 12. 14. 18.
4. Point Gaze, 10. 12.50 15. 18. 22.50 25. 30. 33. 35. 42. 47.50.

BARBETTES.

1. Breton, $0.38 .45
2. Point Duchesse, .25. 65 .75 1. 1.25 1.50 2.25 2.75 3.50 4.
3. Point Gaze, 3.75 5. 6.50 7.25 8.50 9.

VEILS.

1. Thread, round, $4.50 7.50 9. 12.50 14. 18.

FAN COVERS.

1. Point Duchesse, $12.50 18. 20. 25.
2. Point Gaze, 20. 25. 30. 45. 50.
3. Thread, 18. 20. 25. 30.

PARASOL COVERS.

1. Llama, $3. 5.
2. Tatting, 10. 12.50
3. Point Appliqué, 18.50 20. 28.
4. Point Duchesse, 30. 45. 65
5. Thread, 15. 18. 22. 25. 27. 35. 38. 45.

HANDKERCHIEFS.

1. Valenciennes, $2.50 3. 4. 5.50 7. 11. 15.
2. Point Duchesse, 4.50 7.50 8.50 10. 12.50 14. 16. 18. 20. 25. 30.
3. Point Gaze, 10. 12. 15. 18. 22.50 25. 30. 32. 35. 40. 47. 50.
4. Point Appliqué, 3.75 5.75 7.50 9. 12. 15. 18. 20. 22. 25.

MADE ARTICLES.

FICHUS.

1. Imitation Breton, $0.50 .65 .75 .85 1. 2.25 2.50
2. Breton, 1. 1.25 1.56 2. 2.25 2.50 3.75 4.50 7. 11.
3. Languedoc, 1.75 2. 2.50 4.
4. Point d'Esprit, 1.25 1.50 1.75 2. 3.50 3.75 4.
5. Italian Valenciennes, 2. 2.25 2.75 3.50 4.50

CAPES.

1 Breton, $4. 6.50 7. 9. 10. 11.
2 Valenciennes, 10. 12.50 18. 25. 30.
3 Point Duchesse, 22.50 25. 30. 35:
4 Point Appliqué, 18.50 27.50 30. 35.
5 Point Gaze, 75. 95. 125. 150.
6 Black Thread, 12.50 13. 22.50 25. 30.
7 Guipure, 7. 10. 14. 18. 20.

CRAVATS.

1 Muslin, embroidered, $0.20 .25 .35 .45 .50
2 Muslin, hemstitch, .45 .55 .65 .75 95
3 Muslin-and-lace, .25 .30 .35 .45 .50 .60 .75 1.00 1.20 1.40 1.60 1.75 2.
4 Crêpe de Chêne, .40 .50 .60
5 Silk, plain, .25 .35 .40 .45
6 Silk, embroidered, .50 .65 .75 1. 1.25 1.50

COLLARS.

1 Point Appliqué, $2. 4. 8. 9. 11.
2 Point Duchesse, 4.50 7.50 9. 12. 15 20. 30.
3 Point Gaze, 2. 5. 7. 10. 15. 18. 20. 25.
4 Point Gaze sets (collar and cuffs), 25. 30. 35. 40. 50. 65.

COLLARETTES.

1 Breton, $3.25 3 75 4.50 5. 6. 6.50 7.
2 Point d'Esprit, 1.75 1:90 2.25 2.60 3. 3.75 4.25
3 Italian Valenciennes, 1. 1.25 1.40 1.65 1.75 2. 2.20 2.50 2.75
4 Brabant, 2.25 2.75 3. 3.50 4. 4.50

JABOTS.

1 Crêpe de Chêne and lace, $1. 1.50 1.95 2. 2.25 2.75 3.
2 Valenciennes, 1. 1.50 2. 2.75 3.50 4.
3 Breton, 75 .85 .95 1. 1.35 1.55 1.75 2.25 2.50
4 Point Duchesse, 2.75 2.95 3. 3.75 4.25 5.

HANDKERCHIEFS.

1 Imitation Valenciennes, $0.75 .95 1. 1.25 1.40 1.65 2.
2 Imitation Breton, 1.25 1.75 2. 2.25 2.50 2.75

BELTS

1 Breton-lace, satin and roses, $2.50
2 Point d'Esprit-lace and roses, 2.50

SLEEVES.

1 Spanish, $3.75 5.00

BIBS.

1 Italian-Valenciennes, $0.65 .75 85 1. 1.25 1.40 1.65 1.75 2. 2.25 2.50
2 Breton, 1.20 1.25 1.45 1.65 1.85 2.25 2.60 3.

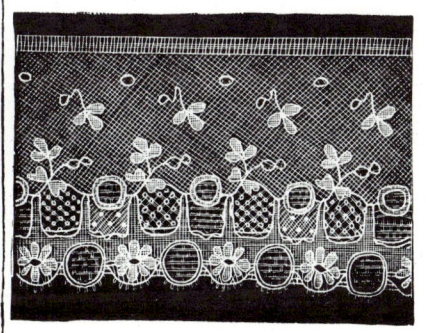

Imitation Point, 2 inches, 0.35

Imitation Point Rose, 2 inches, 0.31

Point d'Esprit, 0.15

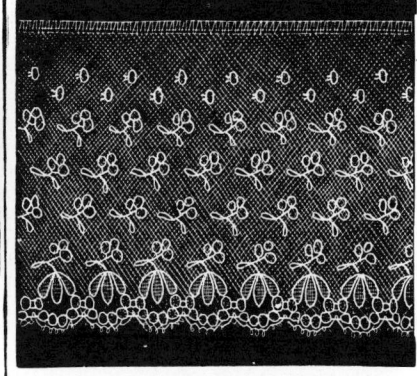

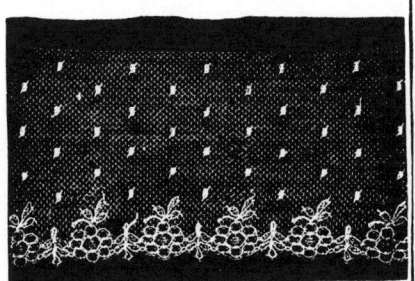

Point d'Esprit, 0.22

Imitation Mechlin, 3 inches, $1.10

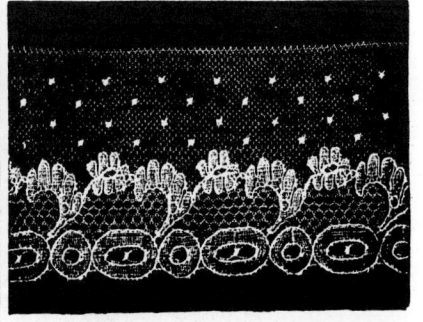

Imitation Mechlin, 2½ inches, 0.40

Imitation Mechlin, 2½ inches, 0.40

Imitation Mechlin, 2½ inches, 0.27

LORD & TAYLOR, NEW YORK.

Languedoc, 2 inches, 0.31

Mechlin, 2 inches, 0.60; 3 in., 0.75

Guipure Net, 27 inches, 1.75

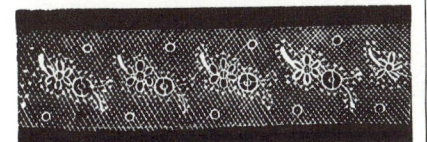

Coralina, 1½ inches, 0.10

Pearl de Lily, 3 inches, 0.35.

Mechlin, 1½ inches, 0.56; 2½ in., .85; 3 in., 1.25; 4 in., 1.40

Imitation Mechlin, 1¾ inches, 0.20

Coralina, 2 inches, 0.14; 2½ in. .18

Black French, 2 inches, 0.25.

Black French, 3 inches, 0.25; 4½ in., .31

Black French, 3½ inches, 0.25; 4 in., 28; 5 in., .35

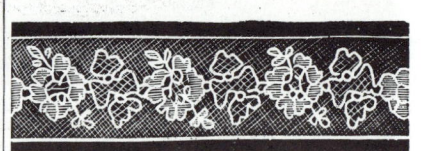

Vermicelli and Mirecourt, 1½ inches, 0.14

Black French 2 inches, 0.30

Black French, 3 inches, 0.38; 4 in. .50; 5 in., .70

Spanish, black and cream, 2 inches, 0.27; 3 in., 37; 4 in., .44; 5 in., .56

LORD & TAYLOR, NEW YORK.

Guipure Net, 27 inches, 2.25

Torchon, ½ inch, 0.15

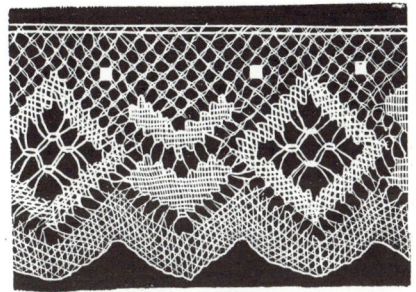

Torchon, 2½ inches, 0.25.

Torchon, 1¼ inches, 0.30.

Spanish, black, 3½ inches, 0.31

Spanish, black, 3 inches, 0.40

Spanish, white or black, 3 inches, 0.35; 4 in., .45
5 in., .62

Spanish, white or black, 2 inches, 0.75; 4 in., 95.

82   LORD & TAYLOR, NEW YORK.

Torchon, 1¾ inches, 0.25

Breton, 1¾ inches, 0.18

Breton, 1¾ inches, 0.18

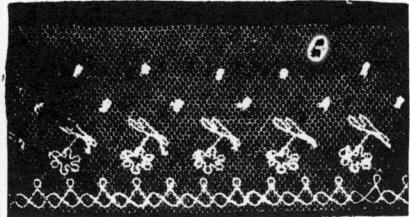

Breton, 1½ inches, 0.14

Breton, 4 inches, 0.30

Spanish, white, 4 inches, 0.80

LORD & TAYLOR, NEW YORK. 83

Vermicelli, 1½ inches, 0.19; 2 in., .25; 2½ in., .35; 3½ in., .40

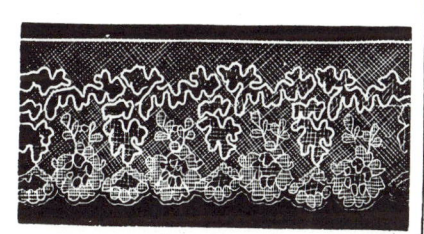

Vermicelli and Mirecourt, 1½ inches, 0.16; 2 in., .25; 3½ in., .37

Point de Newport, 2 inches, 0.21; 2½ in., .25; 3 in., .35

Mirecourt, 2 inches, 0.28; 2½ in., .35; 3 in., .40

Spanish, black, 5 inches, 0.65

Torchon, 1½ inches, 0.18.

Torchon 1½ inches, 0.20.

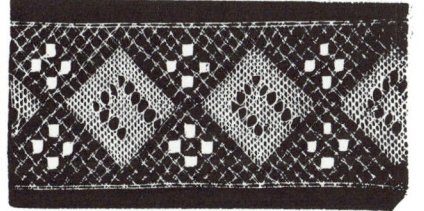

Torchon 2 inches, 0.28.

Torchon, ½ inch, 0.09

Torchon, ½ inch 0.15

Torchon, 1 inch, 0.25; 2 inches, 0.50.

Fine Torchon, 2¼ inches, 0.70.

Torchon, ¾ inch, 0.08.

Torchon 1¾ inches, 0.22.

Torchon, ¾ inch, 0.15.

Torchon, 1¼ inches, 0.22.

Torchon, 1 inch, 0.12.

LORD & TAYLOR, NEW YORK.

85

Spanish, 2½ inches, 0.35

Spanish, 3½ inches, 0.50

Spanish Net, 27 inches, 3.75

Spanish Net, 27 inches, 3.75

Spanish Net, 27 inches, 2.00

Spanish Net, 27 inches, 3.00

86 LORD & TAYLOR, NEW YORK.

Spanish Net, 27 inches, 2.50.

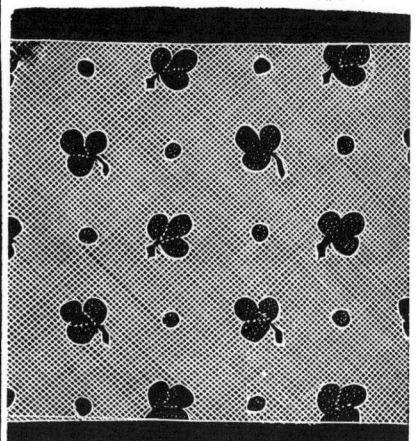

Black Spanish Net, 27 inches, 2.65.

Spanish Net, 27 inches, 3.00.

Spanish, black, 3¼ inches 0.35

Spanish, black, 3½ inches, 0.35

Torchon, 2½ inches, 0.28.

Torchon, 2 inches, 0.35.

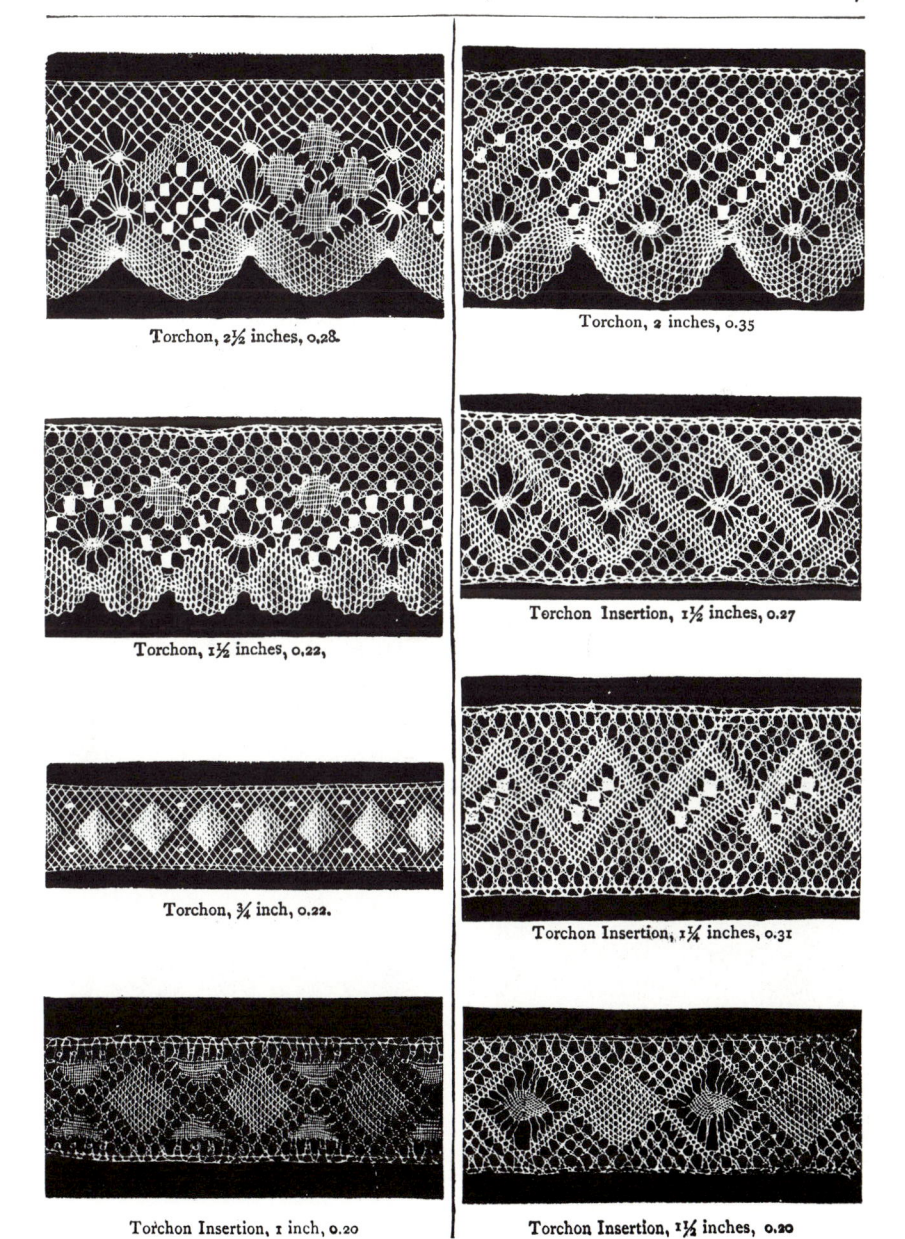

Torchon, 1½ inches, 0.22.

Torchon Insertion, 1½ inches, 0.27.

Torchon, ¾ inch, 0.22.

Torchon Insertion, 1¼ inches, 0.31.

Torchon Insertion, 1 inch, 0.20.

Torchon Insertion, 1½ inches, 0.20.

88   LORD & TAYLOR, NEW YORK.

Torchon, 1½ inches, 0.18.

Torchon, 1¼ inches, 0.33.

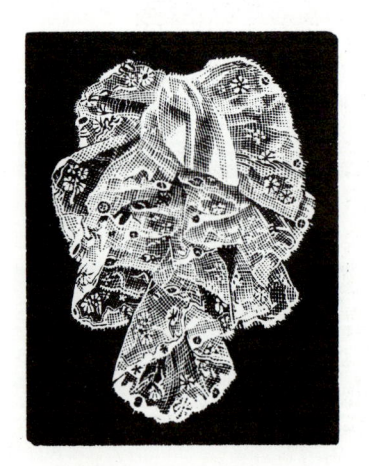

Caroline Jabot, 1.75.

Newport Point Jabot, 1.35.

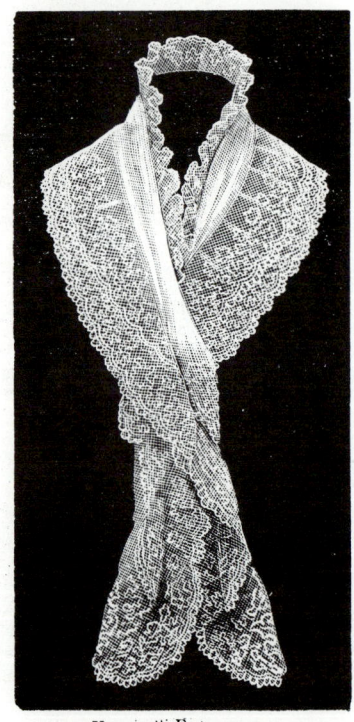

Vermicelli Fichu, 2.50.

Coralina Lace Jabot, 0.65.

Languedoc Jabot, 1.25

Duchesse Scarf, $14.00

90   LORD & TAYLOR, NEW YORK.

Breton Fichu, 0.85

Languedoc Chemisette. 1.25

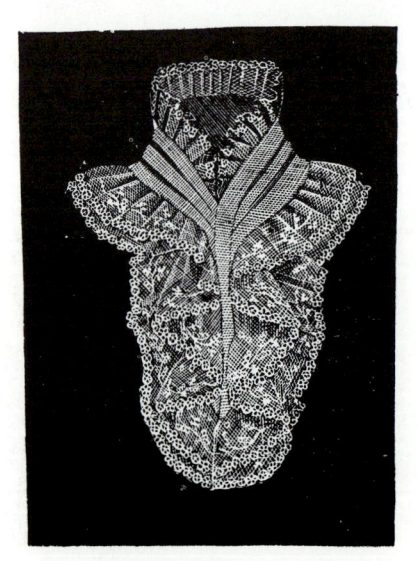

Languedoc Fichu, 2.00

Mirecourt Lace and Mull Fichu, 3.00

LORD & TAYLOR, NEW YORK.

Mirecourt, 1.50

Vermicelli Jabot, 1.00

Spanish Scarf, 2.50

Guipure Scarf, 3.25

92 LORD & TAYLOR, NEW YORK.

Mirecourt, 1.75.

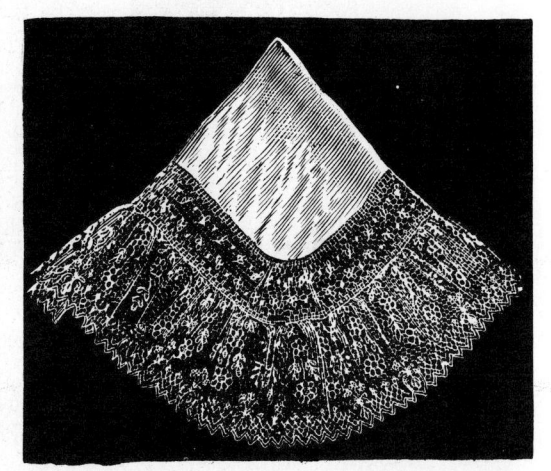

Imitation Breton Handkerchief, 1.75

Languedoc Jabot, 1.15.

Valenciennes Handkerchief, 11.00

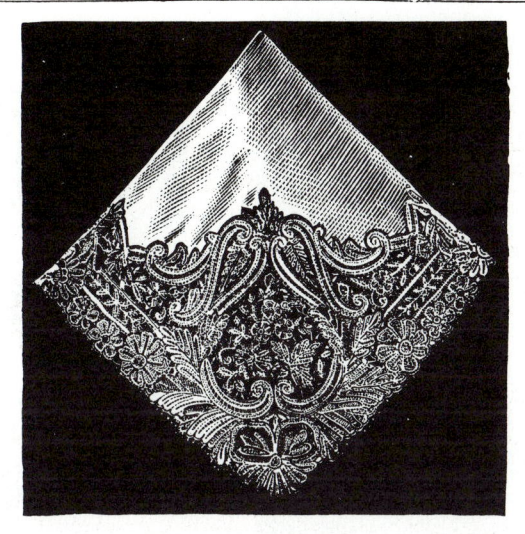

Duchesse Handkerchief, 16.00

Point Gaze, 22.50

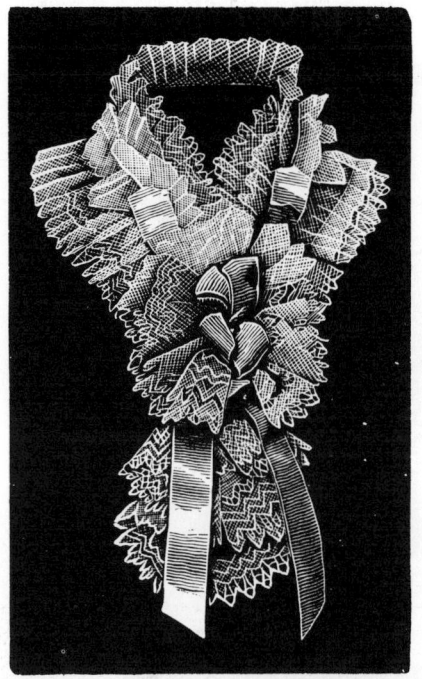

Fancy Lace Collarette and Satin Ribbon, 2.25

Caroline Fichu, 1.00

Languedoc Jabot, 0.95

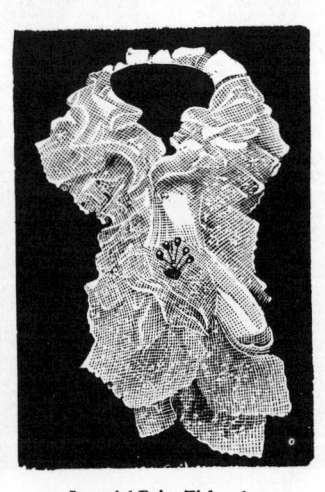

Imperial Point Fichu, 6.50.

Spanish, 3.75

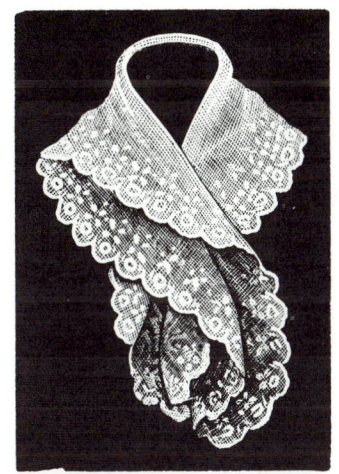

Mirecourt and Mull Fichu, 1.90.

Point d'Armour Jabot, 5.00.

Mirecourt and Mull, 4.50.

Pearl de Lily, 3.50.

EMBROIDERIES.

Embroidery this season is either wrought in showy open patterns, or close eyelets mingled with thickly worked scrolls, flowers and fine leaves in patterns whose exquisite delicacy and beauty have never been exceeded.

Fayal embroidery does not wear well, and is superseded by canvas work which is equally effective. All widths of all patterns are furnished in the new embroideries with inserting to match.

Embroidery for batiste muslin dresses is furnished on écru muslin to match the tint of the material, which now resembles in color and appearance the ancient pineapple cloth, though it is not so sheer. Embroidery is shown in silk and cotton, and in blue, rose and other colors to trim these dresses, but the work in écru thread will probably be most used, as it will not lose its beauty in washing.

Hamburg Edgings.

1. ½ inch, 0.05 .08 .10 .15 .17 .18 .20
2. 1 inch, 0.10 .15 18 .20 .25 .28
3. 1½ inches, .15 .21 .20 .22 .25 .27 .30 .35
4. 2 inches, .20 .22 .25 .28 .30 .35 .40
5. 2¾ inches .21 .25 .30 .32 .35 .37 .40
6. 3 inches, .25 .30 .35 .40 .50 .55 .60 .65
7. 3½ inches, .35 .40 .45 .50 .60 .90 .95
8. 4 inches, .55 .60 .65 .75 .85
9. 5 inches, .90 .95 1.00 1.25 1.50 1.75

Hamburg Insertions.

1. ½ inch wide, $0.05 .08 .10 .12 .15 .18 .20
2. ¾ .15 .18 .22 .25 .28 .30
3. 1 .12 .15 .18 .20 .25 .30 .35
4. 1¼ .22 .25 .28 .30 .35 .38 .40
5. 1½ .25 .30 .35 .40 .45 .50
6. .40 .45 .50 .55 .60
7. 2½ .50 .60 .75 1.00

Nainsook Edgings.

1. ½ inch wide, .10 .15 .17 .18 .20 .22 .25
2. 1 .15 .18 .20 .25 .28 .30 .35
3. 1½ .25 .28 .30 .32 .35 .40 .45
4. 2 .50 .55 .60 .65 .70 .75
5. 2½ .60 .65 .70 .75 .80 .85
6. 3 .65 .70 .75 .80 .85 1.00 1.15
7. 3½ .95 1.00 1.25 1.50 1.75 2.00
8. 4 1.35 1.45 1.50 1.75 2.00
9. 5½ 2.00 2.25 2.75

Nainsook Insertions.

1. ½ inch wide, .15 .18 .20 .22 .25
2. 1 .20 .25 .30 .35 .40 .45
3. 1¼ .40 .45 .50 .55 .60
4. 1½ .50 .60 .65 .70 .75
5. 2 .90 .95 1.00

LORD & TAYLOR, NEW YORK.

Fayal Edgings.

1	1 inch wide,	0.20	.25	.30	.35	
2	1½		.45	.50	.55	.60
3	2	.45	.50	.60	.65	.70
4	2½	.50				
5	3	.55	.65	.75	.90	
6	3½	1.00	1.15	1.25	1.50	
7	4½	1.75	1.85	1.90		

Fayal Insertions.

1	1 inch wide,	0.20	.25	.30	.35
2	1¼	.30	.35	.40	.45
3	1½	.45	.50	.55	.60
4	2	.60	.65	.70	

Swiss Edgings.

1	½ inch wide,	0.10	.15	.18	.20
2	1	0.20	.25	.28	.30
3	1½	.30	.35	.40	.45
4	2	.45	.50	.55	.60
5	3	.65	.75	1.00	
6	3½	1.00	1.25	1.50	

Swiss Insertions.

1	½ inch wide,	0.10	.12	.15	.18	.20
2	1		.18	.20	.25	.30 .35
3	1½		.40	.50	.60	.75 .90

French Bands.

1 Fine patterns, per half-dozen, 1.35
2 Chemise, .75 .85 1.00

Neck Rufflings.

1 Crêpe-lisse, various styles, 0.25 .30 .35 .40 .45 .50 .55 .60 .75 .90 1.00
2 Lace-edged, various styles, 0.15 .18 .20 .25 .30. .35 .40

Skirt Pleatings.

1 Swiss plaitings with lace edge, .15 .18 .20 .23 .30 .35. 40 .50 .55 .75

Satin Skirt Pleatings.

All colors, .40 .45 .50

Cambric, 1 inch, 0.30

Cambric, 2 inches, 0.60

Cambric, 1 inch, 0.35

Cambric Edge, ½ inch, 0.11

98 LORD & TAYLOR, NEW YORK.

Cambric, 2 inches, 0.60

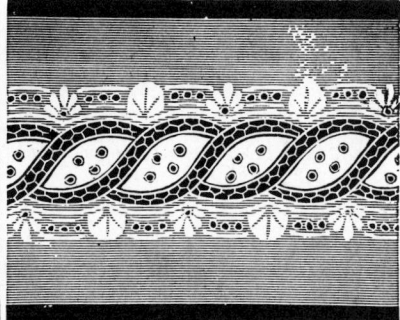

Cambric, 1½ inches, 0.40

Cambric, 1¼ inches, 0.35

Cambric, 1½ inches, 0.45

Cambric, 1½ inches, 0.35

Cambric, 2 inches, 0.55

LORD & TAYLOR, NEW YORK.

Cambric, ¾ inch, 0.20

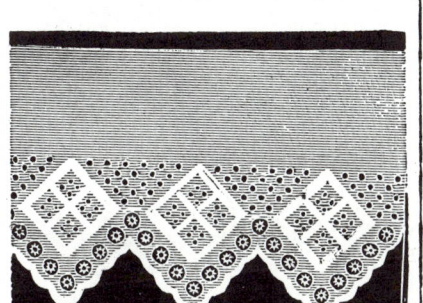

Nainsook, 1 inch, 0.30

Cambric Edge, 2 inches, 0.25

Nainsook, 1½ inches, 0.55

Cambric, 3 inches, 0.75

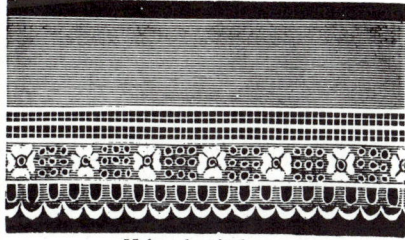

Nainsook, 3 inches, 0.75

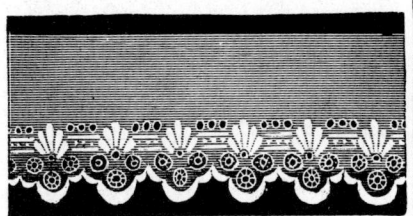

LORD & TAYLOR, NEW YORK.

Nainsook, ¾ inches, 0.22

Nainsook, 1½ inches, 0.40

Nainsook, 1½ inches, 0.45

Nainsook, 2 inches, 0.65

Nainsook, 4½ inches, 1.75

Nainsook, 3 inches, 0.90

Nainsook, 6½ inches, 2.50

Nainsook, 4 inches, 1.10

Cambric Edge, 2 inches, 0.30

Cambric Edge, 2 inches, 0.25.

Cambric Edge, ½ inch, 0.07

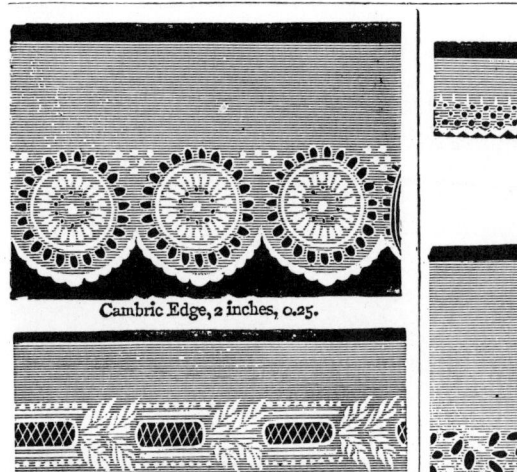

Cambric, ½ inch, 0.20

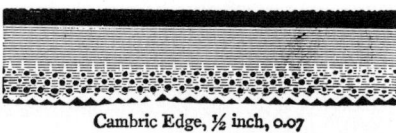

Cambric Edge, 1 inch, 0.13

MUSLIN UNDERWEAR.

The perfection to which lace and embroidery has been brought by manufacturers places handsome underwear within the reach of all. Cambric and fine percale have almost superseded linen for summer use. Fine tucking, embroidery, torchon and Valenciennes laces are the favorite trimming. Puffing is less used than formerly. Good taste demands that all these garments should be made in dainty, simple styles, which may be easily laundered, the greatest care being taken to select fine cambric and delicate patterns of embroidery or lace.

Bridal trousseaux are usually made to order, and include a dozen sets of three pieces each, and six high-necked and six low-necked corset-covers, a dozen cambric skirts and six trained skirts.

A new skirt, which is only made to order, is surrounded by a wide ruffle handsomely trimmed with embroidery or lace, while two or three plain ruffles flounce the back breadth above it, and adds a slight fullness, which forms a moderate bustle.

Flannel skirts are now often embroidered with wool and seeded with silk. This work is handsome, and washes much better than solid silk embroidery. Embroidery in pale-blue, rose and cardinal, is used on such skirts, but pure white is preferred for flannel and for all underwear.

CHEMISES.

Bands, 38, 40, 42, 44, 46 inches.

If other sizes than those enumerated under chemises, drawers, night-dresses, skirts and corset-covers are required, the garments will need to be made; a few days time will be necessary and the price a little in advance.

MUSLIN FOR LADIES.

No. 1, $0.50

1   Corded band, 0.50 .75

No. 3

2   Pointed yoke, three rows insertion, Hamburg edging, 0.75

3   Tucked front, Hamburg ruffle below the band, 0.95

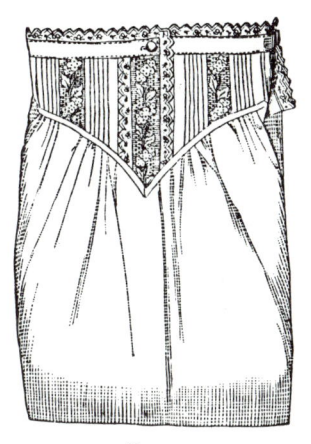

No. 2

4   Corded band, tucked yoke, made from "Pride of the West" muslin, 1.

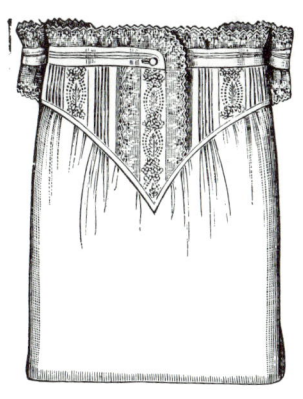

No. 5

5   Corded band, three rows insertion, Hamburg edging, 1.25

6 Tucked yoke, made from "Pride of the West" muslin, Hamburg edging, 1.50

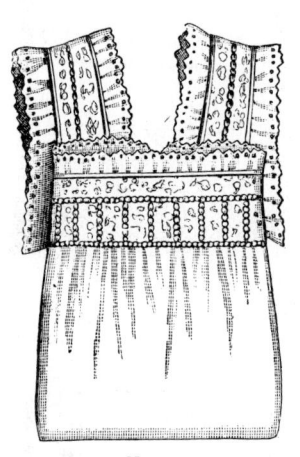

No. 7.

7 Square neck, trimming of Hamburg edging and insertion, 2.40.

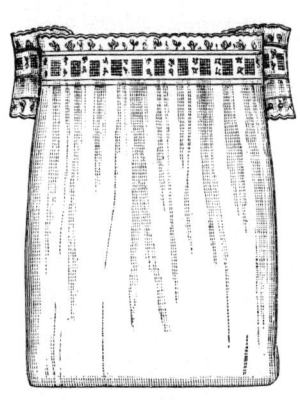

No. 8.

8 Square neck, Hamburg insertion, back and front, 2.75

LINEN CHEMISES.

1 Corded band, $2.50
2 Corded band, Hamburg edging, 2.90
3 Hamburg edging and insertion, 3.25
4 Sacque-chemise, hand-embroidered 4.50 5. 5.50 6. to 10.
5 Sacque-chemise, trimmed with imitation Valenciennes lace, 5. to 10.
6 Sacque-chemise, trimmed with torchon lace, 6. to 10.

CAMBRIC CHEMISES.

1 Corded band, $0.95
2 Corded band, Hamburg edging, 1.35
3 Corded band, Hamburg insertion and edging, 1.75
4 Puffing and torchon insertion, 2.
5 Hamburg insertion, 2.75 to 10.
6 Imitation Valenciennes lace, 2. 2.25 2.50 to 5.

DRAWERS.

Bands, 25, 27, 29 inches.
Lengths, 25, 27, 29 inches.

MUSLIN, FOR LADIES.

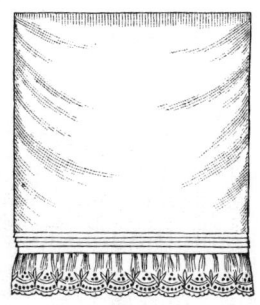

No. 1

1 Hamburg ruffle, tucked above, $0.50
2 Tucked ruffle, tucked above, 0.60

LORD & TAYLOR, NEW-YORK. 105

No. 3

3 Tucked cambric ruffle, Hamburg edging, 0.65
4 Hem, tucked above, 0.50

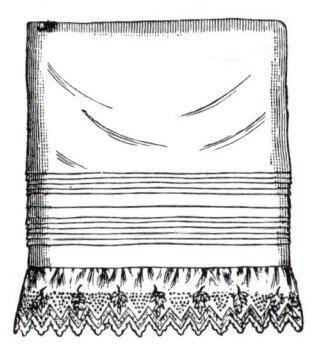

No. 5

5 Hamburg edging, cluster of tucks above 0.75

No. 6, $1.10

6 Deep Hamburg ruffle, two clusters of tucks above, 1.10 1.25

No. 7, $1.

7 Hamburg ruffle, two clusters of tucks above with insertion between. 1. 1.10 1.65

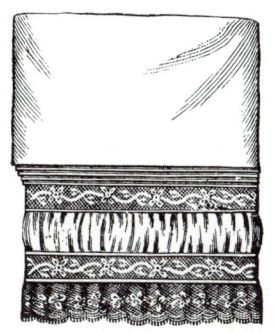

No. 8

8 Valenciennes insertion and edging, with puffing, 1.50

No. 9

106   LORD & TAYLOR, NEW-YORK.

9   Valenciennes and Hamburg insertion, Valenciennes edging, 1.75

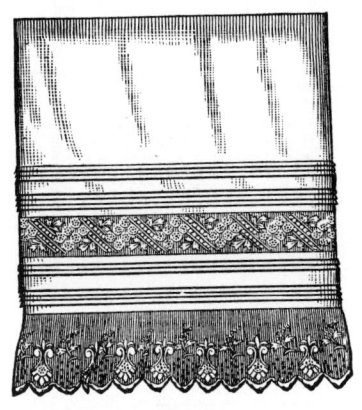

No. 10

10   Hamburg ruffle, two clusters of tucks, with insertion between, 2.00

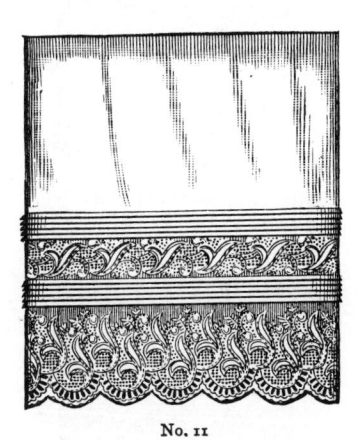

No. 11

11   Deep Hamburg ruffle, two clusters of tucks above, with insertion between, 3.25

NIGHT-DRESSES.
Neck-measure, 14, 15, 16 inches.
MUSLIN, FOR LADIES.

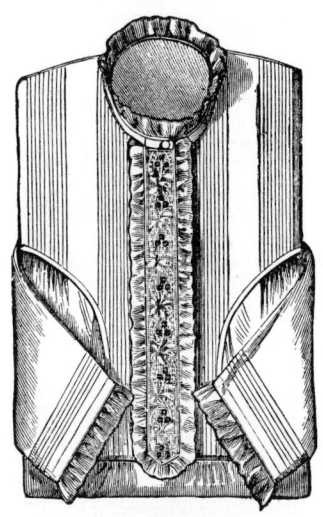

No. 1

1   Tucked yoke with ruffle, 0.75

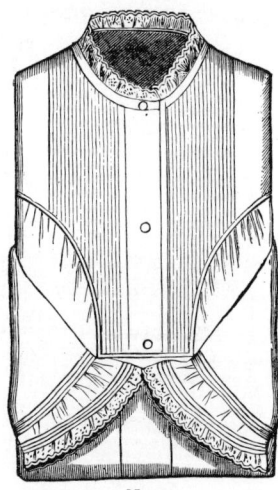

No. 2

2   Cluster-tucked yoke, Hamburg edging on neck and sleeves, 1.

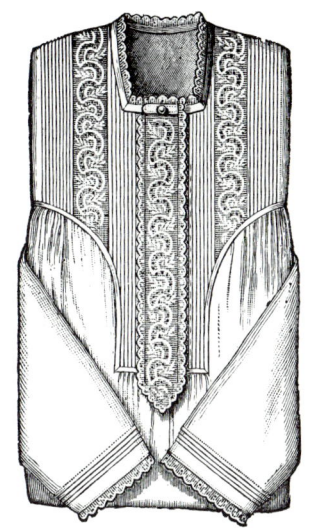

LORD & TAYLOR, NEW-YORK. 107

3 Tucked yoke, three rows of insertion, Hamburg edging, 1.25
4 Square yoke of wide and narrow tucks, three pleats in back, Hamburg edging on front, 1.50

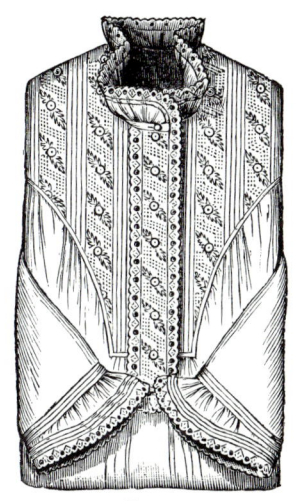

No. 3

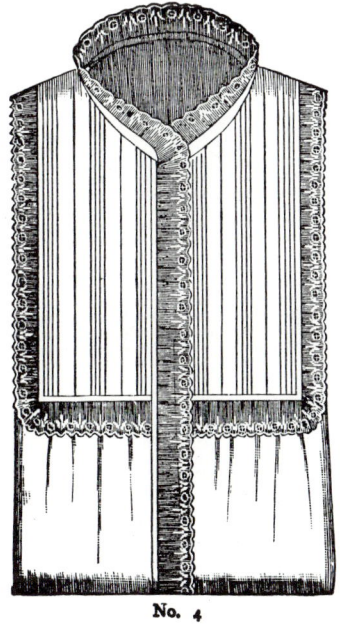

No. 4

No. 5

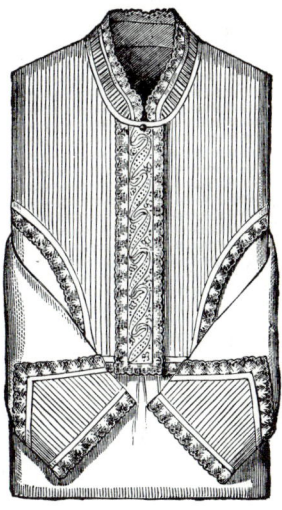

No. 6

5 Cluster-tucked yoke, five rows of insertion, Hamburg edging, ruffle around neck and cuffs, 1.40

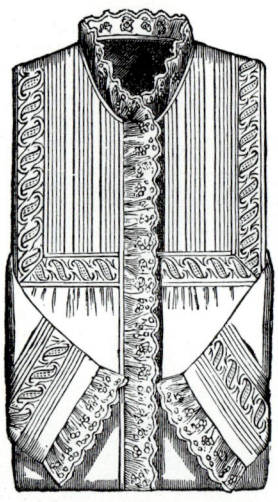

6 Solid-tucked yoke with insertion, edging all around, 1.75

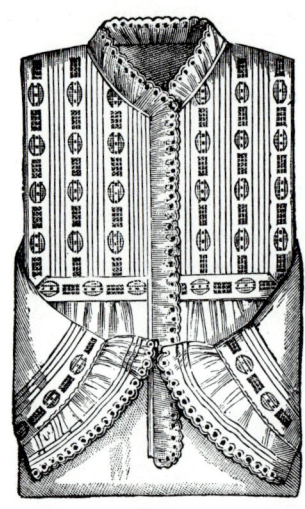

No. 7

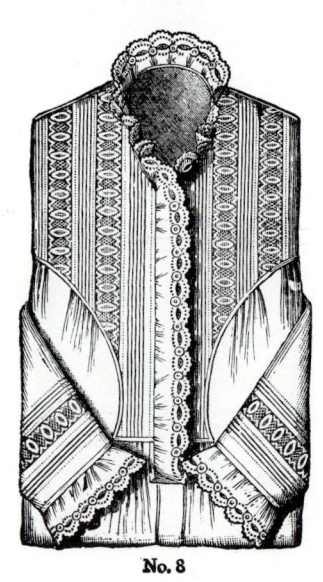

No. 9

No. 8

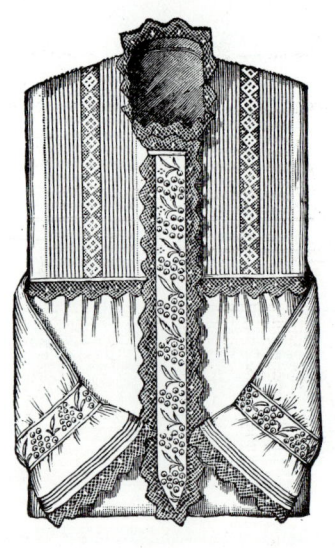

No. 10

LORD & TAYLOR, NEW-YORK.

7 Square yoke, one row of insertion around yoke, Hamburg ruffle on neck and sleeves, 1.75
8 Yoke of tucks and insertion, ruffle of Hamburg edging, 1.95
9 Square yoke of tucks and insertion, Hamburg ruffle on neck and sleeves, 2.40
10 Square yoke, torchon insertion and edging, 2.75

WALKING-SKIRTS.
Length, 38 to 40 inches.
MUSLIN, FOR LADIES; Princess back.

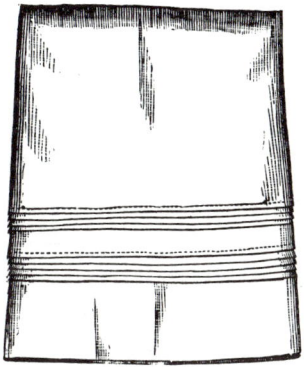

No. 1, $0.60

1 Deep hem, nine tucks above, 0.60 .75.

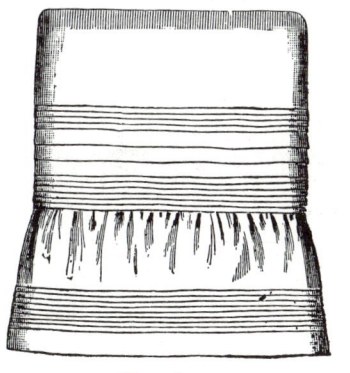

No. 2, $1.00

2 Cambric ruffle, nine tucks in ruffle, tucked above, 0.95 1.00

No. 3

3 Cambric ruffle edged with torchon lace one row insertion on flounce, 1.50

No. 4

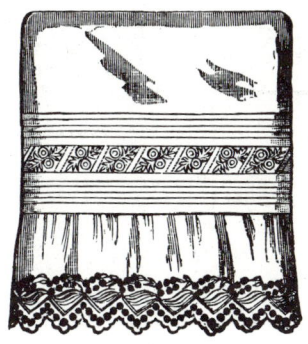

No. 5,

LORD & TAYLOR, NEW YORK.

4 Cambric ruffle, Hamburg edging, 1.60
5 Hamburg ruffle, insertion above, 2.25.

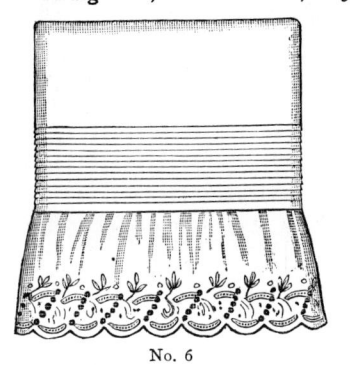

No. 6

6 Hamburg ruffle, tucks above, 2.25

No. 7

No. 8

7 Cambric ruffle, two rows insertion, Hamburg edging on ruffle, cluster of tucks above, 2.50
8 Cambric ruffle, edged with torchon lace, two rows insertion, tucks above, 2.50

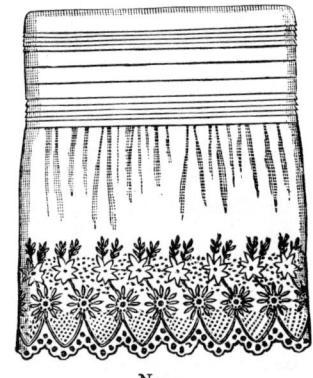

No. 9

9 Deep Hamburg ruffle, tucks above 3.00

TRAIN SKIRTS.

Muslin, for Ladies.
1 Cambric ruffle, deep cluster of three tucks above, $1.00
2 Two cambric ruffles, cluster of three tucks in each, 1.60
3 Two cambric ruffles, Hamburg edging on each ruffle, 2.85
4 Hamburg ruffle, deep cluster of tucks above, 1.75
5 Deep ruffle, insertion and edging of lace on ruffle, cluster of three tucks above, 2.50
6 Deep ruffle, torchon insertion and edging, 2.95
7 Deep ruffle, two rows torchon insertion and edging, 4.15

Flannel.
1 Plain, hem and tucks, $2.40
2 Scolloped 3.00
3 Scolloped with dot, 3.50
4 Embroidered, 4.00 4.50 5.00 6.50 6. to 18.

CHEMISES.

Muslin, for Misses.
1 Plain band :
    size 3, 28 inches, $0.36
        4. 32   .42

LORD & TAYLOR, NEW YORK.

size 5,	34 inches,	.50
6,	36	.55
7,	38	.60

2 Band and sleeves finished with cambric ruffle :

size 3,	28 inches,	0.42
4,	32	.48
5,	34	.55
6,	36	.60
7,	36	.65

3 Hamburg edging on neck and cuffs, center-piece of insertion :

size 3,	28 inches,	0.57
4,	32	.63
5,	34	.68
6,	36	.75
7,	38	.85

DRAWERS.

MUSLIN, FOR MISSES.

1 Trimmed with tucks above the hem :

size 1,	length 10 inches,	$0.31
2,	12	.34
3,	15	.35
4,	18	.40
5,	21	.45
6,	23	.48
7,	26	.54

2 Trimmed with cambric ruffle :

size 1,	length 10 inches,	0.34
2,	12	.37
3,	15	.40
4,	18	.43
5,	21	.48
6,	23	.53
7,	26	.58

3 Trimmed with Hamburg edging :

size 1,	length 10 inches,	0.41
2,	12	.44
3,	15	.48
4,	18	.53
5,	21	.60
6,	23	.65
7,	26	.70

4 Trimmed with Hamburg ruffle :

size 1,	length 10 inches,	0.48
2,	12	.50
3,	15	.53
4,	18	.58
5,	21	.63
6,	23	.65
7,	26	.68

5 Trimmed with Hamburg edging, tucks and insertion :

size 1,	length 10 inches,	0.70
2,	12	.75
3,	15	.80
4,	18	.85
5,	21	.90
6,	23	.95
7,	26	1.00

NIGHT-DRESSES.

MUSLIN, FOR MISSES.

1 Tucks down the front with loom-edging:

size 1,	length 22 inches,	$0.57
2,	27	.65
3,	32	.70
4,	37	.78
5,	42	.85
6,	49	.95

2 One row insertion, Hamburg edging

size 1,	length 22 inches,	0.78
2,	27	.85
3	32	.95
4,	37	1.05
5,	42	1.18
6,	49	1.25

SKIRTS.

MUSLIN, FOR MISSES.

1 Hem and tucks :

size 1,	length 12 inches,	$0.31
2,	14	.35
3,	18	.38
4,	20	.42
5.	24	.48
6,	28	.52
7,	32	.58

2 Cambric ruffle ;

size 1,	length 12 inches,	0.37
2,	14	.40
3,	18	.45
4,	20	.53
5,	24	.55
6,	28	.60
7,	32	.65

3 Hamburg ruffle :

size 1,	length 12 inches	0.67
2,	14	.76
3,	18	.85
4,	20	.92
5,	24	.98
6,	28	1.05
7.	32	1.10

CORSET COVERS.

Bust, 34, 36, 38, 40 inches.

HIGH NECK.

1. Plain. with Hamburg edging, $0.50
2. Tucked yoke, with Hamburg edging, 0.75
3. Tucked yoke, one row insertion, edging, 1.00
4. Three rows insertion, edging, 1.20

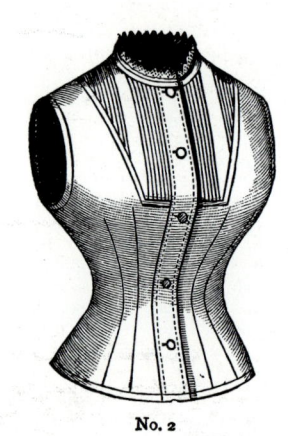

No. 2

5. Three rows torchon insertion, edging, 1.30
6. Hamburg insertion back and front, 1.60

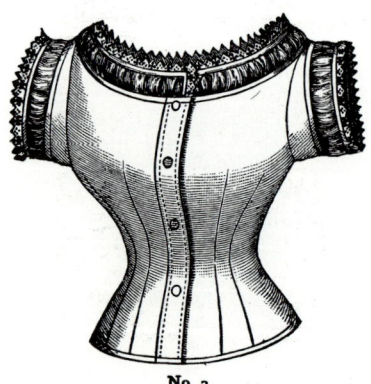

No. 3

LOW NECK.

1. Plain, with Hamburg edging, 0.75
2. Pointed yoke of wide and narrow tucks, with Hamburg edging, 0.95
3. Puffs, Hamburg edging around yoke, 1.00
4. Hamburg insertion, puffing, 1.95
5. Torchon insertion, puffing, 1.90 2.25
6. Corset-cover to match Bridal Set, No. 6, 7.50

BRIDAL SETS.

Each number includes Night-Dress, Chemise and Drawers. The price is for the set.

1. Tucked yoke, with Hamburgh insertions in front, plaits on front of night-dress, $6. 7. 7.50 8. 9.50 10. 12
2. Circular shaped yoke made of Torchon lace and fine tuckings, between, 18.
3. Shirt-bosom front composed of fine tuckings and imitation Valenciennes insertion and edging, the tucking down the entire front, deep flounce around skirt, 19.50
4. Tucked yoke, with imitation Valenciennes lace front and back, insertion between tucks, 12. 14. 16. 18. 20. 22. 25.
5. Square yoke, tucked front and back, trimmed with torchon lace, puffs or tucks between, 16. 18. 20. 22. 24.
6. Square yoke with imitation Maltese lace, puffs front and back, lace between, 15. 18.
7. Entire front of night-dress of imitation Maltese lace, back of yoke of the same, 18. 20. 22. 24.
8. Night-dress with square yoke front and back, entire front of imitation Valenciennes lace and needle-work medallions; chemise and drawers to match, set, 37. ; corset-cover to match, 7.50
9. Yoke front and back, and sleeves of night-dress, trimmed with real Valenciennes lace and bows of white satin ; **ruffle nine inches deep around night-dress, $175**

LORD & TAYLOR, NEW-YORK.

Night-dress of set No. 2, page 112

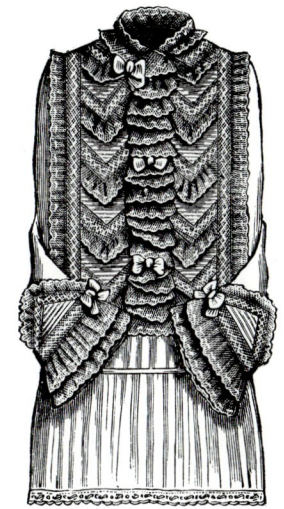

Night-dress of set No. 3, page 112

Chemise of set No. 2, page 112

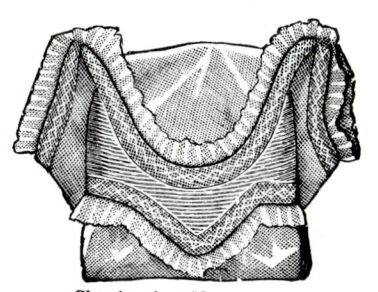

Chemise of set No. 3 page 112

Drawsrs of set No. 2, page 112

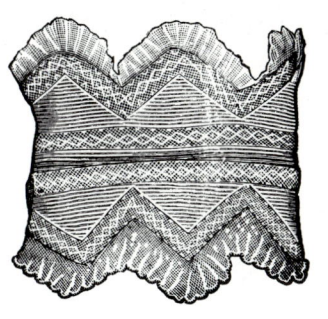

Drawers of set No. 3, page 112

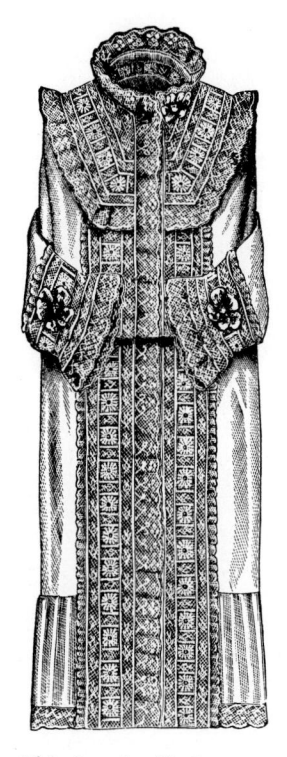

114 LORD & TAYLOR, NEW YORK,

Night-dress of set No. 8, page 112

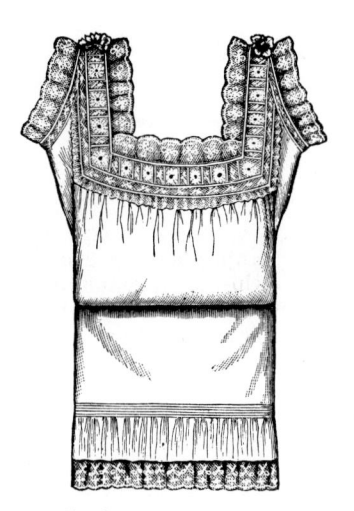

Chemise of set No. 8, page 112

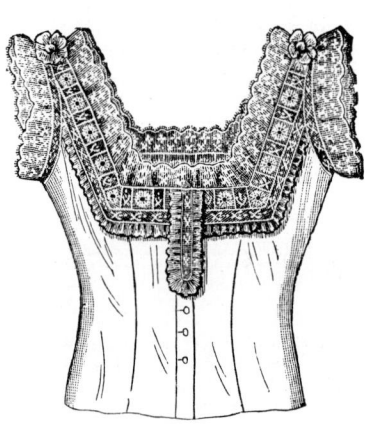

Drawers of set No. 8, page 112

Corset-cover to match set No. 8, page 112

LADIES' AND CHILDREN'S MERINO AND SILK UNDERWEAR.

The use of a light cashmere or silk undergarment during the summer has become the almost universal practice. It is necessary to health in this changing climate. Raw silk is especially recommended by physicians, and its expense becomes a matter of less moment, when its durability and power to resist all injury from washing is known. Crêpe de santé, or crêpe of health, is a thin, light material, usually of silk, which is recommended for delicate persons and for stout figures. Tiny vests of softest cashmere wool, are furnished, open the entire length, for infant's wear.

In this department is furnished the Jersey waist, for costumes, which is knitted of wool or silk, and fits the figure without a seam. Improved Jerseys are now fastened by tiny buttons set so near together that they do not change the clinging fit of the garment while they render the waist as easy to put on or off as any other. In black, prune, and other dark shades, the knit Jersey will be worn this summer for yachting, croquet, and country costumes. It is a most popular garment in England, and all new basques from abroad, though fitted by seams, are modeled by French modistes after its clinging contours.

VESTS.

FOR LADIES.

In ordering vests please state bust-measure. The sizes are as follows:

26 is suited to 30 inches bust-measure.
28   32
30   34
32   36
34   38
36   40
38   42

1 Ladies gauze merino vests, regular-made:
Low neck, ribbed arm—
26 inches, $0.85   34 inches, 1.05
28   .90   36   1.10
30   .95   38   1.15
32   1.00   40   1.20
High neck and short sleeves—
26 inches, .90   34 inches, 1.10
28   .95   36   1.15
30   1.00   38   1.20
32   1.05   40   1.25
High neck and long sleeves—
26 inches, 1.10   34 inches, 1.30
28   1.15   36   1.35
30   1.20   38   1.40
32   1.25

2 Ladies' extra superfine gossamer vests, regular-made:
Low neck, ribbed arm,
26 inches, 1.35   32 inches, 1.65
28   1.45   34   1.75
30   1.55   36   1.85
High neck and short sleeves—
26 inches, 1.50   34 inches, 1.90
28   1.60   36   2.00
30   1.70   38   2.10
32   1.80   40   2.25
High neck and long sleeves—
26 inches, 1.75   32 inches, 2.05
28   1.85   34   2.15
30   1.95   36   2.25

3 Ladies' extra superfine, patent gauze vests, regular-made:
Low neck, ribbed arm
26 inches, 1.50   34 inches, 1.90
28   1.60   36   2.00
30   1.70   38   2.10
32   1.80
High neck and short sleeves—
26 inches, 1.65   32 inches, 1.95
28   1.75   34   2.05
30   1.85   36   2.15

4 Ladies' extra superfine gauze cashmere vests, regular-made:
Low neck, ribbed arm,
26 inches, 1.75   34 inches 2.15
28   1.85   36   2.25
30   1.95   38   2.35
32   2.05
High neck, short sleeves,
26 inches, 1.95   32 inches, 2.30
28   2.05   34   2.45
30   2.20   36   2.60

5 Ladies' gauze vests, not regular-made, all sizes, 0.45 .50 .60

6 Ladies' gauze silk vests, pink, sky-blue, pearl, flesh-color, from 4.00, according to size and style.

7 Ladies' silk vests, super-weight:
High neck, long sleeves, from 5.00
High neck, short sleeves, from 4.85

8 Ladies' worsted Jerseys, black, navy-blue, seal-brown, tan, 4.75, 5. 5.50

CRÊPE DE SANTÉ FOR LADIES.

A new article very light and thin, but very warm; highly recommended for delicate persons, also specially for stout figures. The sizes are as follows:

    1 is suited to 30 and 32 bust-measure.
    2   34   36
    3   38   40

1 Crêpe de santé, silk; low neck, without sleeves:
    size 1 $3.60   size 3 4.80
         2   4.20   4 5.40

2 Crêpe de santé, silk; high neck, short sleeves:
    size 1 4.20   size 3 5.60
         2   4.90   4 6.50

3 Crêpe de santé, silk; high neck, long sleeves:
    size 1 4.90   size 3 6.70
         2   5.80   4 7.60

4 Crêpe de sante Union suits, wool:
28 inches, $6.00   32 inches, 7.00
30   6.50

5 Crêpe de santé Union suits, silk-and-wool:
28 inches, 7.50   32 inches, 8.50
30   8.00

FOR CHILDREN.

1 Children's extra-superfine gauze cashmere vests, regular-made
Low neck and short sleeves,—
16 inches, $ .90   24 inches, 1.15
18   .95   26   1.25
20   1.00   28   1.35
22   1.05

High neck and ¾ sleeves—
16 inches, 1.25   26 inches, 1.50
18   1.30   28   1.55
20   1.35   30   1.60
22   1.40   32   1.65
24   1.45

2 Children's extra-superfine gossamer vests, regular-made:
High neck and short sleeves—
16 inches, .85   24 inches, 1.05
18   .90   26   1.10
20   .95   28   1.20
22   1.00
High neck and long sleeves—
16 inches, .95   24 inches, 1.25
18   1.00   26   1.30
20   1.15   28   1.40
22   1.20

3 Children's gauze vests, regular-made:
Low neck and short sleeves—
16 inches, .45   24 inches, .65
18   .50   26   .70
20   .55   28   .75
22   .60
High neck and short sleeves—
16 inches, .50   24 inches, .70
18   .55   26   .75
20   .60   28   .85
22   .65

4 Children's gauze vests, not regular-made, 0.25 .35. 40 .45 .50 .55. 60 according to size.

5 Children's worsted Jerseys, 4. 4.25 4.50

DRAWERS.

FOR LADIES.
1 Ladies gauze drawers, regular-made:
Band 28 inches, 1.45
    30   1.60
    32   1.75
    34   1.95
    36   2.05
    38   2.10

2 Ladies' extra fine gauze drawers, regular-made, from 1.60, according to size.

FOR CHILDREN.
1 Children's pantalettes, regular-made, band 18 to 28 inches, from 0.95 according to size:

2 Children's pantalettes, not regular-made, band 18 to 28 inches, from 0.50 according to size.

COLORED SKIRTS.

Colored skirts are almost always worn with promenade dresses. In Paris white skirts are entirely discarded, except for evening costumes. New skirts are of fine farmer's satin in solid gold color or in cardinal, and are edged with fine knife-pleatings, and finished with or without a heading of embroidery. Striped petticoats of gold color and turquoise-blue are edged with bias ruffles of box-pleating. Steel colored mohair skirts are bordered by rows of pleating and bands of embroidery in red, peacock-blue and other colors. Some mohair skirts are flounced up the back breadth with pleatings lined with crinoline which form a moderate bustle.

Blue and white seersucker in fine stripes and checks makes the most serviceable plain skirt, and always washes and wears excellently.

We have large assortments of these skirts at each price. We shall fill orders without reference to the pattern in the Illustration, unless instructed to the contrary.

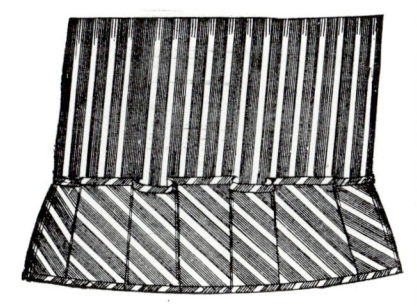

No. 1, Poplin, striped, $0.50

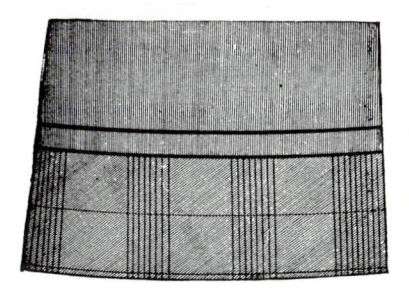

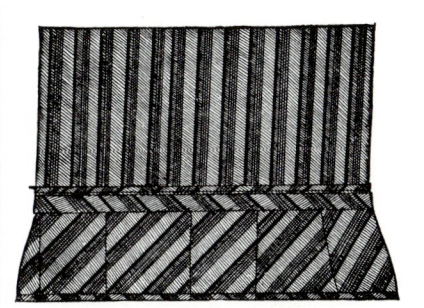

No. 3, Poplin, striped, 0.75

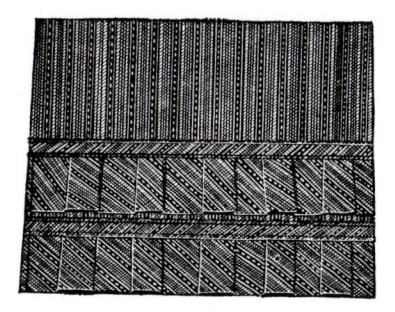

No. 2, Poplin, with colored piping, washable, 0.70

No. 4, Poplin, striped, 0.95

118   LORD & TAYLOR, NEW YORK.

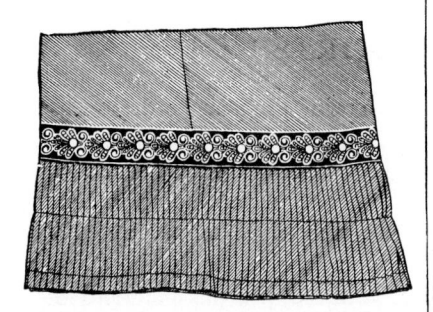

No. 5, Poplin, with embroidered band, washable, 1.00

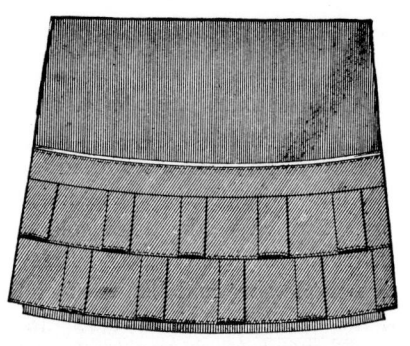

No. 8, Poplin, with colored piping, washable, 1.25

No. 6, Poplin, with colored piping, washable, 1.00

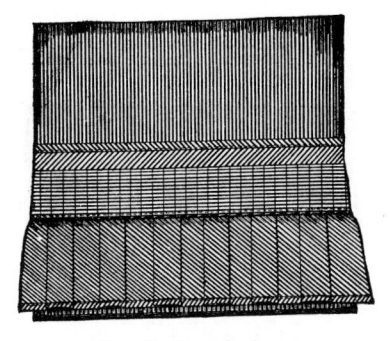

No. 9, Poplin, striped, 1.25

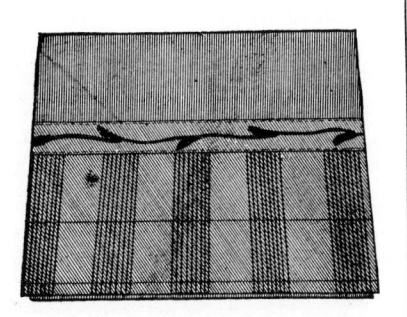

No. 7 Poplin, with embroidered band, washable, 1.20

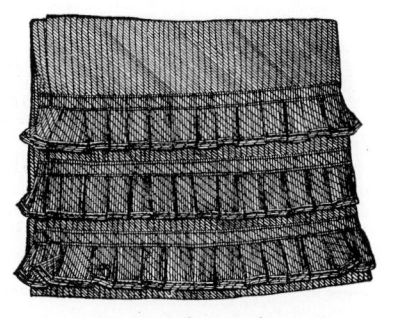

No. 10, Poplin, striped, 1.35

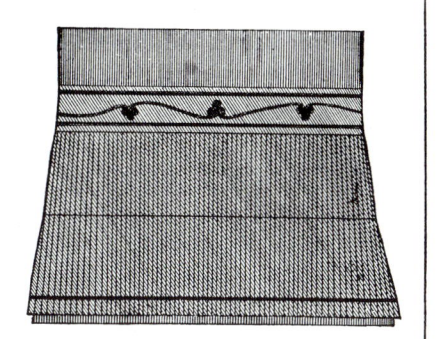

No. 11, Poplin, with embroidered band, washable, 1.50

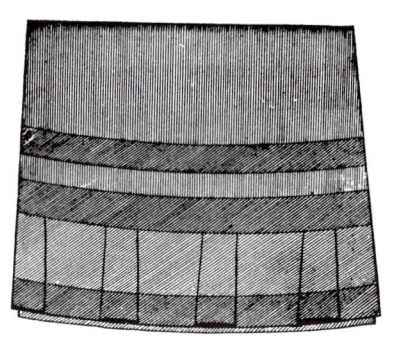

No. 12, Mohair, grey, 1.60

13 Mohair, grey, with four box-pleated ruffles up the back, forming a bustle, 1.75 2.
14 Seersucker, with one and two flounces, 1.25 1.35 1.50 1.75
15 Seersucker, with one flounce of box-pleating or knife-pleating with narrow embroidered flounce above, 1.75 2.00 2.75
16 Farmer's satin, black, with one side-pleated flounce, 1.00 1.25 1.50 1.75 2. 2.25
17 Farmer's satin, black, with side-pleated flounce, headed with an embroidered band in different colors, 1.50 1.75 2. 2.25 2.50 3. 3.50
18 Farmer's satin, black, with two box-pleats or knife-pleats, 1.75 2.25 3.00
19 Farmer's satin, black, with one box-pleated flounce, 1. 1.25 1.50 1.75 2. 2.25 3.50

CORSETS, Etc.

The greatest care is now taken to ensure perfectly-fitting corsets. It has been the aim of the manufacturer to mold them to the figure, and make them as soft and pliable as possible. They are rather longer on the hips than formerly, to ensure the careful fit of the long-clinging princess shaped basques that are now worn.

Those in London cord, in which the bones are superseded by heavy stitched cords, are used by ladies who like a very soft corset. Similar garments with shoulder straps are shown for children.

Small low bustles are still worn, and are especially necessary to support full-trained evening dresses.

The measurements needed are: around waist, hips, and bust, length under arm to waist, and length at back and front. An old corset that is satisfactory is a good measure. Measures should be taken over the corsets under the dress.

1 Lord & Taylor's "Imperial," made to order; especially suited to stout figures, $10.

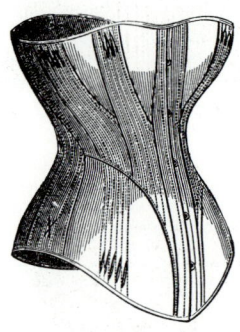

2 French coutil ("Bernhardt"), abdominal, with narrow clasps, extra heavy bones, and side steels, 6.00

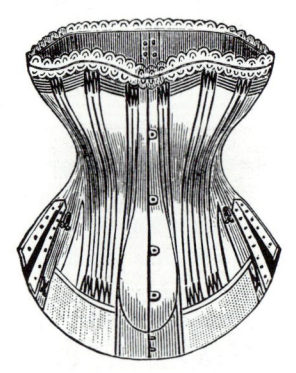

3 French coutil, narrow clasps, extra long, 3.00 3.25.

4 French coutil ("Lord & Taylor's Belt"), abdominal, broad side steels, laced, and with deep band of webbing for stout figures, 4.50.

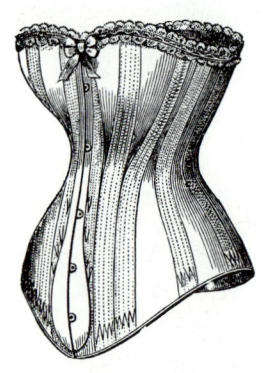

5 French coutil ("The Jersey"), broad steels, 4.00

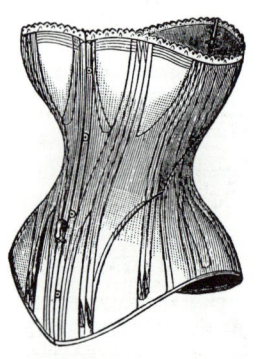

6 French coutil, according to quality and weight of bones, 1.75 2.50 3.75 4.50 5.

LORD & TAYLOR, NEW YORK. 121

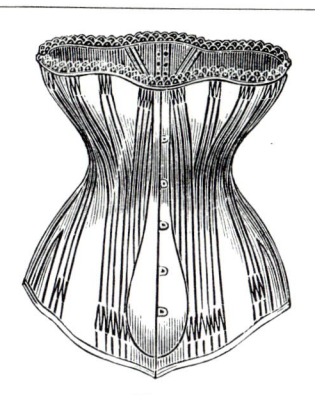

No. 7
7 French coutil, broad steels, white or grey, 2.35

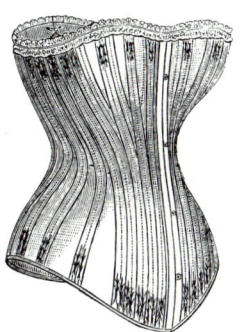

No. 8, $4.
8 Thompson's glove-fitting, 1.25 1.50 1.75 4.

No. 9, $2.25

9 French woven, according to quality, 1. 1.35 1.75 ; embroidered, 2.25.

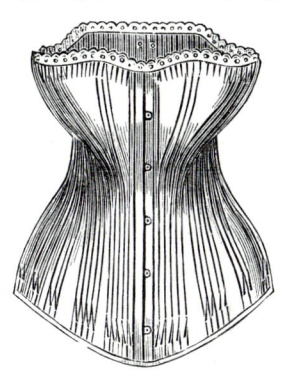

No. 10, $2.25

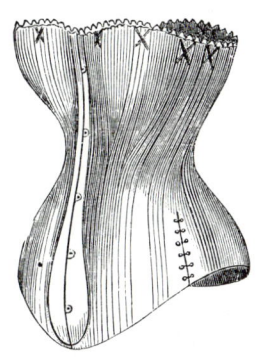

No. 11, $2.35

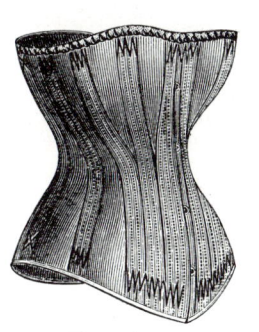

No. 12, $3.00

10   French woven, extra long, 1.50 1.90
     2.25 2.50.
11   French woven, broad steels, for stout
     figures, 2.35.
12   French corset of red rep, stitched in
     black or old-gold, 3.00.

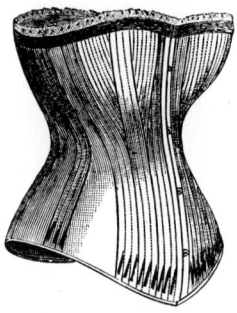

No. 13, $2.75

13. French Momie-Cloth, in pink, blue, buff
     and white, $2.50; a finer quality, more
     elaborately trimmed, 2.75.

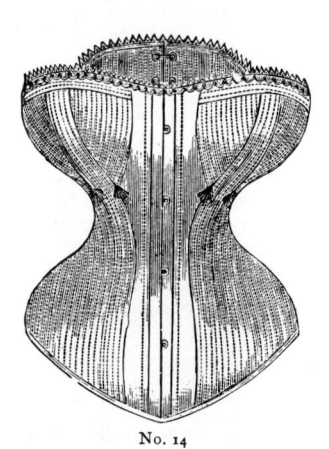

No. 14

14   "Our own," a good domestic corset, 1.00
15   French woven; short, for evening dress
     or riding,
         About forty bones,   1.00
         Shorter,   1.75
         Six hundred bones,   2.00

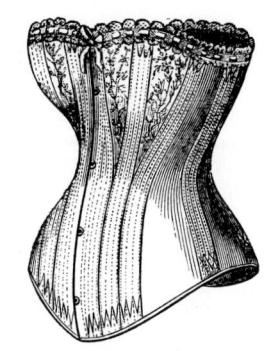

No. 16, $3.25

16   Bridal: white with embroidery, or white
     with colored gores and embroidery,
     3.25.
17   French woven ("Zonare"), nursing, 1.75.
18   Boston comfort waist: a corset for invalids with shoulder-straps and rows of very stiff cords, in place of bones, to give support and still yield readily to the movements of the person, laced at the side, 1.80.
19   Boston comfort waist for children, with attachment for stocking and skirt supporter, buttoned at the back, 0.85.

Boston comfort waist: each waist is stamped with two numbers, the first is size of waist and the second is the size around the shoulders. In ordering for children please state age, whether slender, etc.

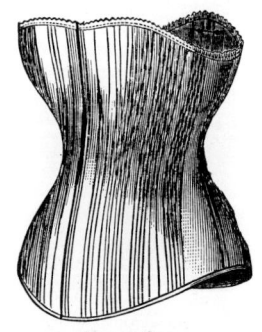

No. 20, $0.95

20   Misses' corset, ordinary clasp, lacing at
     the back, cords instead of bones, 0.95.
     1.15

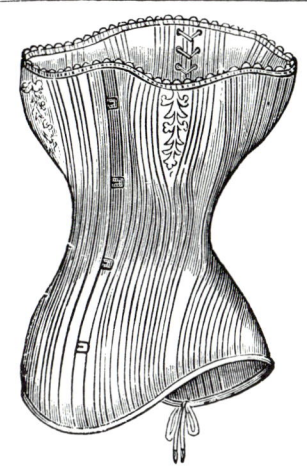

LORD & TAYLOR, NEW YORK. 123

No. 20, $1.15

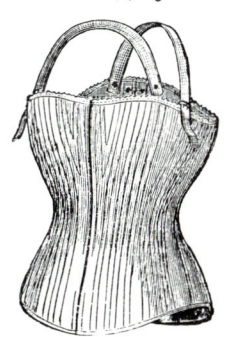

No. 21

No. 21. with bones, $0.85

21 Children's corset, ordinary clasp, lacing at the back, cords instead of bones, shoulder-straps, 0.85.

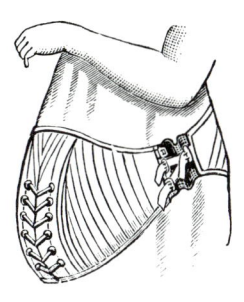

No. 22, $2.00

22 Abdomen-supporter: elastic bands, front and back, support in the most comfortable manner; buckles and slides nickel-plated; attachment for stocking-supporter, 2.

The webbing at the front, elastic and non-elastic, when worn out may be easily replaced with the extra webbing supplied for that purpose.

No. 23

23 Shoulder-braces:
sizes 1 and 2 for children under 16, 0.85
size 3 for misses and ladies, .85

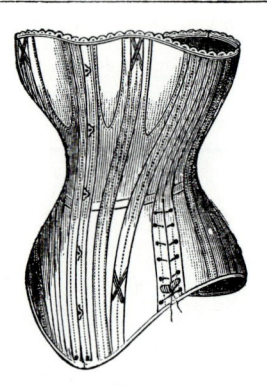

No. 24.

24 Moody's abdominal : French coutil, white and drab, with "Welcome" clasp,
19 to 30 inches, 3.50
31   36   3.75

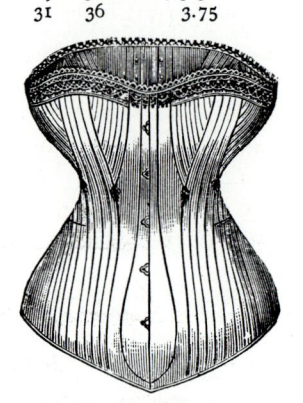

No. 26, $1.25

25 Moody's abdominal: domestic sateen, white and drab.

19 to 30 inches, 2.00
31   36   2.25

26 Coutil, spoon steel, perfect fit, white and drab, 1.25

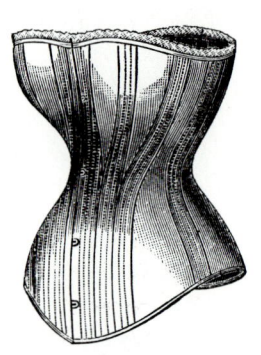

No. 27.

27 French coutil, "Olivette," medium length, narrow steel, and a perfect fit : extra good, 1.45, (real value, 2.)

28 Domestic: hand made, well boned, double steel, white and drab, 0.50

29 Domestic : hand made, spoon steel, white and drab, with or without side lacings, 0.75.

INFANTS' CLOTHING.

Infants' dresses are made for ordinary occasions in simple yoke-slips of French cambric or nainsook, high in the neck with long sleeves, and trimmed with soft lace or fine embroidery. Long dresses measure about a yard. Tiny, close-fitting caps are worn by small babies, embroidered by hand with dainty sprigs and edged with fine Valenciennes lace. Sashes of the material of the dress usually begin at the side seams. Blankets and flannel skirts are hand-embroidered to match, with wool or silk, and flannel skirts are often ornamented with an insertion of torchon lace above the embroidery. Hand-knitted jackets and sacks of soft, fleece-like Zephyr wool are usually worn. Rich christening robes have solid fronts of Valenciennes lace mixed with medallions of fine embroidery, a narrow, cream-white satin ribbon is used as a sash, a bib of handsome Valenciennes is furnished with the dress, and the shirt of linen cambric is trimmed with the same lace. White cashmere cloaks are trimmed with embroidery and fringe or lace. White piqué cloaks are embroidered by hand or trimmed with open work patterns of Hamburg.

Baby baskets are now often furnished without a standard and are placed on any handsome little table. They are made of baby-blue satin, trimmed with real lace or of dotted Swiss muslin over white, pale-blue or pink silesia. The first short dresses are French slips twenty inches in length, and finished with or without yokes, and trimmed with tucking and embroidery or with torchon or Valenciennes lace.

The wrap to be worn with these dresses is a sacque with a short cape, and is of soft, snowy wool or matelassé trimmed with Irish crochet, imperial-point or torchon lace. It is considered the best taste to use no color for children under a year old. After this age pale tints of rose color or baby-blue are used on the caps and in sashes when worn. At two years of age the child puts on a little coat of écru, grey or any light tint, which does not quite reach to the bottom of the dress, and is often finished with a tiny hood and corded with satin or trimmed with gay plaid silk.

INFANTS' CLOTHING.

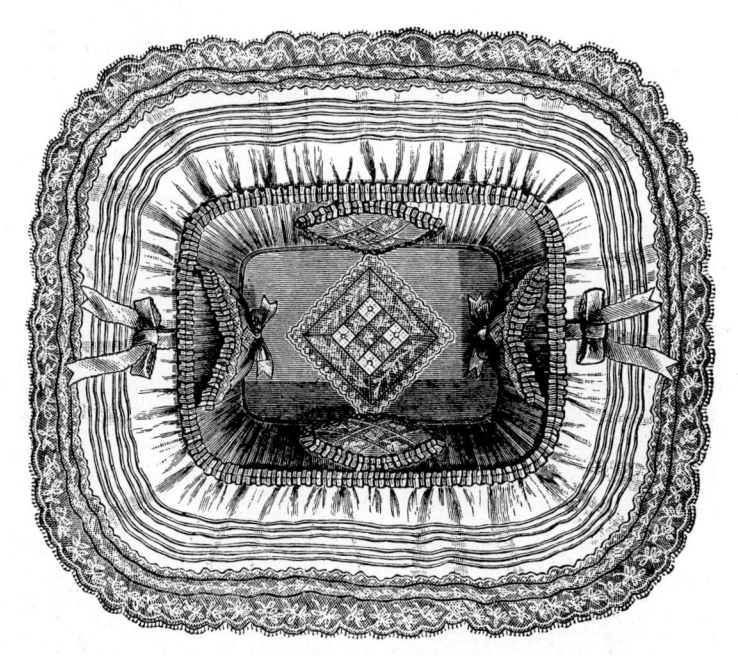

Dotted Swiss over colored Silesia, $6.50

BASKETS.

1. Trimmed with colored muslin, embroidered in white or colors, $4.50
2. Trimmed with Swiss muslin and imitation Valenciennes lace lined with colored silesia, 5.50 5.75 6.50 7.50 9. 10. 15. 20. 25
3. Trimmed with Valenciennes lace and lined with satin, 20. 25. 30. 35. 40. 50.
4. Light-blue silk, figures painted in colors, trimmed with imitation Valenciennes lace, 50.

SHIRTS.

1. Linen, trimmed with imitation Valenciennes lace, 0.45 .55 .60 1.50 2. 2.25 2.50 2.75 3.50
2. Linen, embroidered by hand, 1.50 2. 2.25 2.50
3. Linen, trimmed with real Valenciennes lace, 7.50 8.50 9.50 10. 11. 12,

Shirt No. 3, $7.50

BIBS.

1 Quilted, trimmed with narrow edging,
$0.25 .30 .35 .45 .50 .60 .70 .75
2 Embroidered by hand, 1. 1.25 1.50 1.75

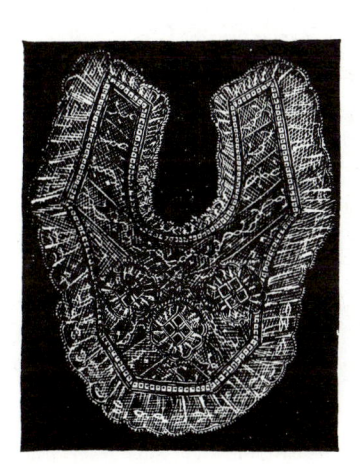

No. 4, $7.

LONG SLIPS.

No. 3, $2.

3 Imitation Valenciennes lace with Hamburg insertion, 1.75 2. 2.25 2.50 2.75 3.
4 Valenciennes lace with medallions of lace and embroidery, 4. 4.75 5. 6.50 7. 8. 9.

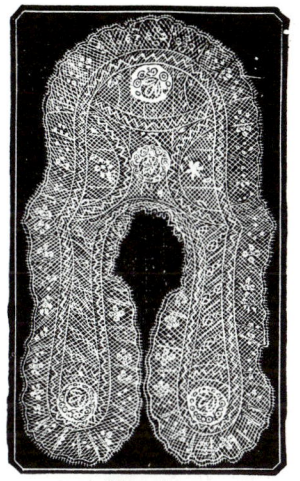

No. 8, $11.50.

1. Cambric slip, box-pleat in centre, Hamburg edging on neck and cuffs, $0.65
2. Cambric slip, three box-pleats in centre, five tucks in skirt, 0.80

Imitation Valenciennes Lace, $45.

3. Solid-tucked square yoke, Hamburg edging on neck and cuffs, five tucks in skirt, 1. 1.25 1.50 1.75
4. Square yoke, tucked, two rows of Hamburg insertion in yoke and skirt, cluster of three tucks between, 2. 2.25 2.50
5. Tucked yoke, insertion between, Hamburg edging on ruffle around skirt, 2.50 3.
6. Tucked yoke with Hamburg insertion, two clusters of fine tucks around skirt, 3.50 3.75
7. Tucked yoke with Hamburg insertion, cluster of fine tucks around skirt, Hamburg ruffle, 3.75 4. 4.50 5. 6.50 7.50
8. Yoke of imitation Valenciennes lace insertion and edging; skirt of same with narrow puffing and a bias trimming of lace finished with deep Valenciennes lace, 11.50
9. Yoke and skirt trimmed with imitation Valenciennes lace, insertion and edging, 6.50 7.50 9. 10. 12. 15.
10. French nainsook, yoke of Hamburg insertion and edging, skirt trimmed with two rows of fine tucks one row of insertion and deep Hamburg edging, 15.
11. Robe, entire front of Hamburg insertion with fine tucks between, Hamburg edging around skirt, 10. 12. 16. 18. 20.

No. 12.

12. French nainsook; robe front trimmed with alternate rows of imitation Valenciennes insertion with Hamburg insertion between and loops of narrow white satin ribbon; Hamburg embroidery, edged with Valenciennes lace, around bottom of skirt, 27.
13. Robe, entire front of real Valenciennes lace, trimmed with lace and appliqué medallions, 50. 65. 75. 80 125. 145.

LORD & TAYLOR, NEW YORK.

SHORT DRESSES.

Sizes, one to two years.

No. 1,

No. 5, $3.75

7 Front of Hamburg insertion, and bias tucking; back has a yoke with skirt gathered on, sash of same material, 10.50
8 Fine-tucked yoke, trimmed with imitation Valenciennes lace, Hamburg insertion between tucks in yoke and around skirt, 5.50 6.50 7.50 8.50 9 10. 12. 15. 18. 20. 25.

1 Circular and square yokes, back and front, finished with narrow Hamburg edging; skirt, plain hem with fine tucks above, 1.25.
2 Tucked yoke with narrow Hamburg edging, cluster of nine tucks in skirt, 1.25
3 Square-tucked yoke, with Hamburg edging around neck and cuffs, two clusters of fine tucks in skirt, trimmed with deep Hamburg edging, 2. 2.25
4 Square-tucked yoke, Hamburg insertion between two clusters of fine tucks, around skirt one row of Hamburg insertion and edging, 2.50 3. 3.50
5 Four rows tucks, and three rows Hamburg insertion down the front, two ruffles with Hamburg edging and tucks on skirt, 3.75
6 Fine-tucked yoke with insertion between, two cambric ruffles, Hamburg edging on skirt, five tucks above, 6.50 7.50 8.50 9.

No. 9, $35.

9 Robe, entire front of imitation Valenciennes lace, the same around skirt, 12. 15. 18. 20. 22. 25. 30. 35. 40.

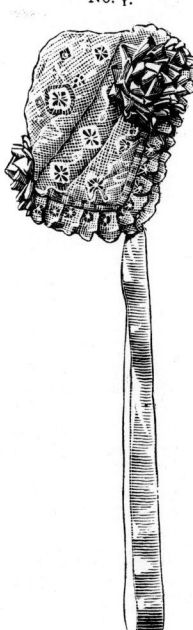

CAPS.

No. 1.

No. 4.

1 French-cap, close-fitting, nainsook, trimmed with imitation Valenciennes lace, $1.50
2 French-cap, imitation laces, 1.50 1.75 2. 2.25 2.50 2.75 3. 3.25 3.50 3.75 4. 4.25 4.50 4.75 5. 5.50 6. 6.50 7. 7.50
3 Quilted satin, all colors, 2.25 to 4.00
4 Torchon lace and imitation Valenciennes lace, trimmed with narrow satin ribbon, 5.00
5 French-cap, real laces, 5. 6.50 7. 7.50 8. 8.50 9. 9.50 10. 10.50 10.75 11. 12. 12.50
6 Infant's cap, Valenciennes lace and insertion with lace medallions, 9.

BLANKETS.

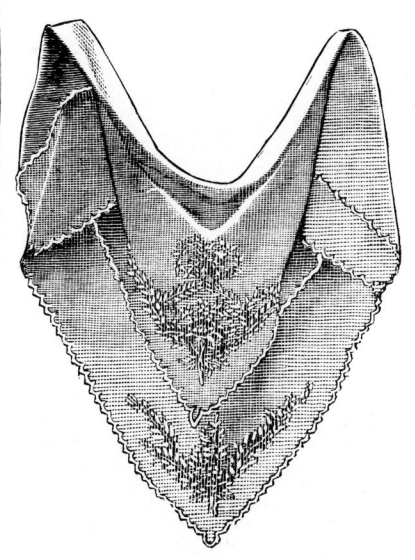

No. 3, 5.50.

1 Flannel, scolloped, flannel binding, $1.50 1.75 2.
2 Flannel, embroidered, 2.50 2.75 3.50 3.75
3 Cashmere embroidered, 3.50 3.75 4.25 4.50 5.50 7.00 8.00 10.00 15.00 18 00 22.00.

LORD & TAYLOR, NEW YORK. 131

WORSTED SOCKS.

1   All colors, per pair, $0.30 .45 .50 .75 1.

No. 1.

No. 3, $30.

SHORT SACQUE.

1   Child's first size short cloak, white damassé trimmed with Breton lace $25.00 30.00 35.00 40.00 45.00

INFANTS' CLOAKS.

1   Cashmere, fold of white satin on upper cape, $8.

2   Cashmere, fold of white satin on both capes, 12.

3   Cashmere, embroidered, 17. 20. 25. 30. 35. 40. 50

4   Damassé and white cord, made to order, 50. 65. 75

5   Cashmere, embroidered with silk by hand chenille-and-silk fringe, 65.00.

6   A complete line of long cloaks, cashmere, piqué and nainsook, 5.00 to 75.00.

INFANTS' WARDROBES.

Prices are for single articles as well as for the whole.

1 Wardrobe:

two flannel bands, .37½,	$0.75
two flannel skirts, 1.50,	3.00
two flannel barrows, 1.10,	2.20
two cambric skirts, 1.10,	2.20
six linen shirts, .45,	2.70
one day dress,	4.50
one day dress	2.00
four day dresses, 1.50,	6.00
four night dresses, 0.80,	3.20
one calico wrapper,	1.40
one piece diaper,	1.80
one rubber diaper,	.40
one pair socks,	.35
one basket,	4.50
	$35.00

2 Wardrobe:

two flannel bands, .37½,	$0.75
two flannel barrows, 1.10,	2.20
two flannel skirts, 1.50,	3.00
six linen shirts, .50,	3.00
two cambric skirts, 1.50,	3.00
four day slips, 1.25,	5.00
two day slips, 1.50,	3.00
one day dress,	3.50
four night dresses, 1.00,	4.00
one day dress,	7.50
one calico wrapper,	1.40
one piece diaper,	2.00
one rubber diaper,	.40
four pairs socks, .30,	1.20
one lace cap,	3.75
one basket,	5.50
one quilted bib,	.30
two " " .25,	.50
	$50.00

HANDKERCHIEFS.

A handkerchief in fine snowy linen is now preferred. Initials are not much used, but an elaborate border of fine French embroidery is wrought inside of the hem. A few handkerchiefs in the sheerest linen cambric are embroidered in pale-blue and red, and finished by sharply accented scollops, but these handkerchiefs are often preferred in pure white.

LINEN.

For Ladies.

1. Hemmed :

each	dozen	each	dozen
$0.08	0.90	0.15	1.75
.10	1.15	.18	2.00
.13	1.50	.20	2.30

2. Hemstitched :

each	dozen	each	dozen
0.13	1.50	0.30	3.50
.15	1.75	.40	4.50
.20	2.30	.50	5.50
.25	2.90	.55	6.00

3. Hemstitched, colored border :

each	dozen	each	dozen
0.20	2.30	0.35	4.00
.25	2.90	0.50	5.75
.30	3.50		

4. Hemstitched, sheer :

each	dozen	each	dozen
0.50	5.75	1.00	11.50
.65	7.50	1.25	14.50
.75	8.50	1.50	17.50

5. Initial, hemstitched :

each	dozen	each	dozen
0.25	2.90	.75	8.00
.50	5.75		

6. Scolloped, embroidered in white :

each	dozen	each	dozen
.35	4.00	1.25	14.00
.50	5.75	1.50	17.00
.60	7.00	2.00	22.50
.75	8.50	2.50	28.00
1.00	11.50	2.75	32.00
1.15	13.50	3.25	38.00

7. Scolloped, embroidered in colors :

each	dozen	each	dozen
0.25	2.90	0.75	8.50
.30	3.50	1.00	11.50
.35	4.00	1.25	14.00
.40	4.50	1.50	17.00
.50	5.75	2.00	22.50
.60	6.75	2.50	28.00
.70	8.00		

8. French-embroidered, hemstitched :

each	dozen	each	dozen
1.25	14.00	2.50	28.00
1.50	17.00	2.75	31.00
1.75	20.00	3.00	34.00
2.00	22.50	to	to
2.25	25.50	8.00	92.00

For Children.

1. Hemmed, colored border :

each	dozen	each	dozen
0.07	0.80	0.10	1.15
.08	.90	.13	1.50

2. Hemstitched :

each	dozen	each	dozen
.15	1.75	.20	2.30

3. Hemstitched, colored border :

each	dozen	each	doxen
0.18	2.00	.25	2.90
.20	2.30		

For Gentlemen.

1. Hemmed :
   21 inches—

each	dozen	each	dozen
0.15	1.75	0.30	3.50
.20	2.40	.35	4.00
.25	3.00	.40	4.50

23 inches—

each	dozen	each	dozen
0.25	3.00	0.50	5.75
.30	3.50	.60	7.00
.35	4.00	.65	7.50
.40	4.50	.75	8.50
.45	5.00		

27 inches—

each	dozen	each	dozen
0.30	3.50	0.55	6.50
.35	4.00	.60	7.00
.40	4.50	.65	7.50
.45	5.00	.75	8.50
.50	5.75		

2 Hemmed, colored border:

each	dozen	each	dozen
0.25	3.00	.35	4.00
.30	3.50		

3 Hemstitched:

23 inches—

each	dozen	each	dozen
0.25	3.00	0.60	6.75
.30	3.50	.65	7.50
.35	4.00	.70	8.00
.40	4.50	.75	8.50
.45	5.00	.85	9.50
.50	5.75	1.00	11.00
.55	6.25	1.25	14.00

27 inches—

each	dozen	each	dozen
0.50	5.50	0.80	9.25
.60	6.75	.90	10.00
.70	8.00	1.00	11.00

4 Hemstitched, colored border:

each	dozen	each	dozen
0.35	4.00	0.60	7.00
.40	4.50	.75	8.50
.50	5.50	1.00	11.50

5 Initial, hemmed:

each	dozen	each	dozen
0.35	4.00	0.60	7.00
.50	5.75		

6 Initial, hemstitched:

each	dozen	each	dozen
0.50	5.50	1.00	11.00
.75	8.00		

SILK.

1 White, twilled, hemmed, $0.50 .75 1. 1.25
2 White, pongee, hemmed, 0.75 1. 1.25 1.50 1.75 2. 2.50 3.
3 Novelties, all colors and shades, 0.50 .75 1. 1.25 1.35 1.50 1.75 2. 2.50
4 India, hemstitched, 0.75 1. 1.25 1.50 1.75 2. 2.25

LINEN COLLARS AND CUFFS.

COLLARS.

Prices each.

1 Plain, $0.07 .08 .09 .10 .12 .13
2 Hemstitched, 0.15
3 Cape-collars, plain, 0.15 .17 .18 .20. 25
4 Cape-collars, hemstitched, 0.30
5 Sailor collars, plain, 0.10 .12 .15
6 Sailor collars, embroidered, 0.20 .30 .40 .50 .60
7 Hemstitched, fancy, 0.35 .50 .60 .85 .90 1.00
8 Children's embroidered collars, extra deep, 0.50 .65 .75 1. 1.15 1.25 1.50 2. 2.50 3.
9 Linen chemisettes, 0.30 .40 .62 .75

CUFFS.

Prices per pair.

1 Plain, $0.20 .22 .25 .30 .35
2 Hemstitched, 0.28 .50 .65

(Collar and cuffs.)

Prices per set.

1 Embroidered, $0.25 .30 .35 .40 .50 .60 .75
2 Embroidered, extra deep, for children 2.50 2.75 3. 3.75
3 French-embroidered, 1.75 1.85 2. 2.50

TRIMMINGS AND ORNAMENTS FOR DRESSES AND CLOAKS; FANCY-GOODS, Etc.

Never has the Orient poured forth so freely her gorgeous colors and graceful models as in the glittering beaded garniture which now add a final touch to handsome costumes. Art and practical manufacture have united to furnish the drooping palms, fuchias, roses and ferns of the East, in the graceful forms and glowing varied colors of nature, yet strong, light and durable in texture.

Wreaths of leaves are wrought in shades of olive, with pendant fuchias showing brilliant tints of crimson and rose-pink, and wreaths of exotic ferns and roses in natural tints, will form gorgeous flower garlands of crystal for summer dresses.

Again peacock plumes are shown in natural colors, touched with gilt or bronze, and formed in strips of beaded garniture.

More beautiful than all is the Spanish lace, whose quaint lilies and roses are wrought in the most brilliant shades and colors in solid cashmere beads; whole breadths of Spanish lace is similarly wrought and form the most beautiful draperies for the front of handsome dresses. The same lace is similarly wrought in jet in edging and net and will form the trimming of black silk and fine grenadines. New fringes and passementeries are often in solid beads of steel, or of steel and jet. There is a touch of steel in nearly all garnitures.

Crochet silk passementeries, all revised and all in the most graceful patterns, outlined by jet or steel. The jet now used is called "hollow" jet, and is nearly as light as silk. Lightness and purity of fabric are the special marks of the new garniture. The same graceful pendant palms, fuchias and other ferns seen in colored crystal are repeated in black silk, and accented by the glitter of jet.

New buttons to match passementeries are formed of cashmere cut steel beads and of jet in open and close figures. They are round and furnished with a shank. Gold surface buttons are set with steel points, and silver buttons are similarly ornamented. Jet is mingled with steel in all kinds of fanciful ways, and buttons are often as finely finished as jewelry.

TRIMMINGS.

Price per yard.

BLACK SILK FRINGES, three to six inches deep.

1. Chenille and crimped tape, $0.85 to 4.
2. Chenille, twist and tape, 0.95 to 3.75
3. Braid and twist, 0.50 to 3.75
4. Knotted, one to six knots: medium, 0.50 to 1.75; heavy, 1. to 2.50
5. Crimped braid, one to six inches deep, 0.55 to 2.
6. Mourning fringes in great variety, 0.75 to 5.00
7. Novelties, as they are produced, 2. to 5.

JET FRINGES, three to ten inches deep.

1. With chenille, 0.75 to 15.
2. With tape, 1.00 to 7.50
3. With twist, 1.00 to 3.
4. With chenille and tape, 1.00 to 7.50
5. With twist and tape, 1.25 to 7.50
6. With twist and chenille, 0.75 to 15.
7. Twist background, with chenille and tape overskirt, 1.00 to 7.50
8. Twist and chenille, with satin drops, 1.25 to 7.50
9. Passementerie-fringes, made in sections which can be cut and used as ornaments, 2.95 to 20.
10. Solid-jet fringes, one to ten inches deep, 1.50 to 21.
11. Fringe-aprons of chenille and jet, 15.00 to 35.
12. Novelties as they are produced, 2.50 to 50.00

STEEL FRINGES.

1. Plain, from two and one-half to five inches deep, 1.25 to 7.50.
2. With netted headings, from two and one-half inches deep, 2.25 to 15.00.
3. With jet, from two and one-half to seven inches deep, 1.25 to 18.
4. With chenille and twist, from three to eight inches deep, 1.25 to 20.

COLORED-SILK FRINGES, three to six inches deep.

1. Chenille, plain, 1.50 to 3.50
2. Chenille and twist, 0.75 to 3.
3. Chenille and braid, 0.95 to 3.25
4. Tassel-fringes of chenille, twist and tape, 1.90 to 3.75

5. Cashmere-fringes in combinations of twist, chenille, tape and braid, with cashmere beads, to match all colors in dress goods, 3.00 to 25.
6. Bead fringes, in white and colors, 4.75 to 12.
7. Novelties in great variety, four to twelve inches deep, 2.00 to 12.

MARABOUT TRIMMINGS, one to four inches wide.

1. Crimped tape and chenille, 0.75 to 5.
2. Crimped twist, tape and chenille, 0.75 to 7.50
3. Chenille, tape, chenille-flies and jet, 5.75 to 10.00
4. Crimped tape and chenille, all colors, 1.50 to 5.

Colored marabouts are kept in stock to a limited extent, but are mostly made to order to match fabrics.

GIMPS AND PASSEMENTERIES, one to four inches wide.

1. Gimps, plain, 0.15 to 3.
2. Gimps with jet, 0.25 to 15.
3. Gimps with drops, 0.50 to 7.50
4. Gimps with jet and drops, 0.50 to 7.50
5. Insertion gimps, plain, 0.15 to 3.
6. Insertion gimps with jet, 0.50 to 7.50
7. Insertion gimps with drops, 0.35 to 8.
8. Insertion gimps with drops and jet, 0.35 to 8.00
9. All steel, and steel with black cords, one-half inch to six inches, 0.75 to 35.
10. Novelties in black or colored passementeries to match combinations of colors in dress materials.

GALLOON TRIMMINGS.

1. Embroidered bands of all colors on satin or silk, for dress trimmings, 1.50 to 3.50
2. Made to order to match dress-fabrics.

ORNAMENTS.

1. Plain loops, each, $0.15 .20 .22 .25 .28 .35 .40 .45 .50 .55 .60 .65 .70
2. Gimp-cord loops, each, 0.40 to 1.50
3. Tassel-loops, each, 0.60 .70 .75 .85 .90 1. to 3.50

LORD & TAYLOR, NEW YORK.

4 Loops for dressing-gowns, each, 1.25 to 3.
5 Loops for smoking-jackets, each, 1.25 to 3.
6 Ornaments with jet beads, each, 0.35 to 3.75
7 Tassel-ornaments, with chenille and tape, each, 0.85 to 4.50
8 Tassel-ornaments with braid and twist, each, 0.50 to 3.
9 Small ornaments for trimming: drops, per dozen, 0.18 to 2.50; olives, per dozen, .18 to 2.50
10 Jet tassels, 0.50 to 5.
11 Ornaments with steel beads, each, 0.75 to 15.
12 Steel drops, balls, crescents. in shades and colors to match passementeries and fringes, 0.50 to 10.

CORDS AND TASSELS.

1 Gimp-cord with bullion tassels, two-and-a-half yards long, $0.85 .95 1. 1.15 1.25 1.50 1.75 2.
2 Gimp-cord with twist-and-braid over-skirt tassels, 1.00 1.25 1.50 1.75 2. to 4.
3 Gimp-cord, three yards long, with flat tassels of tape, chenille and twist, 1.25 1.50 1.65 1.75 1.85 2.
4 Crape cord, with tassels of tape and chenille, 1.50 to 5.
5 Crape cord, with twist-and-silk-ruff tassels, 0.85 to 2.50
6 Paris cord-and-spike girdles: black or colored, 2.50 to 4.50; with beads, 3. to 6.
7 Paris cord-and-tassels, for dressing-gowns, 0.75 to 3.50
8 Paris cord-and-tassels for smoking jackets, 1.25 to 3.50
9 Black silk cord-and-tassels, 0.85 to 2.50
10 Colored silk cord-and-tassels, two to three yards long, all colors and shades, 1.25 to 2.75
11 Chenille cord-and-tassels, three yards long, 1.25 1.65 1.75 2. 2.25 2.50
12 Steel beaded in diffferentt length of cords and sizes of tassels, 2.25 to 8.
13 Cord-and-tassels for cushions, all colors, set, 1.50 1.75 2. 2.25 2.50
14 Silk cords, all sizes and colors, yard, 0.02. .03 .05 .06 .07 .08 .09 .10 .11 .12 .14 .15 .18 .20 .22 .25 .30 .35 .40 and .50

15 Eye-glass cords, yard, 0.02 .03 .04 .05 .06
16 Woven cords, yard, 0.08 .09 .10 .12
17 Tubular cords, yard, 0.12 .14 .16 .18 .20
18 Lacing cords, yard, 0.02 .03 .04 .05
19 Chenille cords, yard, 0.15 .18 .20 .25
20 Silver cords, yard, 0.10 .12 .14 .18
21 Gold cords, yard, 0.10 .12 .14 .18
22 Silk dress-tassels, black or colored, one-and-a-half to four inches deep; according to size, each, 09. .10 .15 .20 .25 to .75
23 Cable cord: ball, .02; box of 16 balls, .20
24 Cable cord: dozen yards, 0.06; box of one pound .48

BUTTONS.

Prices per dozen; varying generally according to both size and quality.

LINES FOR MEASURING DIAMETERS (AMERICAN STANDARD).

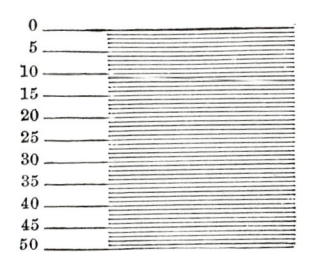

```
0  ————————————————
5  ————————————————
10 ————————————————
15 ————————————————
20 ————————————————
25 ————————————————
30 ————————————————
35 ————————————————
40 ————————————————
45 ————————————————
50 ————————————————
```

1 Black-silk crochet, 12 to 50 lines:
   plain, $0.18 to 2.50
   round and flat, 0.25 .28 .30 .35 .40 .48 .50 .55 .60 .65 .75 1.00 1.25 1.50 to 2.50
   beaded, 0.25 to 1.25
2 Black silk crochet, 36, 40, 45, 50 lines 0.50 to 2.50
3 Colored silk crochet, all colors, shades and styles, 24 to 32 lines, 0.18 .20 .25 .30 .35 to .60
4 Velvet, black, 18 to 50 lines, .06 .07 .08 .09 .10 .11 .12 .13 .14 .15 .16 .18 .20 to .60
5 Satin, black, 18 to 50 lines, 0.10 .12 .15 .18 .20 .22 .25 .28 .30 .32 .35

6 **Gros-grain silk,** black, 18 to 50 lines, 0.05 .07 .08 .10 .12 .13 .14 .15 .18 .20 .22 .25 .30 .35
7 Gros-grain silk, all colors and shades: 24 lines, 08; 26, .10; 28, .12
8 Gilt or silver, all shapes and sizes, 0.08 to 0.75
9 Black-beaded crochet, 0.30 to 2.25
10 Black bombazine, 0.06 .07 .08. .09 .10 .12 .14 .16
11 Black mohair, .06 .08 .10 .12 .14 .16 .18
12 Steel, 0.05 .06 .08 .10 .12 .14 to 3.
13 Jet, 0.10 .12 .14 .16 .20 .25 .30 .35 .40 .45 .50 .55 .60 .65 .70 .75 to 1.75
14 Jet, cut novelties, 0.85 to 2.75
15 Garnet, cut novelties, 1.50 to 2.75
16 Bronze: dress sizes, 0.50 to 2.75 ; cloak sizes, 0.95 to 3.50
17 Paris and Vienna novelties in pearl or metals; trimming, dress and sacque sizes to match, 1.00 to 12.
18 Fancy glass, 0.08 .10 .12 .14 .16 .18 .20 .25
19 Black, inlaid with pearl, gold, silver, colored pearl, rose pearl, etc., 0.18 to 3.
20 Black, inlaid with birds, leaves, sprays, Japanese figures, etc., .18 to 3.
21 Horn, .05 .06 .09 .10 .12 .13 to .75
22 Rubber, 0.05 .06 .07 .08 .10 .11 .12 to .50
23 Ivory, black or colored, 0.06 .08 .10 .12 .14 .16 .18 .20 .22 .25 .30 .35 to .65
24 Composition, various styles, for cloaks, 0.25 to 1.25
25 Gentlemen's trouser, 0.02.
26 Agate, white, black or colors, card of six dozen, 0.04 .05 .06 .07 .08

PEARL.

1 White, "fine super" :

18 lines,	$0.12	32 lines,	$0.28
20	.13	34	.37
22	.15	36	.39
24	.17	38	.49
26	.19	40	.63
28	.21	42	.72
30	.24		

2 White, "extra fine super":

18	0.15	26	0.27
20	.18	28	.32
22	.22	30	.38
24	.24	32	.45

3 Natural-black (smoked) "super-natural":

24 lines,	$0.22	32 lines,	$0.38
26	.24	34	.45
28	.28	36	.49
30	.32		

4 Natural black (smoked), "extra super natural":

22 lines,	$0.24	30 lines,	$0.45
24	.27	32	.50
26	.32	34	.58
28	.38	36	.65

5 Rose. 0.20 to .50
6 Fancy, 0.18 to 1.50
7 Shaded, 0.18 to .50
8 Engraved, white, natural-black, or rose ; dress or cloak sizes, 0.75 to 8.
9 Vest, 0.65 to 1.
10 Shirt, .08 .10 .12 .14
11 Small, for infants' or children's clothing 0.06 .07 .08 .10

BRAIDS.

1 Alpaca, black: yard, $0.02 .03. 04 ; piece of 24 yards, 0.38
2 Alpaca, all colors, yard, 0.04
3 Skirt braids, black or colored, piece of four yards, 0.05 .07 .08
4 Skirt braids, Goff's, all colors and shades, roll, 0.06
5 Silk bindings, according to width, yard : black, 0.05 .06 .07 .08 .10 .12 all colors and shades, 0.87
6 Mohair braids, according to width, yard: black, 0.08 to .28 colored, 0.08 to .28
7 Hercules braids, black or white, yard, 0.05 .06 .07 .08 .10 .12 .14 .16 .18 .20 .24
8 Trimming braids, fancy, one-half inch to two inches wide; according to width, yard, 0.10 to .65
9 Piqué braids, yard: white, 0.03 to .15 ; fancy, 0.03 to .15
10 Feather-edged braids, piece of five yards:

No. 00 Price, 0.04		No. 3 Price, .06
0	.04	4 .07
1	.04	5 .08
2	.05	

11 Serpentine braids, linen or cotton, piece of three or four yards, 0.07 .08 .09 .10 .12

12	Soutache braids, black or colored: yard, 0.05 .06; piece of about 30 yards, 1.25
13	Coronation braids, white : piece of six yards, 0.05; dozen, .50
14	Flannel bindings, white silk; according to width, yard, 0.04 .05 .06 .07
15	Flannel bindings, cotton, yard, 0.04 .05 .06 .07
16	Bed-tick bindings, blue-and-white or red-and-white, piece of about ten yards, 0.15 .18 .20
17	Carpet-bindings, piece of about ten yards, 0.25 .30

SEWING-SILK AND TWIST.

1	Button-hole twist, black. white or colored: spool of 16 yards, $0.05
2	Sewing silk or machine silk, black, white or colored: spools of 100 yards, 0.10; spools of quarter oz., .19; spools of ½ oz., .35; spools of one oz., .75
3	Embroidery silk, black, white or colored : skein, 0.02; hundred skeins, 1.30; tablets, each, $0.02; doz., 0.20
4	Saddler's silk, black or white; skein, 0.02 hundred skeins, 1.60
5	Filling silk, plain colors or shaded: skein, 0.05; hank of ten skeins, .45
6	Silk yarn, black, white or colored: ball, 0.45; dozen, 5.00; pound, 10.00 spool.

COTTON AND THREAD.

1	Linen floss: skein, $0.04; dozen, .40
2	Linen thread, skein, 0.04 .05
3	Linen thread: spool, 0.09; dozen, 1.
4	Carpet thread: skein, 0.04; pound, .85
5	C. B. embroidery cotton, all colors: skein, 0.03; dozen, .35
6	Marking cotton, all colors: ball or skein, 0.02; dozen, .20
7	Dexter's knitting cotton, Nos. 6, 8, 10, 12: ball, 0.07; pound, 60.
8	Dexter's knitting cotton, Nos. 14, 16, 18, 20: ball, 0.09; pound, .65
9	John Clark's cotton, white, black or colored: spool, 0.05; dozen, .55
10	O. N. T. cotton: spool, 0.05; dozen, .55
11	Willimantic six-cord cotton: spool, 0.05 dozen, 55
12	Willimantic three-cord cotton: spool, 0.04; dozen, .40

13	Brooks' cotton: spool, 0.05; dozen, .55
14	Coats' cotton: spool, 0.05; dozen, .55
15	Basting cotton, dozen, 0.05

PINS AND NEEDLES.

1	Jet-head shawl pins, dozen, $0.02 .03 .04 .05 .06
2	Jet-head hat pins, dozen, 0.10 .12 .15
3	Blanket-pins, paper, 0.05 .06 .07 .08

PINS.

1	English book pins, paper, 0.12
2	Ne-plus-ultra, paper, 0.04 0.05 .06 .07
3	American & Howe, paper, 0.05 .06 .07 .08 .09
4	Mourning pins: English, box, .10 ; French, box, 0.05 and 0.4

SAFETY-PINS.

1	Rowley's, black or white, box, .06 .08 .09 .10
2	Stewarts, dozen, 0.05 .06

HAIR-PINS.

1	Kirby's, No. 50, box, 0.08
2	Kirby's, No. 100, box 0.10
3	Invisible, No. 50, box 0.08
4	Invisible, No. 100, box, 0.10
5	Rubber box, 0.08 .10 .12
6	Kirby's hair-pins, English, paper, 0.03
7	Steel hair-pins, paper, 0.03
8	American hair-pins, paper, 0.03 to 10

CROCHET-NEEDLES, ETC.

1	Nickel-plated : each, 0.06. dozen, 0.55
2	Bone, each, 0.04 .05 .06 .07 .08
3	Knitting-needles, bone, pair, 0.04 .05 .06 .07

NEEDLES.

1	Milward's, sharps, betweens or milliner's, paper, 0.05
2	Robert's, sharps or betweens, paper. 0.05

ELASTICS.

1	Hat-elastic, cotton, black or white, yard, $0.03 .04 .05 .06
2	Hat-elastic, silk, black or white, yard 0.04 .06 .08 .10

LORD & TAYLOR, NEW YORK.

3 Garter-elastic, silk, white, pink, cardinal, blue, ¾ to 1 inch wide, yard, 0.25 to .45
4 Cord-elastics, all sizes.
5 Cotton elastics, white, yard, 0.04 .06 .07 .08 .10 .12
6 Cotton-elastics, black, ¼ to 1 inch wide, yard, 0.04 .06 .07 .08 .10 .12
7 Cotton-elastics, colored, ¼ to 1 inch wide, yard, 0.04 .05 .06 .08 .10
8 Silk-elastics, white or black and colored, yard, 0.12 .14 .16 .18 .20 to 40.

MISCELLANEOUS.

1 Cotton stay-bindings, white or black, each, $0.03 .04 .05 .06 .07 .08 .09 .10 .11 .12
2 Scotch stay-bindings, each, 0.04 .05 .06 .07 .08 .09 .10 .11 .12 .14 .16 .18 .20 .22 .25
3 Linen tapes, piece, according to width, 0.02 .03 .04 .05 .06 .07 .08 .09 .10 .11 .12
4 Whalebone, ¼ to ⅜ inch wide, 30, 33 or 36 inches long; according to size, each, 0.06 .07 .08
5 Short corset-bones, each, 0.04 .05 .06 .07
6 Button-rings, hundred, 19
7 Hair-nets.
8 Tape-measures.
9 Glove-hooks.
10 Linen-bobbins.
11 Cotton-bobbins.
12 Hose-supporters:
   ladies'.   children's.
13 Oil-silk.
14 Rubber-cloth.
15 Rubber-diapers.
16 Scissors, pair, 0.40 to 1.75
17 Garters:
   ladies',   children's.
18 Corset-laces.
19 Dress-laces.
20 Corset-steels, in kid or muslin.
21 Side-steels, in kid or muslin.
22 Shoe-laces, round or flat, pair, 0.01 .02 .03 .05 .06
23 Pen-knives, each, 0.20 to .75
24 Stocking-darners, each, 0.10 .12 .15 .18

HOOKS AND EYES.

1 No. 4:
   card, $0.03   box, 0.15
2 No. 3:
   card, 0.02   box, 0.12

3 Military, No. 10:
   dozen, 0.04   box, .35
DRESS-SHIELDS.
1 Rubber-cloth, pair:
   medium, 0.18   large, .24
2 Pure-rubber, 0.24
3 Chamois-skin, 0.35
4 Cotton, rubber-lined, 0.20 .23 .26
5 Seamless pair:
   medium, 0.22   large, .28

GARTER-BUCKLES.
1 Steel, pair, 0.02 .03 .05
2 Gilt, pair, 0.03 .04 .06
3 Silver, pair, 0.03 .04 .05
4 Nickel, pair, 0.04 .05 .06

THIMBLES.
1 Coin-silver, each, 0.35 .40 .50
2 Silvered, each, 0.02 .03 .04 .05
3 Steel, each, 0.02 .03 .04 .05
4 Gilt, each, 0.06 .08 .09 .10

JEWELRY.

BRACELETS—For Ladies and Children.
1 Roman.
2 Enameled.
3 Gold-plated.
4 Whitby-jet.

MISCELLANEOUS.
1 Shawl-pins.
2 Cuff-pins.
3 Hat-pins.
4 Pins, English-garnet.
5 Pins, silver.
6 Ear-drops.
7 Neck-chains.
8 Medallions.
9 Charms.
10 Watch-chains.
11 Chatelaine-watches.
12 Chatelaine-chains.

COMBS.

DRESSING-COMBS.
1 Rubber, $0.10 to .50
2 Imitation-shell.
3 Shell.
4 Celluloid, $0.69 .75 .80

LORD & TAYLOR, NEW YORK.

FINE-COMBS.

1. Celluloid.
2. Ivory, 0.18 .20 .22 .25 .35 to .50

BACK-COMBS.

1. Imitation-shell.
2. Shell.
3. Rubber.
4. Horn.
5. Celluloid.
6. Ivory.
7. Coin-silver.
8. Metal.

LEATHER GOODS.

SATCHELS.

1. Imitation-leather, sizes 9, 10, 11, 12, 13, 14 inches, $0.75 to 7.
2. Leather, sizes 9, 10, 11, 12, 13, 14 inches, 1.50 to 12.
3. Railroad, for gentlemen, black, brown, red or natural-leather; sizes 14, 16, 18, 20 inches, 3. to 10.

POCKET BOOKS.

1. Russia, 0.50 .60 .70 .75 .80 .85 .90 1. 1.25 to 4.
2. Russia, with memorandums, 2.00 2.25 2.50 3. 3.50
3. American Russia, 0.30 to 3.
4. Sealskin, 0.50 .60 .70 .85 .90 1. to 3.
5. French calfskin, 0.25 .30 .35 .40 .45 .50 .55 .60 .65 to 3.50
6. Plush, 0.28 to 1.25
7. Side-pocket-books, gentlemen's, 0.75 to 3.50

BELTS.

1. Imitation-leather, black, brown, red or écru; two to four inches wide, 0.25 to 1.50

MISCELLANEOUS.

1. Bags with belts, 0.75 to 5.
2. Music-rolls, 0.75 to 2.50
3. Shawl-straps, 0.20 to 1.25
4. Cigar-cases, 0.40 to 5.00
5. Card-cases, Russia or morocco, 0.50 to 2.
6. Dressing-cases, furnished, 3. to 12.

HAND MIRRORS.

1. Initial.
2. Leather-back.
3. Wood-back.
4. Diatite-back.
5. Celluloid-back.
6. Celluloid sets (mirror, brush and comb in boxes, 3.75 to 15.

BRUSHES.

HAIR-BRUSHES.

1. Wood-back, $0.50 to 2.50
2. Celluloid-back, 2.00 to 3.50
3. Metal, 0.40 .50 .60 .70
4. Florence, 0.50 to 1.75
5. Inlaid, 0.50 to 2.50

MISCELLANEOUS.

1. Tooth-brushes, 0.10 .12 .15 .18 .20 .25
2. Nail-brushes, 0.25 .30 .35 .40 .45 .50
3. Flesh-brushes, 0.50 to 1.50
4. Hat-brushes, 0.40 .50 .60 .70
5. Clothes-brushes, 0.30 to 1.

FANS.

1. Japanese, $0.02 to .50
2. Linen, black or colored, 0.25 to .75
3. Silk, black or white, 0.40 to 3.
4. Feather, black or white, 1.00 to 5.
5. Pearl-stick, 3.00 to 25.
6. Ivory-stick, 1.00 to 12.
7. Bone-stick, 0.50 to 5.
8. Gilt-stick, 0.50 to 2.50
9. Silver-stick, 0.50 to 2.50
10. Ebony-stick, 0.75 to 5.
11. Shell-stick, 0.15 to 50

TOILET ARTICLES.

1. Vaseline.
2. Bandoline.
3. Hair-oils.
4. Pomades.
5. Hair-tonics.
6. Toilet-vinegar.
7. Dentifrice.
8. Nail-powders.
9. Smelling-salts.

SOAPS; prices per cake.

1. French, $0.10 to 1.
2. American, 0.10 to .50
3. English, 0.11 to .50

PERFUMES.
ALFRED WRIGHT'S.
EXTRACTS.

½ ounce, $0.30		3 ounces,	$1.15
¾	.37	4½	1.75
1¼	.55	½ lb.,	3.00
2	.85	1	6.00

1. Mary Stuart
2. Bouquet
3. Frangipani
4. Jockey Club
5. Carnation Pink
6. Mignonette
7. New-Mown Hay
8. Orange Flowers
9. Patchouli. A musky perfume
10. Geranium Leaf
11. Stephanotis
12. Jasmine
13. Tea Rose
14. Tuberose
15. West End
16. White Rose. Very lasting
17. Wild Olive
18. Wood Violet, only in 4½ oz. size, $1.75

19. Ilang-Ilang
20. Heliotrope
21. Lily of the Valley
22. Millefleur
23. Musk
24. Ocean Spray
25. Gloriosa

EXTRACTS, Special.

1. Double-Ten, ¾ ounce bottle, 0.90
2. Extracts in bottles in paper boxes, except Double-Ten, 0.70

TOILET WATERS.

1. Lemon-leaf Water. New; distilled from the lemon leaf and slightly modified; sold at a low price for introduction; bottle contains about eight ounces, $0.60
2. Bay Rum. Distilled with rum from the leaf of the Bay Laurel; bottle contains a little more than a pint, 0.50

UMBRELLAS.

NOVELTIES in handles of silk umbrellas, such as agate, silver, buckhorn, waxel-wood, etc., are continually being produced; they are too transient to be particularly described.

UMBRELLAS.

TWILLED SILK.

1. 26 inches, horn handle, $3.00 3.50 5.
2. 26   ivory handle, 4.00 5. 6. 7.50 8.50
3. 28   ivory handle, 8.50 to 10.
4. 28   natural handle, 3.00 3.50 4.50 5. 6. 7.

ALPACA.

1. 26 inches, $1.75 to 4.
2. 28   2.00 to 5.

SCOTCH GINGHAM.

1. 26 inches, $0.60 to 2.50
2. 28   .85 to 2.50

SHOES.

EVERY article is suited to the purpose for which it is made ; some are designed for durability, others for elegance, others for softness, etc., etc. All are well made of proper stock and are as elegant as is consistent with their various uses. The same patterns are used for cutting out the high-priced and low-priced goods of the same shape, so that there is no difference in the fit except what may be due to the nature of the material used. If the instructions for measuring are carefully followed, a good fit may almost always be obtained. If, however the foot be of uncommon shape or of unusual proportions, a good fit requires the shoe to be made to measure : in this case the price is one dollar more than the list price.

INSTRUCTIONS FOR MEASURING.—When sitting, not standing, place the foot on the blank space at the bottom of the sheet, "Order for Shoes," and draw a pencil-line around it to give the length, breadth, and natural shape of the foot, thus : The pencil should be held vertically, or the outline will not represent the size of the foot.

Take the following measures:

1. Ball of foot,
2. Instep,
3. Heel,
4. Ankle,
5. Top.

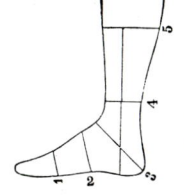

State the size usually worn, and whether a close or loose fit is wanted. The size, and the letter indicating the width, will usually be found marked on the lining of the old shoe, thus : $\frac{2}{B}$, meaning size 2, width B. We keep these particulars for your future use.

LADIES' BOOTS.

1. Prunella congress-gaiter, $1.
2. Prunella congress-gaiter, hand-made, 1.75 2.
3. Prunella button-boot, morocco foxing, 2.
4. Pebble-goat button-boot, worked buttonholes, English extension-sole, medium-plain toe, low square heel, (has been named "common-sense walking-boot"), 3.
5. Pebble-goat button-boot, double cork-soles, worked buttonholes, medium toe, plain heel, 4.
6. Pebble-goat button-boot, double cork-soles, worked buttonholes, medium toe, plain heel, 3.50
7. Pebble-goat button-boot, worked button holes, plain toe and heel, 2.
8. Oil-straight-grain button-boot, English extension-sole, low square heel, hand-made, 5.

No. 4, $3.

9 Kid-top button-boot, morocco foxings, low vamp, small round box-toe, half-concave heel, 3.50
10 Kid-top button-boot, straight-grain foxings, English extension-sole, low square heel, ("common-sense walking-boot"), 4.

No. 9, $3.50

11 Calf-kid-top button-boot, oil-straight-grain foxings, low vamp, waterproof double cork-soles, medium-round box-toe, plain heel, 4.50
12 Mat kid-top button-boot, French-kid slipper tie-foxings, small round low soft box-toe, medium high heel, hand-made, 8.
13 Curaçoa-kid button-boot, low vamp, extra-arched instep, small round box-toe, concave heel, 4.
14 Curaçoa-kid button-boot, worked button-holes, plain toe and heel, 2.00
15 Curaçoa-kid button-boot, worked button-holes, round box-toe, concave heel, 2.50

No. 16, $3.50

16 Curacoa-kid button-boot, plain toe and heel, "common-sense walking-boot," 3. 3.50
17 Curaçoa-kid button-boot, low vamp, box-toe, concave heel, 3. 3.50 3.75

18 Glove-kid front-lace boot, (for tender feet), 2.
19 Glove-kid congress-gaiter, hand-made, 2.50
20 French-kid button-boot, box-toe, concave heel, 4.25
21 French-kid button-boot, plain toe and heel, "common-sense walking-boot," 5.

No. 22, $5.

22 French-kid button-boot, low vamp small round box-toe, concave heel, 5.
23 French-kid button-boot, medium toe and heel, hand-made, 6.
24 French-kid button-boot, small round soft box-toe, low vamps, high concave heel, hand-made, 8.
25 French-kid button-boot, small round soft box-toe, low vamps, low square heels, hand-made, 8.

No. 26, $5.

26 French-kid button-boot, low vamp, extra-arched instep, small round box-toe, high concave heel, 5.
27 Diagonal-cloth top button-boot, curaçoa-kid foxings, concave heel, 2.50
28 Diagonal-cloth-top button-boot, curaçoa-kid foxings, box-toe, concave heel, 3.
29 Diagonal-cloth-top button-boot, plain toe and heel "common-sense walking-boot," 3. 3.50

LADIES' BOOTS—Continued.

30 Diagonal-cloth-top button-boot, curaçoa-kid, small round box-toe, broad half-concave heel, 3.50
31 Diagonal or basket-cloth-top button-boot, French-kid, low foxings, extra-arched instep, small round box-toe, concave heel, 4.

No. 28, $3.

32 Cloth-top button-boot, French-kid slipper-tie foxings, small round low soft box-toe, medium high heels, hand-made, 8.
33 Black-satin button-boot, small round toe, medium heel, 9.
34 White satin button-boot, small round toe, medium heel, 10.
35 French-kid sandal-boot, velvet bows, steel buckles, French heel, 4.

LADIES' LOW SHOES.

36 Goatskin buskin, laced with three holes, low square heel, $1.
37 Curaçoa-kid Newport-tie, plain toe and heel, 1.50

No. 38, $2.

38 Curaçoa-kid Newport-tie, opera toe, medium heel. 2.
39 Curaçoa-kid Newport-button, medium-round toe, concave heel, 2.00
40 Curaçoa-kid tie-walking-shoe, medium toe, low square heel, 2.50
41 French-kid button-walking-shoe, medium-round toe, low square heel, 3.75
42 French-kid tie-walking-shoe, medium-round toe, low square heel, 3.25
43 Curaçoa-kid Newport button-shoe, box-toe, concave heel, 2.
44 Curaçoa-kid Newport tie-shoe, plain toe and heel, 1.85

No. 45, $2.

45 Curaçoa-kid sandal-shoe, 2.

No. 46, $2.50

46 Camille sandal-shoe, trimmed with black velvet and steel buckles, 2.50
47 Over-gaiter, of cloth to match any dress, (worn over a low shoe or slipper, giving the appearance of a cloth-top boot), 2.

LADIES' SLIPPERS.

48 Prunella (serge) slipper, elastic at instep broad sole and heel, $1.
49 Curaçoa-kid slipper, leather bows, broad stout sole, low heel, 1.

No. 50, $1.50

50 Curaçoa-kid slipper, box-toe, high heel 1.25   1.50

LORD & TAYLOR, NEW YORK.

51 Curaçoa-kid sandal-slipper, trimmed, round box-toe, high heel, 2.
52 Curaçoa-kid slipper, small round box-toe, concave heel, 1.75 2.
53 French-kid slipper, pointed vamp, medium toe:
   with low square leather heel, 1.75
   without heel, 1.50
54 French-kid slipper, arched instep, small round box-toe, high concave heel, 2.50

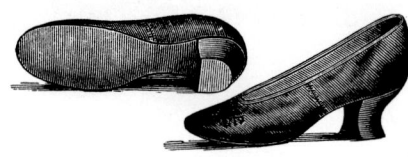

No. 55, $3.

55 French-kid slipper, box-toe, concave heel, embroidered with beads, 3.
56 French-kid slipper, low vamp, medium-round toe, Louis XV. heel, 3.50
57 Curaçoa-kid slipper, low leather heel, trimmed with small leather bows, 1.25
58 Curaçoa-kid low button-walking-shoe, medium-round toe, concave heel, 2.50

MISSES' BOOTS, ETC.

Sizes 11 to 2

59 Pebble-grain button-boot, plain toe and heel, $1.50.
60 Pebble-goat button-boot, worked buttonholes, broad sole, medium toe, low square heel, 2. 2.50
61 Straight-grain button-boot, spring-heels, sizes 11 to 2, 2.75
62 Pebble-goat calf-skin-foxed button-boot, English extension-sole, low square heel, 2.75
63 Pebble-goat button-boot, plain toe and heel, 1.75
64 Pebble-goat button-boot, worked buttonholes, low heel, (for school), 2.
65 Oil-straight-grain button-boot, worked buttonholes, low square heel, 2.75
66 Curacoa-kid button-boot, spring-heels, sizes 11 to 2, 2.75
67 Curaçoa-kid button-boot, low vamp, extra-arched instep, small round box-toe, low concave heel, 3.
68 Curaçoa-kid button-boot, worked button holes, plain toe and heel, 2.50
69 Brush-kid button-boot, worked buttonholes, medium heel, 1.90
70 French-kid button-boot, medium-round toe, concave heel, 4.00
71 Curaçoa-kid French sandal-boot, plain heel, trimmed with black-satin bows and steel buckles, 3.50
72 White-kid button-boot, 2.75
73 Curaçoa-kid slipper, low leather heel, leather bows, 1.25

CHILDREN'S SHOES.

Sizes 4 to 10½

74 Pebble-goat button-boot, spring heel, (sizes 4 to 8½), $1.
75 Pebble-goat button-boot, low broad heel, extension-sole, 1.25
76 Pebble-goat button-boot, spring heel, (sizes 5 to 10½), 1.60 1.75
77 Pebble-goat button-boot, broad sole, low flat heel, (sizes 7 to 10½), 1.75
78 Pebble-goat button-boot, worked buttonholes, extension-sole, spring heel, 1.75
79 Pebble-goat button-boot, worked buttonholes, full English extension-sole, hand-made, 2.25
80 Curaçoa-kid button-boot, spring-heel, worked buttonholes, (sizes 4 to 8), 1.25
81 Curaçoa-kid button-boot, worked buttonholes, broad sole, spring heel, (sizes 8 to 10½), 1.75
82 Curaçoa-kid button-boot, worked buttonholes, full extension-sole, low square heel, (sizes 7 to 10½), 1.75
83 Kid-top morocco-foxed button-boot, English extension-sole, spring heel, hand-made, 2.75
84 French-kid button-boot, full extension-sole, spring heel, hand-made, 2.75
85 French-kid button-boot, extension-sole, low square heel, (sizes 8 to 10½), 2.75

BOYS' SHOES.

Sizes 10 to 5½

86 Calfskin button-boot:
   sizes 11 to 2, $2.50
   2½ to 5½, 3.00
   2½ to 5½, 3.50
87 Buff button-boot:
   sizes 11 to 2, 1.75
   11 to 2, 2.00
   2½ to 5½ 2.50
88 Calfskin button-boot, (sizes 11 to 2), 2.50

INFANTS' SHOES.

89 Soft-sole button-boot, black, blue, pink bronze, or pearl, (sizes 0 to 3), (first shoes), $0.36

No. 89, $0.35

90 Morocco button-boot, black, (sizes 1 to 6), 0.50
91 American kid button-boot, black, (sizes 1 to 6), 0.75 .90
92 Kid button-boot, black, bronze, blue, pink, or pearl, (sizes 1 to 7), 1.25
93 Straight-grain button-boot, (sizes 4 to 7), 1.

GENTLEMEN'S SLIPPERS.

94 Goatskin, $1.25 1.50
95 Goatskin, trimmed with patent leather, 2.

No. 96, $3.

96 Cloth and velvet, embroidered, 2. 2.50 3.
97 Cloth and velvet, hand-embroidered, 4. 5.
98 Silk velvet, made to order, 7.
99 Silk velvet, with monograms embroidered to order, 8.
100 Boys' and youths' slippers from 1. to 2.50

FURS AND FUR GARMENTS.

At this season and continuing throughout the spring and summer until cold weather again, we are engaged in preparing the skins, already bought, and manufacturing fur garments for the fall and winter of 1881–2.

The selection of skins and their preparation requires care and time—care that only good ones be chosen, and time that they may be well cured and dressed. If these precautions are not observed, furs quickly wear out and prove unsatisfactory to their owners. The ability to sell at a price less than that of a reputable house, is usually proof that these precautions have not been observed.

We make over old fur garments to conform to new shapes, and receive furs on storage.

The new styles for the next season will be shown in our September catalogue.

LINENS.

Snowy double-damask table linen is furnished in the finest qualities with landscape centers and many other graceful patterns, with double borders and napkins in corresponding design. Pompeiian designs are almost plain in the center with a broad border showing a Grecian band entwined with a laurel wreath. Hunting scenes are surrounded by double borders of copse with quail and other designs. A cloth with a group of woodland flowers and ferns for its center-piece has a double border of ferns, harebells and leaves. Snowdrop and lozenge patterns are still a favorite design. The Queen's own pattern of block checks is always in good taste and may be chosen in a lower priced linen as it does not display the quality as readily. The same is true of the running patterns of trellis vine and grapes which are furnished in medium-priced goods. Dinner napkins are from three-quarters to nearly a yard square. Smaller napkins are for breakfast or lunch. Lunch cloths are in white, gold-color, grey and écru, with double Grecian borders of ruby-color. Red cloths have similar borders in black or white. Doylies or fringed napkins are furnished to match.

Huckabuck and damask towels are both used. Fine huckabuck are shown in large sizes with gay borders and deep knotted fringe. Pure white damask towels have handsome centers in basket designs, with broad border of fine arabesques and deep knotted fringe. Momie towels with crape-like centers have gay border ornamented with lines of drawn work and embroidered in Pompeiian design with rose-color, pale-blue, ecru and navy-blue. Handsome large crape-like towels have double borders of lace work, and are finished with fringe. Towels with ornamental borders are often used for bureau covers. Turkish bath towels are in an endless variety of fancy colors. To persons with rheumatism or weak circulation, who need a rough friction towel, Cash's tape towels are recommended.

Linen sheeting is much cheaper than formerly, and heavy, coarsely-woven qualities are preferred while finer linen is chosen for pillows.

White shirting linen with tiny dots or sprays of pale blue, red or black in jockey patterns of horseshoe or caps and in odd little Japanese figures is chosen for colored shirting for men and boys. Stylish polka dots of color or fine hair stripes are liked by many ladies for morning-dresses, which are made in simple styles and piped with color or the figure used, and especially for children's dresses as they wash and wear indefinitely.

TABLE DAMASK.

Irish, Scotch, or German.

Prices per yard.

1. Unbleached:
   6-4, about 1½ yards wide, $0.25 .35 .45 .50
   7-4, about 1¾ yards wide, 0.40 .45 .50 .55 .60 .65 .70 .75 .80 .85
   8-4, about 2 yards wide, 0.70 .75 .80 .85 .90 .95 1. 1.10 1.25 1.40 1.50

2. Bleached:
   7-4, about 1¾ yards wide, 0.50 .60 .65 .75 .80 .85 .90 1. 1.15 1.20 1.25
   8-4, about 2 yards wide, .90 1. 1.15 1.20 1.25 1.30 1.35 1.40 1.50 1.60 1.70 1.75 1.80 2. 2.25 2.50
   10-4, about 2½ yards wide, 1.50 2. 2.25 2.50 3.25

3. Turkey-red:
   6-4, about 1½ yards wide, 0.50 .60
   7-4, about 1¾ yards wide, 0.60 .65 .70 .85 1.00

TABLE CLOTHS.

Prices each.

Damask.

1. About 2 × 2 yards, $1.75 2. 2.25 2.50 3. 3.50 4. 4.50 5. 5.75 6.

2. About 2 × 2½ yards, 2. 2.50 2.60 2.70 3. 3.50 4. 4.50 5. 5.50 6. 6.50 7. 7.50 8. 8.50 9. 9.50 10. 11. 12.

3. About 2 × 3 yards, 2.25 2.50 3. 3.50 3.75 4. 4.50 5. 5.50 6. 6.50 6.75 7. 7.50 8. 9. 9.50 10. 11. 12. 13. 13.50 14. 15. 16.50 17. 18.

4. About 2 × 3½ yards, 4.50 4.75 5. 5.75 6. 6.50 7. 7.50 7.75 8. 9. 9.50 10. 11. 12. 14. 15.

5. About 2 × 4 yards, 4. 4.50 4.75 5. 5.75 6. 6.50 7. 7.50 7.75 8. 9. 9.50 10. 11. 12. 14. 15.

6. About 2½ × 2½ yards, 3.50 4. 4.50 5. 5.50 5.75 6. 6.50 6.75 7. 7.50 8. 9.

7. About 2½ × 3 yards, 5. 5.50 6. 6.50 6.75 8. 8.50 8.75 9. 10. 11. 12. 12.50 13. 14. 16. 17.

8. About 2½ × 3½ yards, 7.50 8.50 8.75 9. 9.50 10.50 11. 12. 13. 14.75 15. 18. 19. 20. 21. 22. 25.

9. About 2½ × 4 yards, 7.50 8.50 9.50 10.50 12. 14. 15. 15.50 16. 18. 20. 23. 25. 27.

10. About 2½ × 5 yards, 10. 12. 16. 18. 21. 22. 25. 27. 30. 36. 42.

11. About 2½ × 6 yards, 20. 24. 27. 35.

12. With fringe and colored border: red, blue, buff, brown, etc.
    About 2 × 2 yards, 3.50 4.50
    2 × 2½   4.50 6.
    2 × 3   6. 7. 9. 10.
    2 × 3½   7.50 9. 9.50
    2 × 4   9. 10. 11. 12. 14.

13. Pink, mode, or buff:
    About 2 × 2 yards, 4. 5.
    2 × 2½   5. 6.
    2 × 3   6. 7.

Turkey-red:

1. About 2 × 2 yards, 2.50
   2 × 2½   3.00
   2 × 3   3.50
   2 × 3½   4.50

Cardinal.

1. About 2 × 2 yards, 3.00
   2 × 2½   4.00
   2 × 3   5.00
   2 × 3½   5.50

Blanketing for under table-cloths.

1. Cotton, nearly 2 yds. wide, per yd., 1.

NAPKINS.

Prices per dozen.

1. About ⅝ × ⅝ yard, $1. 1.20 1.25 1.50 1.75 2. 2.25 2.50 2.75 3. 3.25 3.75 4. 4.50 5. 5.50 5.75 6. 6.50 7. 7.50 8. 8.75 9. 10. 10.50 11. 12.

2. About ¾ × ¾ yard, 2.25 2.50 2.75 3. 3.50 4. 5. 5.50 5.75 6. 6.50 7. 7.50 8. 8.50 9. 9.50 10. 11. 12. 13. 14. 15. 16. 16.50 17. 18.

3. About 1 × 1 yard, 7.50 8. 9. 9.50 10.50 12. 13.50 14.50 15. 16.

White d'Oyleys.

1. About ⅜ × ⅜ yard, 0.75 .90 1. 1.25 1.50 1.75 2. 2.50 3. 3.50 4. 4.50 5.

LINEN.

Prices per yard.

PILLOW.
1. 40 inches wide, $0.50 .60 .75 .80 .90 1.10
2. 45 inches wide, 0.50 .60 .62 .65 .80 .85 .95 1.15 1.45
3. 50 inches wide, 0.75 .80 .85 1.
4. 54 inches wide, 0.60 .80 .85 .90 1.

SHEETING.
1. 2 yards wide, 0.60 .66 .85
2. 2¼ yards wide, 0.80 .90 1. 1.25
3. 2½ yards wide, 0.80 .90 1. 1.15 1.20 1.25 1.50 1.60 2. 2.75
4. 2¾ yards wide, 1.25 1.30 1.50 1.75 2.

SHIRTING.
1. 1 yard wide, 0.25 .30 .35 .40 .45 .50 .56 .60 .65 .70 .75 .80 .85 .90 .95 1. 1.10 115 1.20 1.25

PRINTED.
1. A great variety of designs, 1 yard wide, 0.40 .45 .50

DIAPER.

Prices per piece.

1. 18 inches wide, $1. 1.25 1.50 1.75 2. 2.50
2. 20 inches wide, 1.50 1.75 2. 2.25 2.50 2.75 3.
3. 22 inches wide, 2. 2.25 2.50 2.75 3. 3.50
4. 24 inches wide, 2.50 2.75 3. 3.50

COTTON DIAPERS.
1. Per piece of 10 yards, 0.85 1. 1.10 1.25

TOWELS.

Prices per dozen.

1. For glass and silverware, $2.50 3.00
2. Huckabuck, 1. 1.25 1.50 1.75 2. 2.50 2.75 3. 3.25 4. 4.50 4.75 5. 5.50 5.75 6. 6.50 7.
3. Damasks, plain, 2. 2.25 2.50 3. 3.50 3.75 4. 4.25 4.50 4.75 5. 5.50 6. 6.50 7. 7.50 8. 8.50 9. 9.50 10. 11.
4. Damasks, embroidered, 5. 5.50 6. 6.50 7. 7.50 8. 8.50 9. 9.50 10. 11. 12. 13.50 14. 15. 16. 17. 18. 19. 20. 23. 25. 28. 29.50
5. Turkish, brown or white, 3. 4. 5. 5.50 6. 8.50 9. 10. 12. 14. 20.

TOWELING.

Prices per yard.

1. For silver and glassware, $0.12 .15 .16 .17 .20 .26 .30 .35 .40
2. Huckabuck, 0.20 .25 .28 .30 .35 .37 .40 .45 .50 .60 .65
3. Twilled, brown or white, for kitchen use, 0.09 .10 .11 .12 .12½ .14 .15 .16 .18 .20 .22 .25 .28
4. Crash :
 American, 0.10 .12 .14 .16 .18 .20
 Russian, 0.10 .12 .14 .16 .18 .20

DRUGGETS.

CRUMB CLOTHS.
1. About 2 ×2 yards, $1.50 1.85
2. 2½ × 2½ 2.00 2.25
3. 2½ × 3 2.50 2.70
4. 2½ × 3½ 3.00 3.50
5. 3 × 3 2.15 2.25 3.25 3.75

DRUGGET, per yard.
1. About 1½ yards wide, 0.60
2. 2 .75 1.40
3. 2½ .95 1.75 2.00
4. 3 1.15 1.25 2.50
5. 3½ 1.25
6. 4 1.60 3.85

STAIR-CRASH.

1. 18 inches wide, $0.18 .20 .22
2. 20 .22 .25 .28 .30
3. 22 .28 .30 .32 .35

FLANNELS.

Colored French flannels in all the new shades are now shorn of the nap and will not grow rough. In dark colors they are as popular as ever for morning shopping-dresses, which are made in the manner described under the head of "Cloth."

Many new colors and combinations are furnished in all sizes and varieties of plaid and stripes. A great deal of Oriental pink or rose-color is seen in the spring goods mingled with silver-grey and turquoise-blue. A handsome flannel for wrappers shows inch stripes of these three colors side by side. Handsome pale-grey flannels are crossed by fine lines of turquoise-blue in broken plaid. Heliotrope, red, myrtle-green and many other shades are mixed on plaids and checks in these soft goods and chiné effects are often seen. Basket-woven flannels are still used for ladies' breakfast jackets in various colors, and especially in blues and drabs for children's cloaks.

Pure wool flannels are popular, though many ladies prefer silk and wool which are somewhat more expensive. Embroidered flannels wrought by hand and machine in white, pale-blue and red on white and colored goods are furnished, and bands of embroidered flannel are used for skirts and for trimming wrappers. Opera flannel is now found in all the odd and artistic colorings used for fancy work and embroidery.

WHITE.

COTTON-AND-WOOL.

1. Shaker, 31 inches, $0.30 .35 .40 .45 .50
2. Gray, twilled, 27 inches, 0.25 .30

ALL-WOOL.

1. Various:
    27 inches, 0.20 .25 .30 .35 .40 .45 .50 .55
2. G. H. Gilbert Mfg. Co. :
    30 inches, 0.50 to .95
    34   .55 to 1.00
4. Shaker, 32 inches, 0.60 .65 .75 .80
5. Shaker, twilled, 30 inches, 0.80 1.00
6. Shaker, California, 30 inches, 1.00
7. Embroidered by machine, all-wool, 33 inches, 0.90 to 4.00

Samples of embroidered flannel are not sent.

SILK-AND-WOOL.

1. Ballard Vale Co. :
    31 inches, 1.00
    34   1.10

COLORED.

ALL-WOOL.

1. Scarlet, plain :
    27 inches, $0.25 .30 .35 .40 .45 .50
    32   .55 .65 .75
2. Scarlet, twilled :
    27 inches, 0.30 .35 .40 .45 .50 .55 .60 .75
    32 inches, 0.65 .75 .85 .90 1.
3. Scarlet, embroidered by machine, all-wool, 33 inches, 1.25 to 1.55
4. Navy-blue, plain, 36 inches, 0.50
5. All colors, plain, 45 inches, 0.75 1.
6. Navy-blue, twilled :
    27 inches, 0.30 .35 .40 .45 .50 .55 .60
    54   1.25
7. Gray, twilled :
    27 inches, 0.40 .45 .55
    54   1.10 1.25
8. Plaid, 28 inches, 0.45 .55 .65
9. Opera, 25 inches, 0.40 .45 .60
10. French, fancy-striped, for wrappers, 27 inches, 0.60 .65
11. French, basket, for sacques, 27 inches, 0.55 .65
12. Embroidered by machine, 33 inches :
    Navy-blue, 1.50
    Light-blue, 1.45 1.50

DOMESTICS AND BEDDING.

Counterpanes of snow-white Marseilles are now chosen in preference to the various fancy colored bed-coverings in use the last few years. The gay cotton terry and colored Mitcheline counterpanes are liable to fade, and often present a sorry appearance after the first washing. A fine light quality of Marseilles is now used, and new patterns are still in graceful flower and leaf designs.

Handsome bed-coverings are of fine antique lace, with pillow protectors or "shams," to match, or they are often made of sheer cambric with insertions and edgings of Hamburg embroidery, or Valenciennes or torchon lace. The shams may be used either with a coverlet of Marseilles or of lace in corresponding design, except when they are in antique lace, when only a lace coverlet is used. A quilt of satin or silesia is laid under all coverlets of lace, and the pillow protectors are then caught down by bows of ribbon in pale-pink or blue or old-gold to match the color of the quilt. Low-priced shams braided (by machine) in graceful patterns are finished by a plain hem, but ladies after add a frill of lace or embroidery at home, and thus pretty, tasteful shams are secured at a very moderate price. [For Pillow Shams, see Upholstery, page 159.]

The heavy, coarsely-woven Utica sheeting is usually preferred, while pillow and bolster cases are chosen in fine Wamsutta and Fruit of the Loom. A specialty of this house is night-gown cotton; an excellent fabric for warm night garments. It is woven in heavy firm qualities, and does not grow hard or yellow in the washing.

Summer blankets are furnished in light all-wool qualities and woven of yarn that has already been shrunk.

French blankets in many gay fancy colors, also of shrunken yarn, will be welcomed, as they are remarkably pretty and are not so easily soiled as pure white wool.

Down comfortables are furnished in damask silk and plain silk, and a full assortment of these goods in all qualities is always kept in English chintz and Turkey red.

LORD & TAYLOR, NEW YORK.

SHEETINGS.

1. Utica, bleached:
   - 1¼ yards wide   2¼ yards wide
   - 1½   2½
   - 2   2¾
2. Utica, unbleached:
   - 1 yard   2¼ yards
   - 48 inches   2½
   - 58
3. Wamsutta, bleached:
   - 1⅛ yards   2 yards
   - 1¼   2¼
   - 50 inches   2½
   - 1½ yards
4. Wamsutta, unbleached, 3 yards wide
5. Androscoggin, bleached:
   - 2 yards   2½ yards
   - 2¼
6. Androscoggin, unbleached:
   - 2 yards   2½ yards
   - 2¼

SHIRTINGS.

36 inches wide.

MUSLINS, bleached.

1. New York Mills
2. Wamsutta
3. Utica, nonpareil
4. Utica, heavy
5. Fruit of the Loom
6. Fruit of the Loom, 100 threads per inch
7. Masonville
8. Pride of the West
9. Lonsdale
10. Androscoggin
11. Lord & Taylor's nightgown cotton
12. Twilled, for gentlemen's shirts and drawers

CAMBRICS.

1. Lonsdale
2. Wamsutta
3. Grinnell

MUSLINS, unbleached, 36 inches wide.

1. Utica, fine and close-thread
2. Atlantic, A, heavy
3. Atlantic, H, heavy.
4. Continental, C, fine
5. Boot Mills, C, fine and light
6. Boot Mills, F F, heavy
7. Nashua, 40 inches, heavy
8. Boston, 40 inches, heavy
9. Atlantic, V, ⅞ yard, heavy
10. Drilling, fine
11. Drilling, heavy
12. Duck, for mason's over-garments, sail-canvas, and awning:
    - ⅞ yard wide
    - 40 inches

CANTON-FLANNEL.

1. White, unbleached:
   - 27 inches   36 inches
   - 32
2. White, bleached:
   - 27 inches   33 inches
   - 30   36
3. Colored: drab, brown, blue, or slate, 27 to 30 inches, $0.12½ .15 .18.
4. All colors, 29 inches, for curtains and piano covers

BED-TICKING, ETC.

1. Bed-ticking:
   - 27 inches
   - 32   60
   - 36
2. Awning, striped.
3. Denims, blue or brown:
   - Checks,
   - Hickory,
   - Ducks.

WADDING, ETC.

1. Cotton-batting, white, bundles, ½ and pound packages
2. Cotton-wadding, white, sheets
3. Cotton-wadding, white, yards
4. Cotton-wadding, colored, yards
5. Wool-wadding, white, sheets
6. Wool-wadding, brown, sheets
7. Arctic-down, bags, any size
8. Eider-down, bags, any size

No. 1.

HAMMOCKS.

1 Cotton, full size, $1. to 3.50.
2 Cotton, children's size, 0.75 to 2.
3 Manilla, full size, 1. to 3.50.
4 Manilla, children's size, 0.75 to 2.

BEDDING.

MATTRESSES.

HAIR, HUSK, STRAW, FIBRE, RATTAN.
Made to order only. In writing for price state size, material wanted, and whether in one or two parts.

BLANKETS.
Prices per pair.

THE designation of sizes in the trade is by quarter-yards; but blankets said to be of the same "size" vary in actual measurement. In any "size" the finer or heavier blankets are apt to be smaller, while the coarser or lighter may be of near or quite full measure. Different makers also vary as to liberality in measurement. The buyer in ordering may express choice between size on the one hand and quality or weight on the other, and such choice can usually be regarded.

1 Cotton warp, wool filling, white, 10-4, about 2¼ × 2 yards, $1.75
2 Cotton-and-wool warp, wool filling, white:
   10-4, about 2½ × 2 yards, 3.25 4.50 5.50 6.50
   11-4, about 2½ × 2 yards, 3.25 4.50 6.40 8.25
   12-4, about 2¾ × 2¼ yards, 6. 10.
   13-4, about 3 × 2¼ yards, sweat

3 California, all-wool, white, gray, red, blue:

62 × 72 inches	78 × 88 inches
66 × 74	84 × 90
72 × 84	88 × 98
74 × 80	98 × 102

EXPOSITION BLANKETS, single.

1 Plain, 10-4, about 2½ × 1⅞ yards, each 25. 30.
2 White, fancy-colored border, 10-4, about 2½ × 1⅞ yards, each
3 French, white, wide-and-narrow-striped, 70 × 90 inches, each 15.
4 French, white, blue, border, 59 × 82 inches, each

SUMMER BLANKETS; prices per pair.

1 10-4, about 2 × 2¼, 4. to 8.
2 11-4, about 2 × 2½, 5. to 11.50

CRIB and CRADLE, fine and soft; prices per pair.

1 Cotton warp, wool filling, white, 30 × 50 inches, 1.50
2 Wool, white, 36 × 48 inches, 2.
3 Wool, white, 36 × 42 inches, 3.

LORD & TAYLOR, NEW YORK.

4 English, all-wool, white :
    34 × 48, 4.50
    36 × 50, 5.00
    48 × 64, 5.00

5 All-wool, white, embroidered in worsted with the word "Baby," or with figure of a bird, 30 × 40 inches, 3.75

6 California, all-wool, white, embroidered "Baby," or figure of bird, 36 × 50 inches, 4.50

7 White, 32 × 42 inches, each 3.50

8 French, single, white, fancy-striped 32 × 42 inches, each, 3.50 to 5.
    32 × 42 inches, blue, "Baby" and figure of a leaf, 4.25
    32 × 42 inches, pink, "Baby" and figure of a leaf, 4.50

CAMPING, HORSE, RAILROAD.

    Sizes 2 × 1⅞ yards. Prices per pair.

1 Gray, 1.25 1.50 2. 2.50 3.50 4.50
2 Army, 2.50 3.50 4.50
3 Blue, cotton-warp, wool-filling, 5.
4 Red, all-wool, "medicated," 6 to 10
5 Light-plaid, all-wool, strapped, 4. 4.50 6.
6 Dark-plaid, all-wool, strapped, 3.50 4.20 5.50 6.50 7. 8.50 9.
7 Plain-plaid, all-wool, strapped, 4. 5. 6. 7. 8. 9. 10. 12. 14.
8 Stable or storm, dark-plaid.
9 Dust, cotton-and-wool, dark-plaid, 2. 2.25
10 Wagon-and-street, linen, strapped, 1. 1.25 1.50 1.75 2. 2.50 3. 3.50 4.

COMFORTABLES.

COTTON WADDING.

1 Prints, dark :
    for single beds, about 2¼ × 1¼ yards, $1.25
    for ¾ beds, about 2¼ × 1¾ yards, 1.35 to 1.75
    for full-size beds, about 2¼ × 2 yards, 1.85 2. 2.50 3. 3.50

2 Plain-red, about 2¼ × 2 yards, 2.70 ot 4.50

3 Chintz, for full-size beds, about 2¼ × 2 yards, 4.50

4 Chintz, imitation silk, for full-size beds, about 2¼ × 2 yards, 5. 6.

5 Chintz, English, for full-size beds, about 2¼ × 2 yards, 5. 6.

6 Chintz :
    for cradle, 36 × 42 inches, 0.75 .95 1.25 1.50 2.
    for crib, 42 × 54 inches, 2. 2.25 2.50

EIDER DOWN made to order.

ARCTIC DOWN, our own manufacture.

1 Scotch chintz :
    1⅔ × 2 yards, 9. to 18.
    2 × 2 yards, 9. to 18.
2 Silk, 2 × 2 yards, 12. to 25.
3 Chintz, silk, figured, 2 × 2 yards, according to weight, 25. to 100.

    We make to order any size, any material, any combination of colors, and send samples of materials on request with specifications.

QUILTS.

MARSEILLES.

1 White :
    9-4, about 60 × 82 inches, $1.50 2. 2.25 2.50 2.75 3. 3.50 3.75 4.
    10-4 × 10-4, about 90 × 90 inches, 1.50 2. 2.25 2.50 2.75 3. 3.25 3.50 4. 5. 5.50 6. 6.50 7. 7.50 8. 9. 10.
    10-4, about 80 × 90 inches, 1.50 to 7.
    11-4, about 90 × 100 inches, 1.75 to 13.50
    11-4 × 11-4, about 96 × 100 inches, 1.75 2. 2.50 3. 3.50 4. 4.50 5. 5.50 6. 6.50 7. 7.50 8. 8.50 9. 10. 10.75 11.50 12. 13.50

2 Crib and cradle :
    4-4 × 5-4, about 36 × 45 inches, 0.75 1. 1.50 1.75 2.
    5-4 × 7-4, about 42 × 62 inches, 1.50 2. 2.50 3. 3.50
    6×7, about 54 × 64 inches, 1.25 1.50 1.75 2. 2.25 2.50 3. 3.50

3 Empress (white with blue or pink borders and centers), 10-4 × 10-4, about 90 × 99 inches, 4.50 8. 10.

4 Dresden (designs in blue or pink over the whole), 11-4 × 11-4, about 99 × 99 inches, 10.

5 Mitcheline, pink-and-white or blue-and white, 10-4, about 72 × 90 inches 3.75 4.25

HONEYCOMB.

Honeycomb quilts, for single, ¾ and full-sizes, in the following prices: $0.90 1. 1.10 1.15 1.25 1.50 1.75 2. 2.25 2.75 3.25

SHEETS.

Any size made to order.

1 Wamsutta:
    2 × 2½ yards   2½ × 2¾ yards
    2¼ × 2½

2 Utica:
    2 × 2½ yards   2½ × 2¾ yards
    2¼ × 2½

3 Androscoggin:
    2 × 2½ yards   2½ × 2¾ yards
    2¼ × 2½

PILLOW AND BOLSTER CASES.

Various lengths in stock. Any size made to order.

1 Wamsutta:
    40 inches wide   50 inches wide
    45   54

2 Utica:
    40 inches wide   50 inches wide
    45   54

3 Fruit of the Loom:
    40 inches wide   50 inches wide
    45   54

FLOOR-COVERINGS.

The new carpets are in an endless variety of tasteful designs which mingle gay porcelain colors with dull shades of Oriental beauty. The reproductions of Eastern looms are everywhere seen, though the newest Moquettes are in quaint designs, copied from antique French carpets over a hundred years old. They are usually in crimsons, olives, rose, blues and écrus, which are so toned or faded that the beauty of the color is left while its pronounced effect is lost. These carpets, however, need the brilliant surroundings of gay china, bric-a-brac and glittering sconces which cover the walls of the modern parlor, and they should be brightened here and there by a gorgeous Oriental tinted rug, to be seen to their full beauty. Olive brown grounds are mingled with porcelain green and gold color. Primrose yellow grounds are nearly covered by dull red and other shades, in arabesque designs. An écru surface is strewn with pomegranates and leaves in olive, in fade rose and crimson.

English carpets with grounds thickly covered with mottled figures, small basket designs, fine arabesques and patterns of Japanese effect have conventionalized fuchias, palms and other tropical patterns, thrown over them. They are a boon to housekeepers, as they wear much better than plain grounds, and are not so easily soiled.

For cottage parlors there is no more tasteful floor-covering than simple ingrain. It is furnished in durable quality in many patterns of the more expensive moquettes and Brussels. Wild rose patterns, with pearl grounds, are scattered with tangled clusters of pale pink eglantine, and peacock carpets in écru grounds are strewn with graceful peacock plumes in crimson and brown.

Each carpet is now furnished with a border from three-quarters to five-eighths in width in corresponding design. Hall and stair carpets match in color and pattern. It is often the custom to cover the whole stairs with carpet, leaving no space at the side, when stair buttons are used in place of rods. Hall carpets are in small patterns, and either match or contrast with the parlor carpet in color. With a parlor carpet of écru and crimson arabesques, a rich crimson carpet may be used in the hall and stairs. Dark colors are preferred for the hall, narrow borders are used, and the rugs laid about are Turkish or in Turkish coloring.

CARPETS.

Prices per yard.

AXMINSTER, ¾ yard wide.
 Carpet, $2. 2.50 to 2.75
 Border to match :
  ⅝ yard wide, 1.05 2.00 2.25 2.50
  ½   1.25 1.50 1.75 2.25
  ⅜   1.00 1.25 1.50 2.00
  ¼   .75 1.00 1.10

MOQUETTE, ¾ yard wide.
 Carpet, 1.50 1.75
 Border to match :
  ⅝ yard wide, 1.40 1.60
  ½   1.12 1.50
  ⅜   .90 1.00
  ¼   .60   .90

WILTON, best five-frame, ¾ yard wide.
 Carpet, 2.00 to 2.75
 Border to match :
  ⅝ yard wide, 2.25 2.60
  ½   1.75 2.00
  ⅜   1.25 1.50
  ¼   .75 1.00

BRUSSELS, ¾ yard wide.
 The difference in grades is in material, weight, or pattern ; sometimes in all three.
 Carpet, first grade, 1.65
 Border to match :
  ⅝ yard wide, 1.50
  ½   1.25
  ⅜   .75
  ¼   .60 .65
 Carpet, second-grade, 1.50
 Border to match :
  ⅝ yard wide, 1.40
  ½   1.12
  ⅜   .75 .90
  ¼   .50 .60
 Carpet, third-grade, 1.35

TAPESTRY, ¾ yard wide.
 Carpet, first-grade, English, 1.20
 Border to match :
  ¾ yard wide, 1.20
  ½   .90
  ⅜   .70 .75
  ¼   .45 .50
 Carpet, second-grade, 1.15
 Border to match :
  ½ yard wide, 0.90
  ⅜   .60
  ¼   .40
 Carpet, third-grade, 1.00
 Carpet, fourth-grade, .90
 Carpet, fifth-grade, .75

THREE-PLY, 1 yard wide.
  First-grade, 1.25
  Second-grade, 1.10
INGRAIN, 1 yard wide.
  First-grade, 1.00
  Second-grade, .90
  Third-grade, .80
  Fourth-grade, .70
  Fifth-grade, .60
  Sixth-grade, .50
VENETIAN, for stairs and hall.
  Bordered,   ½ yard wide, 0.25 .35 .50
  Bordered,   ⅝   .30 .40 .50 .60
  Bordered,   ¾   .35 .50 .65 .75
  Not bordered, 1   .75 1.10

DRUGGETS.

Prices per square yard.

First-grade, from 2¼ × 3 to 3 × 4½ yards, $1.12½
Second-grade, from 0.90

RUGS.

EUROPEAN AND AMERICAN.
  Berlin   Brussels
  Axminster   Tapestry
  Wilton   Imitation Oriental
  Velvet
TURKISH.
  Ouchak   Yhiordes
PERSIAN.
  Teheran   Bokhara
  Khorassan   Ferahan
  Backshaish   Koula
INDIAN.
  Nepaul   Agra
  Sinde   Masulipatam
  Delhi   Cashmere

MATS.

  Moquette   Brussels
  Wilton   Tapestry
  Velvet   Beam
  Cocoa:
    size 3, 30 × 18 inches, $1.25 1.50
    4, 33 × 20   1.75 2.00
    5, 36 × 22   2.00 2.50
    6, 39 × 24   2.50 3.00
    7, 12 × 26   3.00 3.75
    8, 45 × 28   3.50 4.50

FLOOR-CLOTHS.

All widths: prices per square yard.

The difference in grades is in weight and quality.
OIL-CLOTHS.
  First-grade, $1.15
  Second-grade,   1.00
  Third-grade,   .75
  Fourth-grade,   .65
  Fifth-grade,   .55
  Sixth-grade,   .45
LINOLEUM.
  Substantially an oil-cloth, with ground-cork body instead of paint. It is warm, somewhat elastic, and very durable, 1.10
LIGNUM.
  Substantially linoleum, made of wood instead of cork, 1.15

MATTINGS.

Prices per square yard.

China, $0.20 to .50
Cocoa, ½, ¾, 1, 1¼, or 1½ yards wide 0.50 .60 .75 a square yard.

STAIR-RODS AND BUTTONS.

Prices per dozen.

1 Brass, ¾ inch wide:
    22 inches long, $3.20
    26   3.60
    30   3.90
    36   4.80
    40   6.00
2 Brass, figured, ¾ inch wide:
    26 inches long, 4.30
    30   4.60
    36   6.00
    40   7.20
3 Gilt, ⅞ inch wide:
    26 inches long, 5.40
    30   6.00
    36   7.80
    40   9.00
4 Nickel-plated, ⅞ inch wide:
    26 inches long, 7.60
    30   8.20
    36   10.80
    40   12.00
5 Walnut or oak, acorn ends, with bronze screw-eyes:
    24 inches long, 1.00
    27   1.00
    30   1.00

6 Walnut or oak, ornamental tip, silver-plated or gilt patent fastenings :

    27 inches long, 4.00
    30 4.00
    36 5.00

7 Buttons, fancy : used in place of rods :
    Walnut, with gilt center, 1.00
    Plated : gilt, silver, or nickel, 1.80

STAIR-PLATES.

Prices per dozen.

1 Metal, covered with rubber :
    16 × 4 inches, $5.75
    16 × 5 7.00
    18 × 6 9.35
    20 × 8 14.00
    24 × 8 16.65

2 Metal, covered with linoleum :
    18 × 6 inches, 5.70
    18 × 8 7.60
    22½ × 8 9.60
    27 × 8 11.80

3 Brass, corrugated, per lb., 0.50
4 Zinc, corrugated, per lb., 0.25
    other sizes in proportion.

A zinc plate 18 x 6 inches weighs about 1¾ pounds.

5 Magic Carpet Sweeper, best in use, 2.00

WORK ON CARPETS, ETC.

Prices per yard..

Prices additional to traveling and hotel expenses. An abatement of 2 cents per yard if carpets are not put down.

MAKING AND PUTTING-DOWN.

Axminsters, Moquette, or Wilton, $0.12½
Brussels or Tapestry, .10

Making bordered-carpets 2½ cents additional.

Ingrain, Venetian, or three-ply, .08
Binding, .06
Mitres on border exceeding four :
    ⅜ yard wide, each, 0.10
    ½ .15
    ¾ .25

PUTTING-DOWN.

Stair-carpet, with rods, each, $1.25
Stair-carpet, without rods, each, 1.00
China or cocoa matting, yard, .08
Linoleum, or lignum, square yard, .10
Oil-cloth, square yard, .08

ALTERING and PUTTING-DOWN OLD CARPETS.

Axminster, Moquette, Wilton, Velvet, 0.08
Others, .06

PUTTING-DOWN OLD CARPETS.

Axminster, Moquette, Wilton, Velvet, 0.04
Others, .03
Sewing-woman's time out, per day, 2.50

UPHOLSTERY.

From costly tapestries of silk to the simplest cretonnes are seen the designs and blendings of color which artists and poets have furnished to this branch of manufacture. It has been the effort of the English art designers to provide as beautiful patterns for simple cottages as for stately mansions. Handsome curtains, with centers of batiste or Russian grenadine, have wide insertions and borders of hand-made antique or cluny lace, and are wrought in lines of drawn work, and with stitches simulating hem-stitching in larger designs. Curtains of solid Nottingham lace are no longer woven in huge scrolls and ferns, but in soft, cream-white textures, with stripes of vermicelli pattern surrounding a set stripe in more elaborate design, the whole finished by a broad border in floriated or arabesque pattern. Rich curtains of Saxony lace are chosen for elegant drawing-rooms. Tapestries of various kinds are used for heavy curtains and for furniture covering. They are usually in Oriental designs and colors, and often simulate Turkish rugs in pattern. French and English cretonnes in raw silk effects make the most charming upholstery for country parlors. They are furnished in an endless variety of designs in gay flowers, grasses and leaves, so artistically printed that they seem to have been painted by hand, and in Oriental patterns which are copied from more costly tapestries. A pole and rings has completely succeeded the old box cornice. Folding doors are not used between parlors and the space is draped with curtains. All doors are often done away with on the parlor floor, and graceful *portieres* are substituted. These artistic hangings should harmonize with the furniture, though to avoid sameness they are generally in different designs. The curtains may be crossed by stripes, while the furniture covering is figured. Fashion drapery is a soft material for curtains which comes at a moderate price in all shades of colors.

FURNITURE-COVERINGS AND CURTAIN MATERIALS.

Prices per yard.

1. Raw-silks, 50 inches, $1.50 1.75 2. 2.50 3. 3.50 4. 4.50 5.
2. Worsted-and-silk tapestries, 50 inches, 2.50 3. 3.50 4. 4.50 5. 6. 7. 8. 9. 10.
3. Cashmeres, 50 inches, 3.50 4. 4.50 5. 5.50 6. 7. 8.
4. Jutes, damask, 50 inches, 1. 1.35 1.50 1.75
5. Damasks, worsteds, 50 inches, 1.50 1.75 2.
6. Terries, wool, all colors, 50 inches, 1.50 1.75
7. Momie cloth, all color, 50 inches : cotton, 1. worsted, 2.50
8. Satins, plain, all colors, 64 inches, 7. 8. 9.
9. Satins, brocade, 64 inches, 8. 9. 10. 11. 12. 14. 16.
10. Plush, worsted, all colors, 24 inches, 3. 3.50 4.
11. Plush, silk, all colors, 24 inches, 3.75 4. 4.50
12. Hair-cloth :
    22 inches, 1.00   27 inches, 1.50
    25   1.25   30   1.75
13. Furniture-leather, all colors, per square foot, 0.30
14. Canton-flannel, single-faced, all colors . 27 inches, 0.20   29 inches, 0.25
15. Canton-flannel, double-faced, all colors, for curtains, 32 inches, 0.37½, 63 inches, 0.90

16 Cretonnes, 32 inches, 0.15 .20 .25 .30 .35 .40 .50
17 Crape-cloth, 32 inches, 0.40 .50 .60 .75 1.
18 Serges, cotton, 32 inches, 0.30 .35 .40 .50 .60

LOOSE FURNITURE-COVERINGS.

Prices per yard.

1 Damasks, cotton, white and drab, 32 inches, $0.30
2 Twills, striped, 32 inches, 0.25
3 Linens, 36 inches, 0.40 .50 .60
4 Jacquards, striped and figured, 40 inches, 0.70

LININGS.

Prices per yard.

1 Turkey-red, $0.15 .20 .25 .30 .35 .40 .50 .60
2 Silesia, 0.15 .20 .25
3 Buckram, for lining lambrequins, 0.25

LACE BED-SPREADS,

WITH PILLOW-SHAMS TO MATCH.

Prices per set.

1 Nottingham, $3.50 4. 4.50 5. 6. 7.
2 Guipure, 7. 8. 9. 10.
3 Antique, 15. 20. 25. 30. 40. 50. 60
4 Saxony, 25. 30. 35. 40. 50. 60.

LACE CURTAINS.

Price per window.

1 Nottingham, $1.65 1.75 2. 2.50 3. 3.50 4. 4.50 5. 5.50 6. 6.50 7. 7.50 8
2 Guipure, 8. 8.50 9. 10. 11. 12. 13. 14. 15. 16. 17. 18. 19. 20.
3 Tambour, 8. 9. 10. 11. 12. 13. 14. 15. 16. 17. 18. 19. 20. 22. 25. 28. 30. 35. 40. 45. 50.
4 Antique, 7. 8. 9. 10. 12. 15. 18. 20. 22. 23. 25. 28. 30. 33. 35. 38. 40. 45. 50. 55. 60. 70. 75. 80. 100. 140.
5 Saxony, 30. 35. 40. 45. 50. 55. 60. 65. 70. 75. 80. 90. 100.
6 Lace shades, 3. 3.50 4. 4.50 5. 5.50 6. 7. 8. 9. 10.

LACE FOR CURTAINS.

Prices per yard.

For Windows.

1 Nottingham, $0.15 .18 .20 .25 .30 **.35** .40 .45 .50 .55 .60 .65 .70 .75 .80 .85 .90 .95 1.
2 Muslin, cottage drapery, 0.12 .15 .18 .20 .22 .25 .30 .35 .40

For Vestibules.

1 Tambour :
   22 inches wide, 1.25 1.35
   24   1.50 1.75
   26   1.75 2.00
2 Nottingham :
   18 inches wide, 0.15 .20 .25
   22   .20 .25 .30
   27   .25 .30 .35
   32   .40 .50 .60
   36   .70 .80 .90

LAMBREQUINS.

Prices per window.

1 Nottingham lace, $0.50 .60 .75 1. 1.25 1.50 2.
2 Tambour lace, 7. 8. 9. 10.
3 Cretonne, 6. 7. 8. 9. 10.
4 Raw-silk or tapestries, 10. 12. 14. 16. 18. 20. 25. 30. 40. 50. 60.

WINDOW DRAPERIES.

Prices per window.

1 Long curtains, jute, $9. 10. 12. 14. 16. 18. 20. 25.
2 Long curtains, cretonne, 12. 14. 16. 18. 20. 25.
3 Long curtains, raw-silk, 25. 28. 30. 35. 40. 45. 50. 60. 70. 80. 90. 100.

WINDOW CORNICES.

Prices per window.

1 Black walnut or gilt, plain, $0.80 .90 1. 1.25 1.50 1.75 2.
2 Black walnut or gilt, ornamental, 2.25 2.50 2.75 3. 3.50 4. 4.50 5. 5.50 6. 7. 8. 9. 10. 11. 12. 15. 18. 20.

CURTAIN POLES, ETC.

Prices per window.

1. Walnut, ash or ebonized-wood, with brackets, ornamental ends and rings complete, $2.25 2.50 3. 3.50 4. 4.50 5. 5.50 6. 6.50 7. 7.50 8. 9. 10. 12. 14. 16.
2. Gilt, with brackets, ends and rings complete, 6. 7. 8. 10. 12. 15. 20.
3. Brass, with brackets, ends and rings complete, 4.00 5. 7. 9. 12. 15. 20.
4. Vestibule-curtain rods, set of four, 1. 1.25 1.50 1.75 2. 2.50
5. Curtain-rings, dozen, 0.05 .10 .15 .20
6. Pole-rings, wood, dozen, 1.25 1.50 2. 2.50 3.
7. Pole-rings, brass, dozen, 1.50 2. 2.50 3 4. 5.

TRIMMINGS.

Prices per yard.

FRINGES.

1. Ball-fringe, worsted-and-silk, $0.50 .75 1. 1.10 1.25 1.50 2. 2.50 3. 3.30
2. Bullion, worsted: 5 inches deep, 0.50 .60 .75
3. Bullion, worsted-and-silk:
   4 inches deep, 1.25 1.50 1.75
   5   1.50 1.75 2.00
   6   1.75 2.00 2.25
4. Bullion, silk:
   4 inches deep, 2.50
   5   3.25
   6   4.00
5. Cotton:
   white, 0.10 .15 .20 .25

GIMPS, worsted-and-silk.

1. For curtains, 0.25 .30 .40 .50 .60 .75
2. For lambrequins, 0.25 .35 .50
3. For furniture, 0.05 .06 .08 .10 .12

BINDINGS.

1. For furniture, piece of 18 yards, 0.40
2. For carpets:
   piece of 12 yards, 0.50
   piece of 18   .75

CORDS; prices per yard.

1. For shades:
   usual size,   0.02
   heavy, for large shades .05

2. For pictures:
   worsted, 0.05 .08 .10 .12
   silver wire, piece of 8 yards, 0.20 .25 .35 .45
3. For furniture, 0.10 .12 .15 .20
4. For cushions, 0.12 .15 .20 .25
5. For drapery, 0.20 .25 .30 .40 .50 .60·
6. Picture nails, dozen, 0.15 .20 .25 .30

TASSELS.

1. Centers and loops for long curtains; set, $6. 7. 8. 9. 10. 12. 14. 16. 18. 20. 25.
2. Loops or tassel-and-cord for looping back curtains, each, 0.65 .75 .85 1. 1.25 1.50 1.75 2. 2.50.
3. Tassels for lambrequins, each, 0.75 1. 1.25 1.50 1.75 2.
4. For pillows, each, 0.35 .45 .50 .75
5. For chairs, each, 0.50 .60 .75 1. 1.25 1.50
6. For shades, white or colored, each, 0.10 .12 .15 .20 .25

CURTAIN-BANDS, prices each.

1. Cotton, white, 0.20 .25 .30 .40 .50 .60
2. Worsted-and-silk, colored, 0.30 .40 .50

SHADES.

Prices per window, according to size.

1. Hollands, white, common fixtures, all lengths and widths, $1.50 and upward
2. Hollands, white, wood spring-roller, all lengths and widths, 1.65 and upward
3. Hollands, white, tin spring-roller, all lengths and widths, 2. and upward
4. Gilt band, common fixtures, all lengths and widths, 2.25 and upward
5. Gilt-band, wood spring-roller, all lengths and sizes, 2.50 and upward
6. Gilt-band, tin spring-roller, all lengths and sizes, 2.90 and upward
7. Dado, tin spring-roller, all lengths and sizes, 4. 4.50 5. 5.50 6. 7. 8. 9. 10.

SHADE-MATERIALS.

Prices per yard.

1. Hollands, white:
   24 inches wide, $0.19
   30   .23
   36   .27
   40   .30
   45   .34
   50   .39
   60   .47
   72   .58

SHADE-MATERIALS—Continued.

2 Hollands, green, blue, drab, brown :
   28 inches wide, 0.28
   30   .31
   36   .36
   40   .39
   45   .45
   50   .50
   56   .55
   60   .60
   72   .75
3 Hollands, cardinal :
   30 inches wide, 0.38
   36   .44
   40   .49
   45   .55
4 Painted shading, all colors :
   36 inches wide, 0.25
   40   .30
5 Painted shading, all colors, hand-made, to order, square foot, 0.07

SHADE-FIXTURES.

1 Hartshorn extension tin spring-rollers, all lengths :
   under 2½ feet, each, $0.75
   2½ to 4 feet,   .90
2 Wood spring-rollers, all lengths :
   1 inch diameter, each, 0.40
   1¼   .50
3 Plain wood-rollers and fixtures, set, 0.35

TABLE AND PIANO COVERS.

*Covers two by three are Piano-Covers.
Table-Covers are of various sizes.*

1 Raw-silk, 6-4, about 1½ × 1½ yards, $3. 4. 5. 6. 8. 10. 12.
2 Raw-silk, 7-4, about 1¾ × 1¾, 5. 6. 7. 8. 10. 12. 15.
11 Embroidered, 8-4 × 12-4, about 2 × 3, 3.75 5. 5.50 6. 6.50 7. 7.50 8. 8.50 9. 10. 11. 12. 13. 14. 15. 16. 17. 18. 19. 20.
12 Turkish, 4-4, about 1 × 1, 7.50
13 Turkish, 5-4, about 1¼ × 1¼, 13.
14 Turkish, 6-4, about 1½ × 1½, 17.
15 Turkish, 7-4, about 1¾ × 1¾, 23.
16 Turkish, 8-4, about 2 × 2, 30.
17 Turkish, 8-4 × 12-4, about 2 × 3, 60. 75. 100.

MOSQUITO-NETTING.

1 White, 1¾ yards wide, piece of 7½ yards, $0.50
2 Pink, blue, green, buff, 1¾ yards wide, piece of 7½ yards, 0.60
3 White, 2½ yds. wide, piece of 9 yds. 1.25
4 Pink, blue, green, buff, 2½ yards wide, piece of 9 yards, 1.50

MOSQUITO-CANOPIES.

1 Pink or white, $2.50 3. 3.25 3.50 4.
2 Lace, white or colored, 7. 8. 9. 10.
3 Raw-silk, 8-4, about 2 × 2, 6. 7. 8. 9. 10. 12. 15. 18. 20. 25.
4 Raw-silk, 8-4 × 10-4, about 2 × 2½, 9. 10. 11. 12. 15. 18. 20. 25.
5 Raw-silk, 8-4 × 12-4, about 2 × 3, 10. 11. 12. 15. 20. 25. 30.
6 Embroidered-cloth, 4-4, about 1 × 1, 1.75 2.25 2.75
7 Embroidered, 5-4, about 1¼ × 1¼, 2.25 2.50 3. 3.50
8 Embroidered, 6-4, about 1½ × 1½, 3. 3.50 4. 4.50 5.
9 Embroidered, 7-4, about 1¾ × 1¾, 3.50 4. 4.50 5. 5.50 6.
10 Embroidered, 8-4, about 2 × 2, 4. 4.50 5. 5.50 6. 6.50

GENTLEMEN'S FURNISHING.

A flat folded scarf is the favorite neck-gear for gentlemen during the cool months of spring, but the Windsor scarf in bias silk, which may be tied in a bow or worn with a ring, and the De Joinville cut on the straight which may be tied in a knot or worn with a ring are both popular; these may be had in dark colors of hair stripe, in polka dots and figures.

The newest collars are straight bands like those worn by clergymen. The edges are made to lap or are separated by a space. Cuffs are straight around and are arranged for link buttons. The plain shield shaped shirt bosom is still used to the exclusion of other styles.

SCARFS.

Knots.

1 Prospero, black or colored, $0.50 .75 1
   1.25 1.50 1.75

Flat.

Prospero, No. 1

2 The Atlas, black, 1.50

No. 2

LORD & TAYLOR, NEW YORK.

No. 3

3 Lord Stanley, black, 1.50

No. 4

4 The Claudent, black or colored, 0.85
1.00 1.15 1.25 1.35 1.50 1.65 2. 2.50

5 De Joinville, to be tied in a knot or to wear with a ring, black or colored, in all the newest designs, 0.50 .75 1. 1.25 1.50 1.75 2. 2.25 2.50 2.75 3. 3.50

FOLDED TIES.

1 Black-silk :   No. 1   2   3
   ¾ × 30 inches,   0.25   .35   .60
   ⅞ × 31   .30   .40   .65
   ⅞ × 34   .45   .75
   1 × 32   .35   .45   .75
   1 × 35   .50   .85
   1⅛ × 33   .40   .50   .85
   1⅛ × 36   .45   1.00
   1¼ × 34   .45   .55   .95
   1¼ × 38   1.10

2 Black-satin :   No. 1   2   3
   ⅞ × 31 inches, 0.60   .65   .75
   1 × 31   .70   .85   .90
   1⅛ × 33   .85   .95   1.00

3 White-silk or satin :
                    No. 1   2
   ⅞ × 31 inches, 0.65   .75
   1 × 32   .70   .85
   1⅛ × 33   .85   .95

BOWS.

1 Black, 0.10 .15 .25 .35 .40 .45 .50 .60

BLACK-SILK SQUARES.

1 30 inches, 2.00 to 2.75
2 32   2.25 to 3.00
3 34   2.50 to 3.25
4 36   2.75 to 3.50

STOCKS.

1 Napoleon cravat, black-silk, 1.00
2 Adjustable-spring, black-silk or satin, 1

HANDKERCHIEFS.

LINEN.

1 Hemmed :
   21 inches—
   each   dozen   each   dozen
   $0.15   1.75   0.30   3.50
   .20   2.40   .35   4.00
   .25   3.00   .40   4.50
   23 inches—
   each   dozen   each   dozen
   0.25   3.00   0.50   5.75
   .30   3.50   .60   7.00
   .35   4.00   .65   7.50
   .40   4.50   .75   8.50
   .45   5.00

LORD & TAYLOR, NEW YORK.

HANDKERCHIEFS—Continued.

27 inches—

each	dozen	each	dozen
0.30	3.50	0.55	6.50
.35	4.00	.60	7.00
.40	4.50	.65	7.50
.45	5.00	.75	8.50
.50	5.75		

2 Hemmed, colored border:

each	dozen	each	dozen
0.25	3.00	0.35	4.00
.30	3.50		

3 Hemstitched:

each	dozen	each	dozen
0.25	3.00	0.60	6.75
.30	3.50	.65	7.50
.35	4.00	.70	8.00
.40	4.50	.75	8.50
.45	5.00	.85	9.50
.50	5.75	1.00	11.00
.55	6.25	1.25	14.00

27 inches—

each	dozen	each	dozen
0.50	5.50	0.80	9.25
.60	6.75	.90	10.00
.70	8.00	1.00	11.00

4 Hemstitched, colored border:

each	dozen	each	dozen
0.35	4.00	0.60	7.00
.40	4.50	.75	8.50
.50	5.50	1.00	11.50

5 Initial, hemmed:

each	dozen	each	dozen
0.35	4.00	0.60	7.00
.50	5.75		

6 Initial, hemstitched:

each	dozen	each	dozen
0.50	5.50	1.00	11.00
.75	8.00		

SILK.

1 White, twilled, hemmed, 0.50 .75 1. 1.25
2 White, pongee, hemmed, 0.75 1. 1.25 1.50 1.75 2.
3 Novelties, all colors and shades, 0.50 .75 1. 1.25 1.35 1.50 1.75 2. 2.50
4 India, hemstitched, 0.75 1. 1.25 1.50 1.75 2. 2.25

GLOVES.

KID.

1 Imported, all colors:
   one-button, $1.50
   two   1.90
2 Fisk, Clark & Flagg, embroidered back, two-button, 2.25
3 Fisk, Clark & Flagg, tan, with embroidered back, 2.
4 Fisk, Clark & Flagg, black, for mourning, embroidered back, 2.

LEATHER.

1 Fisk, Clark & Flagg, dogskin, double-thick in the palm for coaching, two-button, 2.25
2 Fisk, Clark & Flagg, dogskin, for mourning, 2.
3 Fisk, Clark & Flagg, heavy, for driving, 2.
4 Fisk, Clark & Flagg, coachman's tan, for driving, 1.60
5 Dent, dogskin, old-gold, for driving, two-button, 2.
6 Castor-beaver:
   one-button, 1.50
   two-button, 1.00 1.40 1.50

MEN'S ALPACA COATS—sizes 33 to 44.

Take the following measures:
  I. Around the chest under the coat.
  II. Length of sleeve from middle seam of back to wrist.
1 Men's plain black alpaca coats, $2.10 to 3.75
2 Men's black serge   2.25   4.00
3 Men's silk alpaca   4.75   6.50

MEN'S DUSTERS AND ROAD ULSTERS— sizes 33 to 44.

Take the following measures:
  I. Chest measure over the coat.
  II. Length of sleeve from middle seam of back to wrist.
1 Men's linen dusters, $2.15 to 3.10
2 Men's alpaca   3.00   6.00
3 Men's road ulsters, 2.75 to 4.50

MEN'S WHITE VESTS.

Take chest measure under the vest.
1 White Marseilles and duck $0.90 to 4.50

WAITER JACKETS of every description.

  I. Take chest measure under the vest.
  II. Length of sleeve from middle seam of back to wrist.
1 Black jackets, jean, $0.95; sateen, 1.20; Italian, 1.25; Albert twills, 1.25.
2 Black alpaca—unlined, 1.60 1.75
3 Black alpaca—lined, 1.75 2.00 2.25
4 Black cloth jackets 5.75 to 8.25
5 White jackets, jean, 1.00; sateen, 1.20; drill, 1.30

THE
DRESS SHIRTS.

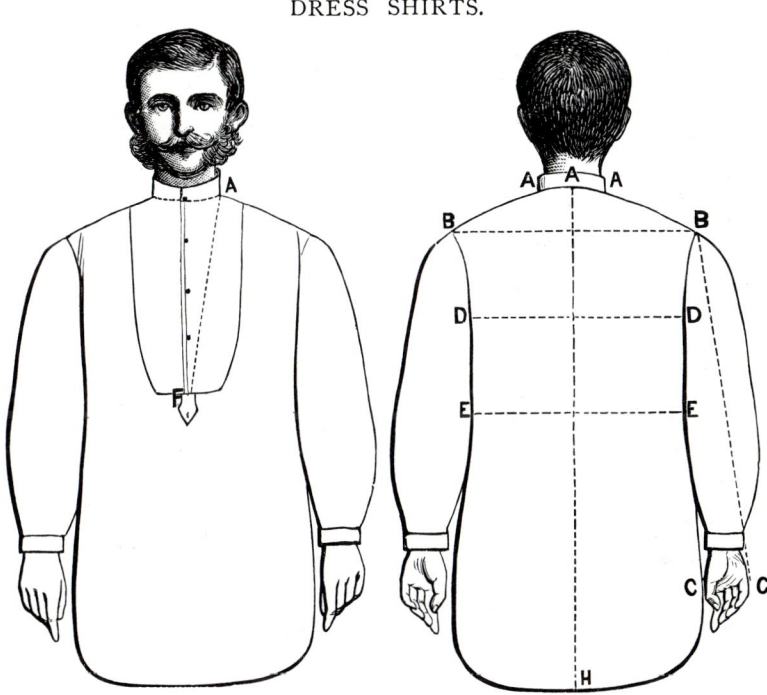

Take the following measures :

1. Around the bare neck, at the collar-band-seam, A A A A.
2. From shoulder-point to shoulder-point across the back, B B.
3. Length of sleeve, from shoulder-point to knuckle, with arm hanging straight down, B C.
4. Around the chest under the arms, and under the waistcoat, D D.
5. Around the waist, under the waistcoat, E E E E.
6. Length of bosom, from shoulder-seam, A F.
7. Length, A H.
8. Around hand at knuckles, C C.
9. To open in front or back, or both?
10. Bosom plain or pleated?
11. Bosom with buttons, stud-holes, or eyelet-holes?
12. Buttons or stud-holes at neck (front and back)?
13. Collar attached?
14. Cuffs attached?
15. Are you round-shouldered?
16. Are you square-shouldered?
17. Are you sloping-shouldered?

DRESS SHIRTS.

READY-MADE, without collar or cuffs, and with plain bosom only ; prices each.
1. Dress-shirts, open-back, unlaundered, $0.75 1. 1.25
2. Dress-shirts, open-back, laundered, 1.25 1.50 2.
3. Dress-shirts, open-front, laundered, 1.50
4. Dress-shirts, colored-cambric ; with two collars and one pair cuffs to each shirt, 1.25 1.50 1.75
5. Night-shirts, unlaundered ; collar attached, 0.75 1.
6. Night-shirts, laundered ; collar attached, 1.25
7. Boys' dress-shirts, unlaundered ; with bands, 0.75 1.
8. Boys' dress-shirts, laundered; with bands, 1. 1.25
9. Boys' dress-shirts, colored-cambric ; with two collars, and cuffs attached, 0.75 1. 1.15
10. Boys' night-shirts, unlaundered ; collar attached, 0.75
11. Boys' night-shirts, laundered; collar attached, 1.

MADE TO MEASURE, prices per dozen.
1. Dress-shirts, plain bosom, 18. 24. 30. 36.
2. Dress-shirts, pleated bosoms, 30. 36.
3. Dress-shirts, percale, colored ; with two collars and one pair cuffs to each shirt, 39.
4. Dress-shirts, percale, colored ; collars and cuffs attached, 36.
5. Boys' dress-shirts, 18. 24.

THE UNDERWEAR.

1. Gauze shirts, $0.50 .75 1.
2. Cartwright & Warner's gauze shirts, according to size and quality, 1. to 2.50
3. Jean drawers, 0.50 .65
   Nainsook (feather weight,) 0.85
   Fisk, Clark & Flagg (P. P. D.) jean drawers, 1.25
   Blue flannel shirts, with small collar, for men, 2. to 3.
7. Blue flannel shirts, for men, for boating, 2. to 3.
8. Blue flannel shirts, for boys, for boating, 2. to 3.
9. Négligé shirts, 1.00 2.00 2.50 3. 3.50
10. Merino, medium weight :
    shirts, sizes 34, 36 38, 40, 42, 44,
    1.50 for size 34, advancing 10c. a size :
    drawers, sizes 30, 32, 34, 36, 38, 40, 42, 44, 46, 48 :
    1.50 for size 30, advancing 10c. a size.

CARTWRIGHT & WARNER'S :
shirts, sizes 34, 36, 38, 40. 42, 44.
drawers, sizes 30, 32, 34, 36, 38, 40, 42, 44, 46, 48
1. Shirts, merino, medium weight :
   No. 11, 1.80 for size 34, advancing 15c. a size.
2. Drawers, merino, medium weight :
   No. 11, 2.30 for size 30, advancing 10c. a size.

HALF-HOSE.

MEN'S.
1. Cotton, unbleached, English, $0.25 .30 .35 .50
2. Cotton, unbleached, French, 0.50 .60 .65
3. Balbriggan, unbleached, 0.25 .35 .40 .50 .60 1. 1.25 1.50
4. Balbriggan, plain colors, 0.35 .50 .75 1. 1.25
5. Fancy-striped, 0.25 .30 .35 .40 .45 .50 .60 .75 .85 .95 1. 1.25
6. Brown-mixed, 0.25 .35 .40
7. Derby-ribbed, unbleached, 0.35 .50
8. Spun-silk, plain or striped, 1.50 1.75 2.50 3.
9. All-silk, plain or striped, 3.75 4.25
10. Lisle-thread, unbleached, 0.50
11. Lisle-thread, fancy or plain, 0.75 1. 1.25

BOYS'.
1. Unbleached, 0.25
2. Fancy and plain, 0.25 .40 .50
3. Brown-mixed, 0.25

SUSPENDERS.

COTTON.
1. Various, $0.25 .40 .60 .75 1.
2. Guyot, 0.50
3. Fisk, Clark & Flagg, 1. 1.25 1.35 1.50
4. Boys', 0.25 .35 .50
5. Shoulder braces, 1. 1.25

SILK.
1. Fisk, Clark & Flagg, 1.50 1.75 2.25 2.50

LORD & TAYLOR, NEW YORK.

JEWELRY.

GOLD.
1. Shirt-studs, spiral or button-back, per set, $3. to 6.
2. Collar-studs, each, 1.50 2. 2.50 3.

PLATED.
1. Sleeve-buttons, 0.50 .75 1. 1.25 1.50 1.75 2.
2. Shirt-studs, spiral or button-back, per set, 0.75 1. 1.25 1.50
3. Collar-studs, each, 0.25 .35 .50 .75
4. Scarf-pins, 0.50 .75 1. 1.25 1.50 1.75 2.
5. Scarf-rings, 1. 1.25 1.50 2. 2.50 3.

PEARL, ETC.
1. Sleeve-buttons, pearl, 0.35 .40 .50 .65 .75 1.

2. Sleeve-buttons, ivory, 0.25 .35 .50 .65 .75
3. Sleeve-buttons, separable, 1. 1.25 1.50

COLLARS AND CUFFS.

1. Collars, all styles:

each	dozen	each	dozen
$0.15	1.50	0.25	2.75
.20	2.40		

2. Boys' collars, all styles:
   each, 0.15   dozen, 1.75
3. Cuffs, all styles:
   pair, 0.25   dozen pairs, 3.00
   .40   4.50
4. Boys' cuffs, all styles:
   pair, 0.25   dozen pairs, 3.00

BOYS' CLOTHING

The first suit put on by boys is a one-piece kilt suit or a kilt skirt and jacket, buttoned to neck or made with an imitation vest front; it is usually made of some fine suiting, cloth or mixed cassimere. Black is employed only for mourning. The kilt skirt may be worn till the age of six, and is often worn longer—the time of changing the style of a boy's clothing being regulated more by the height than the age. The next suit furnished is a blouse with knickerbockers; this blouse is double or single breasted and is made like the engravings; it buttons high in the neck or the collar turns back only far enough to display neck-tie or scarf. The Norfolk blouse is pleated and belted and is a favorite style. Sailor blouses are used more than ever; they are of dark-blue cloth, with sailor collars, trimmed with white or black Hercules braid or narrow braid, and with star or anchor embroidered on corners of collar, and finished with gilt buttons with anchor designs.

Large linen collars are worn by boys with the kilt suits, and by small boys in blouses and knickerbockers who are not old enough to wear a shirt collar and cravat.

Over-coats are long and double or single breasted in mixed or pin-head checked cheviot with velvet collars, cuffs and pocket flaps. Turbans and polo hats are both worn.

The styles described and shown in the engravings are ready-made, embracing the newest designs and choicest selection of fashionable colors

Garments made to measure at a small advance in prices.

LORD & TAYLOR, NEW YORK.

METROPOLITAN.

No. 1

10 to 16 years.

Take the following measures:
1. Around the chest, under the jacket.
2. Around the waist, under the jacket.
3. Length of jacket, E A F.
4. From middle seam of back to sleeve seam, A B.
5. From sleeve seam around point of elbow to wrist, B C D.
6. Length of inside seam of trouser-leg.
7. Length of outside seam of trouser-leg.
8. For kilt suit give length of skirt from E to G.
9. Age.
10. Whether small or large for age, and any peculiarity of form.
11. Color of material.

BOYS' ALPACA COATS—10 to 16 years.
Take the following measures:
 I. Around the chest under the jacket.
 II. Length of sleeve from middle seam of back to wrist.
 III. Age, and state whether small or large for age.
1 Boys' plain black or striped alpaca or black serge coats, $1.40 1.60 2.00 2.50
 Boys' cotton coats, 0.45 .65

1. Coat, vest and long trousers, cutaway straight-front or corners slightly rounded.

Union cassimere suits, 5.85 to 8.75

Fine cassimere or cheviot, 9.50 to 13.50.

Blue flannel, 7.50 to 13.00.

Superfine domestic or foreign cassimeres, cheviots, dark-blue tricots, mixed or plain suitings, 14.50 to 19.50.

Extra trousers, 2.25 to 6.

WINDSOR.

From 5 to 12 years.

Blouse, single-breasted or double breasted, with small rolling-collar and cutaway or button to neck and straight front.

Union cassimere Suits, $2.75 to 4.75.

Fine domestic cassimere or Scotch cheviot suits, 5. to 8.

Blue flannel suits, 5. to 8.

Linen suits, 2.50 to 3.50.

Extra trowsers, 1. to 2.75.

No. 2

CAMBRIDGE.

From 5 to 12 years.

Single-breasted blouse (entirely new,) of fine domestic suitings, $7.50 to 9.

Fine foreign suitings for dress, 9.50 to 12.

Extra trowsers 2.50 to 4.

No. 4

STANDARD.

From 5 to 12 years.

Blouse, double-breasted, short rolling-collar cutaway or straight front.

Fine Union cassimere suits, $4. to 5.50

Domestic or foreign cassimere suits, 6. to 8.50

Extra trowsers, 1.75 to 2.85.

No. 3

HARVARD.

From 5 to 12 years.

Coat, vest and knee trowsers.

Cassimere suits, $5.75 to 8.50

Dress suits of fine domestic cassimeres, granites, tricots, and foreign suitings, 9.75 to 14.75

Extra trowsers 1.75 to 4.75

No. 5

NORFOLK.

From 5 to 9 years.

Norfolk blouse, (very youthful,) button to neck or short rolling-collar, medium or light weight domestic cassimere or Scotch cheviot suits, $6.50 to 8.50
Extra trowsers, 1.75 to 3.

No. 6

KILT SUITS.
ALBERT.

From 2½ to 6 years.

Combination one-piece kilt, blue with white or black trimming, brown or brown mixed and grey flannel, $2.25 3. 3.75 4.50
One-piece kilt, suits of fine domestic or foreign, medium or light weight suitings, 5. to 8.

No. 8

SEA-SIDE.

From 4 to 11 years.

Blue-flannel sailor suits, perfectly plain, or collar and sleeves of jacket and side of pants ornamented with fine braid, $2.50 to 3.
Finer quality, collars ornamented with anchors or stars, 3.50 to 5.75
Superfine with hand embroidered gold star and anchors on collar, 7.75

No. 7.

BRIGHTON.

Two-piece kilt, (very popular style,) of fancy cassimeres, plain or mixed suitings, $4.50 to 8.50

No. 9

NEWPORT.

Two-piece kilt suit of fancy cassimere, plain or mixed suitings, blue cloth, small check or very stylish novelty plaid, 8.75 to 11.

Fine foreign fabrics (special importation,) 11. to 15.

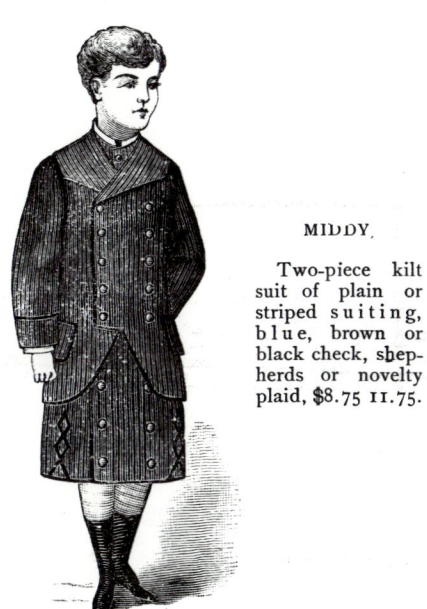

No. 10

CLARENCE.

Two-piece kilt suit of fine, light medium, or dark mixed or striped suitings, $9.50 to 12.75

Superfine foreign fabrics, in a variety of well selected colors and mixtures, 13. to 19.

No. 12

MIDDY.

Two-piece kilt suit of plain or striped suiting, blue, brown or black check, shepherds or novelty plaid, $8.75 11.75.

No. 11

SEA-BEACH.

Two-piece sailor kilt, blue flannel with white or black braid, $5.75 to 8.

Hand embroidered gold stars and anchors on collar, 8.50 and 9.

No. 13

LINEN KILT SUITS.

From 2½ to 6 years.

One-piece linen kilt like engraving, and several other new and very stylish designs.

Plain, fancy blue or brown striped linen drilling, $1.75 1.85 2. 2.15 2.35 2.50 2.75

White Marseilles and Piqué, 3.85 4.50

No. 14

SHIRT WAISTS.

From 4 to 12 years.

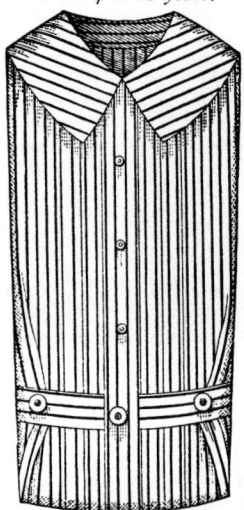

No. 15

15 Colored: .20 .50 .56 .75 1. 1.10 1.25 1.50
White: .43 .67 1. 1.25 1.50 1.75 2.

Waists under 1.00 are made no larger than for boys of 10 years.

BOYS' HATS.

In ordering, please state color, material, and size.

SCALE OF MEASUREMENT.

Size,	6	6⅛	6¼	6⅜	6½	6⅝	6¾	6⅞	7
Inches around head,	19	19⅜	19¾	20⅛	20½	20⅞	21¼	21⅝	22

DERBY.

No. 1
Fine wool felt, $1.25 to 1.50
Fur felt, 1.75 to 2.50

SOFT HAT.

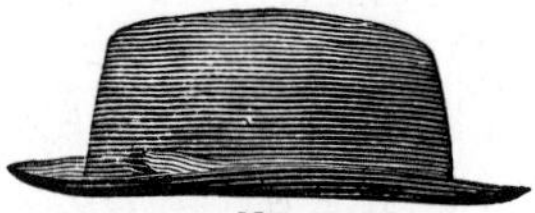

No. 2
Wool felt, $1.00 to 1.75
Fur felt, 2.00 to 2.50

Colors in wool and fur hats, blue, black and beaver.

TURBAN.

No. 3
Wool felt, $1.00 to 1.50
Fur felt, 2.00 to 2.50
Straw turban. 1.25 to 2.50

STRAW HAT.

No. 4
$0.75 to 1.50; 1.75 to 3.00

STRAW HAT.

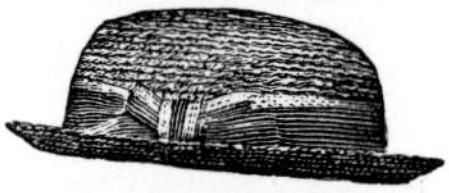

No. 5
$1.00 to 1.50; 1.75 to 2.50

STRAW HAT.

No. 6
$1.00 to 1.50; 1.75 to 2.50

Colors in straw hats, tan, brown, blue and fancy mixed.

INDEX.

	Page.		Page.		Page.
Awnings,	153	Collars, lace,	77	Flannel skirts,	112
		Colored satins,	58	Floor coverings,	158
Barbettes, lace,	76	silks,	58	Flowers, millinery,	51
Barbs, lace,	76	velvets,	59	Fringes, dress-and-cloak,	136
Baskets, for infants,	126	skirts,	117	upholstery,	162
Bedding,	154	Combs,	140	Furniture coverings, 160,	161
Bed-spreads, lace,	161	Comfortables,	155	Furs,	147
ticking,	153	Cords and tassels :			
Belts,	141	dress and cloak,	137	Gentlemen's cloths,	68
lace,	77	upholstery,	162	furnishing goods,	164
Bibs,	127	picture,	162	Gimps, dress-and-cloak,	136
lace,	77	Corduroys,	67	upholstery,	162
Bindings,	139, 140	Cornices, window,	161	Ginghams and prints,	65
carpet,	139	Corset-covers,	112	Gloves, gentlemen's,	166
upholstery,	162	Corsets,	119	ladies' and children's,	71
Black satins,	58	Cotton and thread,	139	Grenadines,	60
silks,	58	Crape,	62		
velvets,	59	made articles,	62	Hamburg edgings,	96
Blankets,	154	Cravats, gentlemen's,	164	insertions,	96
infants',	130	lace,	77	Hammocks,	154
Bonnets and hats,	51	Crêpe de santé vests, ladies'	116	Handkerchiefs,	133
Boots,	143	Crumb-cloths,	150	lace,	76
Boys' clothing,	169	Curtains, lace,	161	Hats and bonnets, ladies',	51
hats and caps,	174	stuff,	162	Horse-blankets,	155
shirt-waists,	174	Curtain-lace,	160	Hosiery, gentlemen's,	168
shoes,	146	materials,	159	ladies' and children's,	68
Braids,	138	poles,	162	Hooks and eyes,	140
Bridal corset-covers,	114				
corsets,	122	Diapers,	150	Imitation laces,	74
dresses,	25, 29	Dolmans,	45	Infants' clothing,	125
sets, underclothing,		Domestics,	152	shoes,	147
etc.,	112	D'Oyleys,	149		
trousseaux,	102	Drawers, ladies',	104	Jabots, lace,	77
Brushes,	141	misses',	111	Jewelry :	
Buttons,	137	Dresses, infants',	127	gentlemen's,	169
Button-sizes,	137	ladies',	7	ladies',	140
		misses',	35		
Canton flannels,	153, 160	Dressing-cases, leather,	141		
Capes, lace,	77	Dress-goods,	59	Kid gloves, gentlemen's,	166
Caps, boys',	174	Dressmaking,	4	Kid gloves, ladies',	71
infants',	130	Dress shirts,	168		
Carpets,	157	Druggets, linen,	150	Laces,	73
work on,	159	wool,	158	Lace curtains,	161
Chemises, ladies',	103			Lambrequins,	161
misses',	110	Eider-down comfortables,	155	Leather goods,	141
Cloakings,	67	Elastics,	139	Lignum,	158
Cloaks, infants',	131	Embroidered flannels,	152	Linens,	150
ladies',	43	Embroideries,	96	Linen collars and cuffs,	134
misses',	48			handkerchiefs,	133
Cloths,	67	Fancy-goods and notions,	135	sheeting,	150
Collarettes, lace,	77	Fans,	141	shirting,	150
Collars and cuffs :		Fan-covers, lace,	76	Linoleum,	158
gentlemen's,	169	Feathers, ostrich,	51	Linings,	161
ladies',	134	Fichus, lace	76		
mourning,	62	Flannels,	151	Mats and mattings,	158

INDEX.

	Page.
Measures for boys' cloth-	
ing,	170
dresses,	4
shoes,	143
shirts,	167
Merino underclothing:	
gentlemen's,	168
ladies',	115
Millinery,	50
Mirrors, hand,	141
Mitts,	72
Mosquito netting,	163
Mourning dress-goods,	61
hosiery,	70
made articles,	62
suits,	28
Muslins,	63, 153
Napkins,	149
Neck rufflings,	97
Neck-wear, gentlemen's,	164
Needles and pins,	139
Négligé shirts,	168
Nets and veilings,	76
Night-dresses, ladies',	106
misses',	111
Night-shirts, boys',	168
gentlemen's,	168
Notions and fancy goods,	135
Oil-cloths,	158
Ornaments:	
dress and cloak,	136
millinery,	51
Ostrich feathers,	51
Overgarments, children's,	48
ladies',	43
Parasol-covers, lace,	76
Passementeries,	136
Perfumes,	142
Piano-covers,	163
Pillow cases,	156
linen,	150
Pins and needles,	139
Pocket-books,	141
prints and ginghams,	65

	Page.
Quilted silks for lining cloaks,	58
Quilts,	155
Ribbons,	54
Robes, infants',	128
Rufflings, neck,	97
Rugs,	158
Sacques, children's,	48
ladies',	45
Sash-ribbons,	54
Satchels,	141
Satins, black,	58
colored,	58
Scarfs, gentlemen's,	164
lace,	76
Sewing-silk and twist,	139
Shades, window,	162
Shawls,	55
Sheetings, domestic,	158
linen,	159
Sheets,	156
Shirtings, domestic,	153
linen,	150
Shirts:	
gentlemen's and boys',	168
infants',	126
Shirt-waists, boys',	174
Shoes,	143
Silks, black,	58
colored,	58
white,	59
Silk handkerchiefs,	134
velvets,	59
Skirts, muslin,	109, 111
colored	117
Skirt flannel,	110
Skirt-pleatings,	97
Sleeves, lace,	77
Slippers, ladies',	145
Slips, infants',	128
Socks and three-quarter hose,	69
infants' worsted,	131
Stair-crash,	150
plates,	159

	Page.
Stair-rods and buttons,	158
Suits, ladies',	7
ready-made,	30
misses',	35
boys',	169
Suspenders,	168
Table-cloths,	149
covers,	163
damask,	149
Tassels, dress-and-cloak,	137
upholstery,	137
Thread and cotton,	139
Tidies,	64
Toilet-articles,	141
Toweling,	150
Towels,	150
Trimmed hats and bonnets,	51
Trimmings:	
dress-and-cloak,	136
upholstery,	162
Ulsters, ladies',	44
Umbrellas,	142
Underwear:	
gentlemen's,	168
ladies' and children's,	102
Union suits,	116
Upholstery,	160
Veilings and nets,	76
Veils, lace,	76
Velveteens,	59, 68
Velvets,	59
Wadding,	153
Wardrobes, infants'	132
Water-proof cloths,	68
White goods,	63
Window-cornices,	161
draperies,	161
shades,	162
Wrappers,	32
Wright's perfumes,	142

Clothing and Furnishings
LORD & TAYLOR
an historical introduction

The female figure had been coerced into a new degree of pencil slimness in 1881, the year that Lord & Taylor issued its 26th catalog. It was an era of rapid change in feminine fashion, in both materials and silhouettes. Such a catalog did not offer only a store's wares to its out-of-town customers, it also provided advice on the latest modes, and subtle judgments on good taste.

To its role as both purveyor and counselor, Lord & Taylor brought some fifty-five years of experience. The firm had been founded as a small dry goods shop in 1826 by a young Englishman, Samuel Lord, and his cousin, George Washington Taylor. Most of the fabrics they handled were imported. The domestic textile industry was in its infancy, the great mills at Lawrence, Mass., having opened only the year before.

For convenience, therefore, Messrs. Lord and Taylor located their store at 47 Catherine Street Slip, near the North River waterfront in New York's Greenwich Village. The business flourished and in six years the partners expanded into the adjoining building. In another six years further growth led to a move to a large four-story building at 61–63 Catherine Street Slip.

In 1852 Taylor retired to England. A year later Lord, as sole proprietor of the firm, opened a new and larger store at Grand and Chrystie Streets, then a fashionable neighborhood. Under its sky-lighted dome, ladies in ever-widening hoop skirts promenaded in the great central rotunda, fingering the silk and laces on display.

Just before the Civil War, Lord opened a second store at the corner of Broadway and Grand St., and took into partnership his eldest son, John T. Lord, and his confidential clerk, John S. Lyle. As New York grew during the booming Reconstruction era, Lord & Taylor added a third store in 1872. This building, at Broadway and 20th St., was constructed with an iron frame which allowed ample space for window displays. It also boasted a steam elevator to carry customers to all five of its floors.

The timing of this latest expansion was, however, unfortunate. In 1873 the country was struck by a severe financial panic. Although Lord & Taylor weathered the subsequent economic depression, some retrenchment was necessary. In 1874 the store at Grand St. and Broadway was closed. A fresh infusion of capital, plus the guidance of Edward P. Hatch, a financial expert who was brought in to direct the firm, enabled the company to maintain its position as one of New York's leading stores, and to prepare for the return of national prosperity in the 1880's.

The relatively steady growth of Lord & Taylor from its modest beginnings was not only due to the general expansion of New York City. The mid-nineteenth century was an era in which a general revolution in merchandising was taking place in both this country and in Europe. Not only in New York and Chicago, but in Paris and Berlin as well, the modern department store was taking form. Stores such as Lord & Taylor, which had started by stocking fabrics, laces and threads, were, by the 1880's, offering both ready-to-wear and made-to-measure clothing for men, women and children, as well as a variety of housewares.

Department stores as we know them today only became possible after the development of a garment industry made a constant supply of ready-made clothing available. Until the middle of the nineteenth century, all clothing was made by housewives or by seamstresses who traveled from house to house, staying with a family for a few weeks to turn out a new wardrobe. For the wealthier city dwellers, there were also seamstresses and mantuamakers who maintained shops where clothing could be made to order.

As a result, most people, except for the very wealthy, owned remarkably few changes of clothing. When the main building of Vassar College was designed just before the Civil War, the specifications called for each student to be supplied with three pegs, one for the everyday dress, one for the Sunday dress, and one for the petticoat.

All this changed very rapidly by the 1860's. In 1848 Elias Howe patented the sewing machine. Three years later Issac Singer brought out a new model, a considerable improvement in that it was operated by a foot treadle, leaving both hands free to manipulate the fabric. By that time ready-made and partly-made men's shirts were already being marketed.

The fledgling garment industry boomed with the government's demand for uniforms during the Civil War. New York and Boston, close to both textile factories and sources of cheap labor, became the country's garment centers. Production was increased in 1865 by the invention of power-run sewing machines. By the end of the war most articles could be bought ready-made.

At about the same time the creation of homemade wearing apparel was also vastly simplified. In 1862 Ebenezer Butterick began to market commercial paper patterns in New England. By 1865 he was established in the mail-order business in New York and was sending his patterns all over the world. No longer did the housewife or the professional seamstress have to struggle to reproduce the intricacies of line and draping illustrated in such publication as *Godey's Lady's Book*. Any woman, with patience and rudimentary skill, could achieve the results promised by Butterick's patterns.

The greater ease of home sewing and the economies achieved through the mass production of ready-made clothes resulted in an acceleration of change in the fashion cycle. Until about 1870, basic silhouettes and lines had remained in vogue for relatively long periods, with major changes occurring after roughly twenty years. In the latter part of the century there were significant variations from year to year, with radical differences in the treatment of the bodice, neckline, sleeve, and skirt emerging every four or five years.

The bustle, which had reached substantial proportions by 1875, declined in both size and position later in the decade. By the late 1870's, any back fullness that was shown had slipped from below the waist to the area of the knees. The popular princess silhouette, slim from top to bottom, was to be rapidly succeeded by the two-piece dress. In the early 1880's, the bustle began to reappear and by 1885 it once more held full sway, sometimes protruding as much as two feet.

The clothes of 1881, as illustrated in the Lord & Taylor catalog, were some of the most anti-anatomical ever designed. Even in evening dress and wedding gowns, where décolletage has almost always been accepted, the figure was encased from throat to toe. The contours of bust, waist and hip were clearly the result of rigid corseting and the boned and padded construction of the outer garment rather than the curves of nature. In fact, the long tight bodice, drawn to a point in the front, was known as the cuirass, a name derived, appropriately enough, from medieval armor.

In order to accommodate the lean, rather spare cut of the bodice and the elaborate draping of the shirt, it became usual to fashion the garment in two parts. Although it hardly seems discernable in the illustrations of this catalog, this fashion foreshadowed a new development, the "man-tailored" suit. These were already being shown in England and, within a few years, would make an appearance in America. There is, perhaps, a hint of things to come in the children's dresses, looser and more comfortable than those for ladies, shown on page 36, or in the walking-jacket on page 45.

The focal point of the costume of 1881 was the skirt. It was elaborately draped, the draperies caught up with bows or fringe or with balls of steel or jet. Pleats and fluting were used extensively. Most characteristic of the year was the hobbled effect around the knees. One contemporary critic wrote disapprovingly, "At the present moment women go about hobbled after the fashion adopted by our forefathers to prevent the straying of their horses and asses when turned out to grass."

Trimmings of all kinds were used lavishly and were offered to the home sewer as well as being displayed on the ready-to-wear and custom-made clothes. The choice of fabrics was also comprehensive. Often two or more fabrics were combined in one costume, as in the dresses illustrated on pages 19 and 24. Manufacturers had evidently learned to make a seemingly endless variety of woven patterns. The descriptions of fabrics stress combinations of materials and colors, including changeable silks. Plaids and stripes were popular. So were such fabrics as brocade, cut velvet, heavy satin and fine wool.

Although fabrics were rich, colors tended to be subdued. Blacks and navies were featured. Browns, greys, and olive tones also were fashionable.

Laces were still much worn, particularly at the throat. But the most extensive use of lace in the late 70's and early 80's was on underclothing. The rise of the tight-fronted dress had produced a corresponding decline in the amount of underwear worn. What fashionable underpinnings lacked in bulk they made up for, however, in a new lavishness. Underwear was produced in delicate fabrics. Fine cottons, linens and silks had superseded flannel. Machine-made lace was by now acceptable and was used with a heavy hand, although the handmade variety was also available at correspondingly higher prices. In fact, the catalog offers a handkerchief, trimmed with point gaze, which costs more than some of the simpler dresses.

Accessories followed the slim lines of the clothes. Hair, for a very brief period, was worn close to the head. Sometimes it was even cropped, and a short, curled fringe was almost universal. On top of this sleek head perched a rakish hat. Bonnets, although still shown, were definitely old-fashioned. Hats might tilt over the eye or cling precariously to the back of the head. Whatever the case, they were trimmed with a profusion of flowers, feathers and laces.

Shoes also were relatively slim. The pointed toe had become fashionable the year before, 1880. Heels were moderate in height. The high buttoned boot, fashionable since the 1860's, continued in vogue. Low-cut shoes, however, fastened with bows or straps, were assuming a new importance. Some of the pumps shown, with their dainty toes and French-court heels, have an amazingly modern appearance.

One item, usually thought of as belonging to an earlier fashion era, continued to be carried in stock. This was the Indian shawl, a status symbol in women's dress since the end of the eighteenth century. Although it was noted that those with antique borders "are especially liked by elderly ladies," thus indicating that the fashion was somewhat passé, Lord & Taylor still offered both paisleys and genuine cashmeres. That the true handwoven shawls were still a luxury item is indicated by the prices, figures which ranged upwards to $1,000.

Proper dress played an important role in Victorian society. It was an era strongly conscious, at least on the surface, of the niceties of good form and the gradations of social position. A contemporary writer on etiquette expressed the prevailing view: "What style is to our thoughts, dress is to our persons. It may supply the place of more solid qualities [sic], and without it the most solid are of little avail. Numbers have owed their elevation to their attention to the toilet. Place, fortune, marriage have all been lost by neglecting it . . . The plainest dress is always the most genteel, and a lady that dresses plainly will never be dressed unfashionably."

To modern eyes even the simplest of the costumes shown in the Lord & Taylor catalog is far from plain. The lavish trimmings and elaborate draperies reflect an era in which women were considered as passive and ornamental. They are a perfect complement to the overstuffed parlors, the plethora of ornament, and rococo richness that characterized nineteenth-century taste.

Broadway and Twentieth Street Store.

Suggestions for further reading

BERNSTEIN, ALINE. *Masterpieces of Women's Costume of the Eighteenth and Nineteenth Centuries.* New York: Crown, 1959.
BRAUN-RONSDORF, MARGARETE. *Mirror of Fashion.* New York: McGraw-Hill, 1958.
CUNNINGTON, C. WILLETT AND PHILLIS. *English Women's Clothing in the Nineteenth Century.* New York: Thomas Yoseloff, 1958.
CUNNINGTON, C. WILLETT AND PHILLIS *Handbook of English Costume in the Nineteenth Century.* London: Faber & Faber, 1959.
Decorum: A Practical Treatise on Etiquette and Dress. New York: Union Publishing, 1880.
LAVER, JAMES. *Taste and Fashion.* London: Harrap, 1945.
PAYNE, BLANCHE. *History of Costume.* New York: Harper and Row, 1965.
VICTORIA AND ALBERT MUSEUM. *Nineteenth-Century Costume.* Introduction by James Laver. London: The Ministry of Education, 1947.
WILCOX, R. TURNER. *The Mode in Costume.* New York: Charles Scribner's Sons, 1958.
WILCOX, R. TURNER. *Five Centuries of American Costume.* New York: Charles Scribner's Sons, 1963.

other trade catalogs:

Lawrence Romaine in *A Guide to American Trade Catalogs, 1744–1900* (New York: R. R. Bowker Co., 1960) lists a number of catalogs issued by such merchants as Lord and Taylor. Some of the more relevant are listed below. These listings also include the name or the names of the institutions where these catalogs can be found. Unfortunately, they have become very rare items.

1879–80. B. Altman & Co., New York. Fall and Winter, catalog #34. 104 pp. Available—Baker Library, Harvard University.
1892. John Wanamaker, Philadelphia and New York. Spring and Summer, catalog #32. 132 pp. Available—Historical Society of Pennsylvania, Philadelphia; *later dates,* Metropolitan Museum, New York.
1893. Hale Brothers & Co., Sacramento, Calif. Spring and Summer, catalog #19. 100 pp. Available—California Historical Society, San Francisco.
1897–8. Jordan, Marsh & Co., Boston, Fall and Winter catalog. 246 pp. Available—Baker Library, Harvard University; *earlier years,* Metropolitan Museum, New York.

Public collections of late nineteenth-century clothing and furnishings

The following public historical and art museums have indicated that they have within their holdings more than a few examples of late nineteenth-century clothing and furnishings. Some of these items will be found on permanent display, others are included in period displays with other historical pieces, and yet others are displayed only from time to time.

Arizona Pioneers' Historical Museum, Tucson, Ariz.
Atlanta Historical Society Museum, Atlanta, Ga.
Brooklyn Museum, Brooklyn, N. Y.
Chicago Historical Society, Chicago, Ill.

Dallas Museum of Fashion, Dallas, Tex.
Delaware State Museum, Dover, Del.
Drexel Museum Collection, Drexel University, Philadelphia, Penn.
El Monte Historical Museum, El Monte, Calif.
Evansville Museum of Arts and Sciences, Evansville, Ind.
Florida State Museum, Gainesville, Fla.
Grand Rapids Public Museum, Grand Rapids, Mich.
Greensboro Historical Museum, Greensboro, N. C.
Henry Ford Museum and Greenfield Village, Dearborn, Mich.
Historical Museum and Institute of Western Colorado, Grand Junction, Colo.
Kansas State Historical Society Museum, Topeka, Kans.
Lane County Pioneer Museum, Eugene, Ore.
Los Angeles County Museum of Art, Los Angeles, Calif.
Maryland Historical Society, Baltimore, Md.
Mattatuck Museum, Waterbury, Conn.
Metropolitan Museum, New York, N. Y.
Michigan Historical Commission Museum, Lansing, Mich.
Missouri Historical Society, St. Louis, Mo.
Monmouth County Historical Society Museum, Freehold, N. J.
Museum of the City of Mobile, Mobile, Ala.
Museum of the City of New York, New York, N. Y.
Nassau County Historical Museum, Syosset, N. Y.
Nebraska State Historical Society Museum, Lincoln, Nebr.
Nevada Historical Society, Reno, Nev.
Newark Museum, Newark, N. J.
New Jersey Historical Society, Newark, N. J.
New Jersey State Museum, Trenton, N. J.
New York Historical Society, New York, N. Y.
North Carolina State Dept. of Archives and History, Raleigh, N. C.
Oakland Museum, Oakland, Calif.
Old Court House Museum, Vicksburg, Miss.
Orange County Historical Museum, Orlando, Fla.
Pioneer Woman Museum, Ponca City, Okla.
San Bernardino County Museum, Bloomington, Calif.
San Diego Historical Society, Serra Museum, San Diego, Calif.
State Historical Society of Wisconsin, Madison, Wis. (*contact Society for information about various exhibit locations*)
Staten Island Historical Society, Richmond, S. I., New York
University of Washington, Costume and Textile Study Center, Seattle, Wash.
Wadsworth Atheneum, Hartford, Conn.
Western Reserve Historical Society Museum, Cleveland, Ohio
William Penn Memorial Museum, Harrisburg, Penn.
Witte Memorial Museum, San Antonio, Texas